THE BEST BUDDHIST WRITING

2·0·0·9

Edited by Melvin McLeod
and the Editors of the *Shambhala Sun*

SHAMBHALA
Boston & London 2009

Shambhala Publications, Inc.
Horticultural Hall
300 Massachusetts Avenue
Boston, Massachusetts 02115
www.shambhala.com

9 8 7 6 5 4 3 2 1

First Edition
Printed in Canada

⊗This edition is printed on acid-free paper that meets the
American National Standards Institute z39.48 Standard.
♻This book was printed on 100% postconsumer recycled paper.
For more information please visit www.shambhala.com.
Distributed in the United States by Random House, Inc.,
and in Canada by Random House of Canada Ltd

ISBN 978-1-59030-734-2
ISSN 1932-393X
2006213739

Contents

Introduction

I remember the first book of Buddhist writing I ever read. It was 1974, and I was working as a police reporter at the local newspaper. Scanning the shelves at my favorite bookstore one day, I spotted a book called *The Tibetan Book of the Dead*. I knew nothing about it— not even that it was about Buddhism—but I bought it because of a serious illness in my family.

I remember opening that book, sitting in the newsroom with a bank of police radios in front of me. Halfway through the first page of the introduction, my life changed. I didn't really understand what I was reading, but I knew it was different from anything else I had ever encountered. I intuited what I can only describe as an unshakable integrity. Whatever this thing called Buddhism was, I somehow knew it would never tell me anything just because that was what I wanted to hear. It would never tell me anything but the truth, and it would never be a crutch. In fact, it would kick the crutches out from under me.

That was thirty-five years ago, and the book of Buddhist writing you're reading now is very different from that one. Evans-Wentz's translation of *The Tibetan Book of the Dead* was one of the few Buddhist texts widely available at the time. Published in 1927, its language was archaic, and its understanding of Buddhism was incomplete at best.

Since then, we have benefited from more than fifty years of great Buddhist teachers who have come to the West and presented Buddhism with accuracy and profundity. In turn, Westerners have practiced with sincerity and dedication, and many are now outstanding

Buddhist teachers in their own right. The work of great writers and artists has been influenced by Buddhism, and Buddhist insight and meditation are being integrated into all areas of mainstream American life—from health care settings to businesses to prisons. While the actual number of Western Buddhists is probably not much higher than it was in 1974, Buddhist influence has quietly seeped into our society, and deep, authentic practice has put down its roots in America.

All these changes are reflected in this year's edition of *Best Buddhist Writing*. But at a deeper level, nothing has changed. Genuine Buddhism will never pander to ego or try to find our favor by telling us what we'd like to hear. It continues to kick the crutches out from under us. Its integrity remains unshakable.

This book contains many different types of writing, in many different voices. Some are personal stories, others are teachings in the traditional sense, and still others apply the wisdom of Buddhist practice to broader issues in our world. Yet all share a dedication to honesty and openness, to telling the truth about our lives as human beings.

The truth, according to Buddhism, is a bad-news-good-news story. From ego's point of view, the news is bad. Buddhism defines ego as our futile struggle to maintain and protect a permanent, ongoing self. This painful struggle is the source of much of our suffering, because we try to deny the truth that everything in this world is subject to change and dissolution. So the bad news for ego—and this is where Buddhism never pulls its punches—is that death is real, suffering is pervasive, we are without a permanent identity or center, and we cause ourselves and others a lot of unnecessary pain. Because of all that, our hearts are, in a sense, permanently broken.

But that broken heart is the good news too. The broken heart is the true heart of love and tenderness. For Buddhism's good news is that if we pause in our struggle against the truths of impermanence and change, we catch glimpses of our true nature, which is always present and unaffected by life's ups and downs. Our true nature is the mind of awareness and wisdom and the heart of compassion and joy. And in its very transience, the world we inhabit is vivid, sacred, and basically good.

Throughout this book, we find Buddhism's rich mix of unflinching clarity, loving heart, and profound insight into the nature of reality. To this is added the knowledge and wisdom of Western thought, all part of the great spiritual and intellectual ferment known as Buddhism in the modern world.

Like all great stories, this one begins with the personal, with how individual practitioners have brought Buddhism into their hearts as they face the challenges of life. These are powerful and inspiring stories that may make you cry and smile simultaneously—Kathleen Willis Morton on the death of her infant son, Olivia Ames Hoblitzelle on a couple's journey through Alzheimer's, Ruth Ozeki's brilliant meditation on writing and her mother's death, Gabriel Cohen on coming to terms with his anger after a divorce, and Calvin Malone's touching story of Christmas in prison. A lot of sadness, certainly, but also open, loving hearts and the genuine benefit of Buddhist practice when times get tough.

As always, the core of Buddhism, its backbone for twenty-five hundred years, is the direct transmission of Buddhist wisdom from the realized mind of the teacher to the open mind of the student. This year's edition of *Best Buddhist Writing* presents an interesting mix of teachings by renowned Asian masters such as the Seventeenth Karmapa, Dzigar Kongtrül, and the Dzogchen Ponlop Rinpoche, and by Westerners such as Pema Chödrön, Martine Batchelor, Phillip Moffitt, Norman Fischer, and Christina Feldman, who offer their deep understanding of Buddhism from a perspective informed and enhanced by their Western intellectual training.

An interesting thread in this year's collection is the discussion of how Buddhist practice, combined with a Western psychological approach, can help us with both our personal issues and our relationships. Jack Kornfield opens this book with a beautiful presentation of basic human goodness, the starting point of Buddhist psychology. The psychotherapist John Welwood is perhaps the best synthesizer of Buddhist and Western psychology, and he shows us how we can use our relationships as the ground of profound spiritual growth. Peggy Rowe-Ward and Larry Ward, married students of Thich Nhat Hanh, offer meditations to help us base our relationships on loving-kindness, compassion, joy, and equanimity, known in Buddhism as the four *brahmaviharas.*

Yet Buddhism, like all spiritual paths, must be about more than just ourselves or our immediate personal relationships. It must be about the relationships among all people, and so it must reflect on, and hopefully influence, the broad issues of the day. Everyone today is looking for wisdom to help them deal with difficult times, and this is, after all, a Buddhist specialty. Here, the Zen teacher Joan Sutherland shows us how the ancient Buddhist masters of China handled their own society's difficulties.

But with all the ups and down the world is going through now, the long-term fate of humanity may hang on what we do about the environment. That's certainly the way many Buddhist teachers and writers see it, and in this year's edition of *Best Buddhist Writing*, they show us how Buddhist teachings and practice go to the heart of the greatest challenge of our time. The Zen teacher Thich Nhat Hanh, founder of Engaged Buddhism, makes a compelling argument that our response to environmental problems must ultimately be spiritual if it is to succeed. The political thinker David Loy analyzes the environmental crisis from a Buddhist viewpoint, and the ecophilosopher Stephanie Kaza explains how we can actually make environmentalism a spiritual path, not just a change in lifestyle. Finally, the Zen gardener Wendy Johnson brings it all back to earth, to our very relationship with the soil.

The basic Buddhist aspiration is that everything we do should be of benefit, both to ourselves and others. And what could be of more benefit than telling the truths the world so often denies—the painful truth of suffering and the equally denied truth of human goodness. The writings in this book will inspire you, provoke you, sometimes make you cry, and sometimes make you laugh. But they were all written with the intention of being of benefit—to the world, to our relationships, and most of all, to the readers. I myself have benefited from each teaching, essay, and memoir in this rich and varied anthology. As I think about it, that's probably how I made my choices. I hope you will benefit from this year's best Buddhist writings as I have.

This is the sixth annual anthology in the *Best Buddhist Writing* series. I'd like to thank Peter Turner, the president of Shambhala Publications, for conceiving the series and choosing the editors of the *Shambhala Sun* to survey each year's Buddhist writings and select what we think are the best. Beth Frankl is the series editor at Shambhala Publications and is a pleasure to work with on it. I'd like to express my deep appreciation for all my colleagues at the *Shambhala Sun* and *Buddhadharma* magazines. The selections in this book reflect our ongoing exploration of what Buddhism means in and to the modern world. Finally, I'd like to thank my wife, Pam Rubin, and my daughter, Pearl. In our lives together as a family I see the benefit of the practice.

Melvin McLeod
Editor-in-Chief
The Shambhala Sun
Buddhadharma: The Practitioner's Quarterly

THE BEST BUDDHIST WRITING 2009

The Wise Heart ☽

Jack Kornfield

Buddhism has all the trappings of institutionalized religion, but no God or external deity. So Western observers have long debated whether it should be classified as a religion, a philosophy of life, or perhaps a psychology. Jack Kornfield is one of America's leading Buddhist teachers and has a PhD in clinical psychology. Here, he looks at Buddhism as a psychology of human goodness with a twenty-five-hundred-year track record of helping people become wise, caring, and fulfilled.

O Nobly Born, O you of glorious origins, remember your radiant true nature, the essence of mind. Trust it. Return to it. It is home.
    —*The Tibetan Book of the Dead*

Then it was as if I suddenly saw the secret beauty of their hearts, the depths of their hearts where neither sin nor desire nor self-knowledge can reach, the core of their reality, the person that each one is in the eyes of the Divine. If only they could all see themselves as they really are. If only we could see each other that way all the time. There would be no more war, no more hatred, no more cruelty, no more greed. . . . I suppose the big problem would be that we would fall down and worship each other.
    —Thomas Merton

In a large temple north of Thailand's ancient capital, Sukotai, there once stood an enormous and ancient clay Buddha. Though not the most handsome or refined work of Thai Buddhist art, it had been cared for over a period of five hundred years and had become revered for its sheer longevity. Violent storms, changes of government, and invading armies had come and gone, but the Buddha endured.

At one point, however, the monks who tended the temple noticed that the statue had begun to crack and would soon be in need of repair and repainting. After a stretch of particularly hot, dry weather, one of the cracks became so wide that a curious monk took his flashlight and peered inside. What shone back at him was a flash of brilliant gold! Inside this plain old statue, the temple residents discovered one of the largest and most luminous gold images of Buddha ever created in Southeast Asia. Now uncovered, the golden Buddha draws throngs of devoted pilgrims from all over Thailand.

The monks believe that this shining work of art had been covered in plaster and clay to protect it during times of conflict and unrest. In much the same way, each of us has encountered threatening situations that lead us to cover our innate nobility. Just as the people of Sukotai had forgotten about the golden Buddha, we too have forgotten our essential nature. Much of the time we operate from the protective layer. The primary aim of Buddhist psychology is to help us see beneath this armoring and bring out our original goodness, called our *buddhanature.*

This is a first principle of Buddhist psychology: see the inner nobility and beauty of all human beings.

Robert Johnson, the noted Jungian analyst, acknowledges how difficult it is for many of us to believe in our goodness. We more easily take our worst fears and thoughts to be who we are, the unacknowledged traits called our "shadow" by Jung. "Curiously," writes Johnson, "people resist the noble aspects of their shadow more strenuously than they hide the dark sides. . . . It is more disrupting to find that you have a profound nobility of character than to find out you are a bum."

Our belief in a limited and impoverished identity is such a strong habit that without it we are afraid we wouldn't know how to be. If we fully acknowledged our dignity, it could lead to radical life changes. It could ask something huge of us. And yet some part of us knows that the frightened and damaged self is not who we are. Each of us needs to find our way to be whole and free.

In my family, it was not easy to see my own goodness. My earliest memories are of a paranoid and unpredictably violent father, a bruised and frightened mother, and four boys who each wondered, "How did we get here?" We would all hold our breath when our father pulled the car into the driveway. On good days he could be attentive and humorous, and we would feel relieved, but more often we had to hide or cower to avoid his hair-trigger anger and tirades. On family trips the pressure might lead him to smash my mother's head into the windshield or to punish his children for the erratic behavior of other drivers. I remember my father's grandmother pleading with my mother not to divorce him: "At least he can sometimes hold a job. He's not so crazy as those ones in the mental hospitals."

Yet I knew this unhappiness was not all there was to existence. I can remember running out of the house on painful days, at age six or seven, while my parents fought. Something in me felt I didn't belong in that house, as if I had been born into the wrong family. At times I imagined, as children do, that one day there would come a knock at the door, and an elegant gentleman would ask for me by name. He would then announce that Jack and his brothers had been secretly placed in this home, but that now their real parents, the king and queen, wanted them to return to their rightful family. These childhood fantasies gave rise to one of the strongest currents of my life, a longing to be part of something worthy and true. I was seeking my real family of noble birth.

In these often cynical times, we might think of "original goodness" as merely an uplifting phrase, but through its lens we discover a radically different way of seeing and being: one whose aim is to transform our world. This does not mean that we ignore the enormousness of people's sorrows or that we make ourselves foolishly vulnerable to unstable and perhaps violent individuals. Indeed, to find the dignity in others, their suffering has to be acknowledged.

Among the most central of all Buddhist psychological principles are the four noble truths, which begin by acknowledging the inevitable suffering in human life. This truth, too, is hard to talk about in modern culture, where people are taught to avoid discomfort at any cost, where "the pursuit of happiness" has become "the right to happiness." And yet when we are suffering, it is so refreshing and helpful to have the truth of suffering acknowledged.

Buddhist teachings help us to face our individual suffering, from shame and depression to anxiety and grief. They address the collective suffering of the world and help us to work with the source of this sorrow: the forces of greed, hatred, and delusion in the human psyche. While tending to our sufferings is critical, this does not eclipse our fundamental nobility.

The word *nobility* does not refer to medieval knights and courts. It derives from the Greek *gno* (as in *gnosis*), meaning "wisdom" or "inner illumination." In English, *nobility* is defined as human excellence, as that which is illustrious, admirable, lofty, and distinguished in values, conduct, and bearing. How might we intuitively connect with this quality in those around us? Just as no one can tell us how to feel love, each of us can find our own way to sense the underlying goodness in others. One way is to shift the frame of time, imagining the person before us as a small child, still young and innocent. Once after a particularly difficult day with my teenage daughter, I found myself sitting beside her as she slept. Just hours before, we had been struggling over her plans for the evening; now she lay sleeping with the innocence and beauty of her childhood. Such innocence is there in all people, if we are willing to see it.

Or instead of moving back in time, we can move forward. We can visualize the person at the end of his life, lying on his deathbed, vulnerable, open, with nothing to hide. Or we can simply see him as a fellow wayfarer, struggling with his burdens, wanting happiness and dignity. Beneath the fears and needs, the aggression and pain, whoever we encounter is a being who, like us, has the tremendous potential for understanding and compassion, whose goodness is there to be touched.

We can perhaps most easily admire the human spirit when it shines in the world's great moral leaders. We see an unshakable compassion in the Nobel Peace Prize winner Aung San Suu Kyi, who remains steadfast and loving in spite of her long years of house arrest in Burma. We remember how former South African president Nelson Mandela walked out of prison with a gracious spirit of courage and dignity that was unbent by twenty-seven years of torture and hardship. But the same spirit also beams from healthy children everywhere. Their joy and natural beauty can reawaken us to our buddhanature. They remind us that we are born with this shining spirit.

So why, in Western psychology, have we been so focused on the dark side of human nature? Even before Freud, Western psychology was based on a medical model, and it still focuses primarily on pathology. The psychiatric profession's *Diagnostic and Statistical Manual of Mental Disorders*, which orients the work of most therapists, clinics, and health care providers, is a comprehensive listing of hundreds of psychological problems and diseases. Categorizing problems helps us study them and then, it is hoped, cure them in the most scientific and economically efficient way. But often we give so much attention to our protective layers of fear, depression, confusion, and aggression that we forget who we really are.

As a teacher, I see this all the time. When a middle-aged man named Marty came to see me after a year of painful separation and divorce, he was caught in the repetitive cycles of unworthiness and shame that he had carried since childhood. He believed there was something terribly wrong with him. He had forgotten his original goodness. When a young woman, Jan, came to Buddhist practice after a long struggle with anxiety and depression, she had a hard time letting go of her self-image as a broken and damaged person. For years she had seen herself only through her diagnosis and the various medications that had failed to control it.

As psychology becomes more pharmacologically oriented, this medical model is reinforced. Today, most of the millions of adults seeking mental health support are quickly put on medication. Even more troubling, hundreds of thousands of children are being prescribed powerful psychiatric drugs for conditions ranging from attention–deficit/hyperactivity disorder (ADHD) to the newly popular diagnosis of childhood bipolar disorder. While these medications may be appropriate, even lifesaving, in some cases laypeople and professionals increasingly look for a pill as the answer to human confusion and suffering. It need not be so.

INNER FREEDOM: LIBERATION OF THE HEART

If we do not focus on human limits and pathology, what is the alternative? It is the belief that human freedom is possible under any circumstances. Buddhist teachings put it this way: "Just as the great oceans have but one taste, the taste of salt, so do all of the teachings of Buddha have but one taste, the taste of liberation."

Psychologist Viktor Frankl was the sole member of his family to survive the Nazi death camps. Nevertheless, in spite of this suffering, he found a path to healing. Frankl wrote, "We who lived in concentration camps can remember the men who walked through the huts comforting others, giving away their last piece of bread. They may have been few in number, but they offer sufficient proof that everything can be taken from a man but one thing: the last of the human freedoms—to choose one's attitude in any given set of circumstances, to choose one's own way."

When we are lost in our worst crises and conflicts, in the deepest states of fear and confusion, our pain can seem endless. We can feel as if there is no exit, no hope. Yet some hidden wisdom longs for freedom. "If it were not possible to free the heart from entanglement in unhealthy states," says the Buddha, "I would not teach you to do so. But just because it is possible to free the heart from entanglement in unhealthy states do I offer these teachings."

Awakening this inner freedom of spirit is the purpose of the hundreds of Buddhist practices and trainings. Each of these practices helps us to recognize and let go of unhealthy patterns that create suffering and develop healthy patterns in their place. What is important about the Buddhist psychological approach is the emphasis on training and practice, as well as understanding. Instead of going into therapy to discuss your problems and be listened to once a week, there is a regimen of daily and ongoing trainings and disciplines to help you learn and practice healthy ways of being. These practices return us to our innate wisdom and compassion, and they direct us toward freedom.

SACRED PERCEPTION

> The saints are what they are, not because their sanctity makes them admirable to others, but because the gift of sainthood makes it possible for them to admire everybody else.
> —THOMAS MERTON

Each time we meet other human beings and honor their dignity, we help those around us. Their hearts resonate with ours in exactly the same way the strings of an unplucked violin vibrate with the sounds of a violin played nearby. Western psychology has documented this phenomenon of "mood contagion" or "limbic resonance." If a person filled with panic or hatred walks into a room, we feel it immediately, and unless we are very mindful, that person's negative state will begin to overtake our own. When a joyfully expressive person walks into a room, we can feel that state as well. And when we see the goodness of those before us, the dignity in them resonates with our admiration and respect.

This resonance can begin very simply. In India, when people greet one another, they put their palms together and bow, saying, "*Namaste* [I honor the divine within you]." It is a way of acknowledging your buddhanature, who you really are. Some believe that the Western handshake evolved to demonstrate friendliness and safety, to show that we are not holding any weapon. But the greeting *namaste* goes a step further, from "I will not harm you" to "I see that which is holy in you." It creates the basis for sacred relationship.

When I began my training as a Buddhist monk, I found a taste of this sacred relationship. Around my teacher, Ajahn Chah, was an aura of straightforwardness, graciousness, and trust. It was the opposite of my early family life, and though it initially felt strange and unfamiliar, something in me loved it. Instead of a field of judgment, criticism, and unpredictable violence, here was a community dedicated to treating each person with respect and dignity. It was beautiful.

In the monastery, the walking paths were swept daily; the robes and bowls of the monks were tended with care. Our vows required us to cherish life in every form. We carefully avoided stepping on ants; we valued birds and insects, snakes and mammals. We learned to value ourselves and others equally. When conflict arose, we called on practices of patience, and in seeking forgiveness, we were guided by councils of elders who demonstrated how to approach our failings with mindful respect.

Whether practiced in a forest monastery or in the West, Buddhist psychology begins by deliberately cultivating respect, starting with ourselves. When we learn to rest in our own goodness, we can see the goodness more clearly in others. As our sense of respect and care is developed, it serves us well under most ordinary circumstances. It becomes invaluable in extremity.

One Buddhist practitioner tells of being part of a group taken hostage in a bank in St. Louis. She describes the initial confusion and fear that spread through the hostages. She remembers trying to quiet her own racing heart. And then she tells how she made a decision not to panic. She used her meditation and her breath to quiet her mind. Over the hours, even as she helped others in her group, she addressed her captors respectfully and expressed a genuine concern for them. She saw their desperation and their underlying needs. When she and the other hostages were later released unharmed, she gratefully believed that the care and respect they showed to their captors had made their release possible.

When we bring respect and honor to those around us, we open a channel to their own goodness. I have seen this truth in working with prisoners and gang members. When they experience someone who respects and values them, it gives them the ability to admire themselves, to accept and acknowledge the good inside. When we see what is holy in another, whether we meet them in our family or our community, at a business meeting or in a therapy session, we transform their hearts.

The Dalai Lama embodies this sacred perception as he moves through the world, and it is one of the reasons so many people seek to be around him. Several years ago His Holiness visited San Francisco, and we invited him to offer teachings at Spirit Rock Meditation Center. The Dalai Lama is the head of the Tibetan government-in-exile, and the State Department had assigned dozens of Secret Service agents to protect him and his entourage. Accustomed to guarding foreign leaders, princes, and kings, the Secret Service agents were surprisingly moved by the Dalai Lama's respectful attitude and friendly heart. At the end, they asked for his blessing. Then they all wanted to have a photo taken with him. Several said, "We have had the privilege of protecting political leaders, princes, and prime ministers, yet there is something different about the Dalai Lama. He treats us as if we are special."

Later, during a series of public teachings, he stayed at a San Francisco hotel famous for hosting dignitaries. Just before he departed, the Dalai Lama told the hotel management that he would like to thank the staff in person, as many as wished to meet him. So on the last morning a long line of maids and dishwashers, cooks and maintenance men, secretaries and managers made their way to the circular driveway at the hotel entrance. And before the Dalai Lama's motorcade left, he walked down the line of employees, lovingly touching each hand, vibrating the strings of each heart.

Some years ago, I heard the story of a high school history teacher who knew this same secret. On one particularly fidgety and distracted afternoon she told her class to stop all their academic work. She let her students rest while she wrote on the blackboard a list of the names of everyone in the class. Then she asked them to copy the list. She instructed them to use the rest of the period to write beside each name one thing they liked or admired about that student. At the end of class she collected the papers.

Weeks later, on another difficult day just before winter break, the teacher again stopped the class. She handed each student a sheet with his or her name on top. On it, she had pasted all twenty-six good things the other students had written about that person. They smiled and gasped in pleasure that their classmates had noticed so many beautiful qualities about them.

Three years later, this teacher received a call from the mother of one of her former students. Robert had been a cutup, but also one of her favorites. His mother sadly passed on the terrible news that Robert had been killed in the Gulf War. The teacher attended the funeral, where many of Robert's former friends and high school classmates spoke. Just as the service was ending, Robert's mother approached her. She took out a worn piece of paper, obviously folded and refolded many times, and said, "This was one of the few things in Robert's pocket when the military retrieved his body." It was the paper on which the teacher had so carefully pasted the twenty-six things his classmates had admired.

Seeing this, Robert's teacher's eyes filled with tears. As she dried her wet cheeks, another former student standing nearby opened her purse, pulled out her own carefully folded page, and confessed that she always kept it with her. A third ex-student said that his page was framed and hanging in his kitchen; another told how the page had become part of her wedding vows. The perception of goodness invited by this teacher had transformed the hearts of her students in ways she might only have dreamed about.

We can each remember a moment when someone saw this goodness in us and blessed us. On retreat, a middle-aged woman remembers the one person, a nun, who was kind to her when, as a frightened and lonely teenager, she gave birth out of wedlock. She has carried her name all these years. A young man I worked with in juvenile hall remembers the old gardener next door who loved and valued him. The gardener's respect stuck with him through all his troubles. This possibility is voiced by the Nobel Laureate Nelson Mandela: "It never hurts to think too highly of a person; often they become ennobled and act better because of it."

To see with sacred perception does not mean we ignore the need for development and change in an individual. Sacred perception is one half of a paradox. Zen master Shunryu Suzuki remarked to a disciple, "You are perfect just the way you are. And . . . there is still room for improvement!" Buddhist psychology offers meditations, cognitive strategies, ethical trainings, which form a powerful set of practices that foster inner transformation. But it starts with a most radical vision, one that transforms everyone it touches: a recognition of the innate nobility and the freedom of heart that are available wherever we are.

Light Comes Through ☽⟩

Dzigar Kongtrül

*At our core as human beings is a deep but vague longing—for happiness,
for meaning, for love, for something we're not exactly sure of—and according to Buddhist teachers, that longing is the very expression of our inherent
goodness. So why are our lives so often marked by anxiety, suffering, and
lack of fulfillment? According to the Tibetan teacher Dzigar Kongtrül, the
problem is not the happiness we wish for, but whom we wish it for.*

Our human search for happiness and freedom from suffering expresses itself in everything we do. We emerge from the womb with
a primordial instinct to find comfort through suckling our mother's milk. Our instinct for fulfillment drives us—it is not something
we need to cultivate. Throughout our countless lifetimes, we have
searched for happiness and freedom from pain. We have always
been sentient; therefore we have always had this longing. It lies at
the very core of our being.

Animals long for happiness too. We see it in their propensity to
frolic. Play doesn't simply fulfill an evolutionary function; it is an
expression of pleasure and joy. As human beings, we understand the
joy and freedom that comes from play. We also witness animals'
desire for freedom from suffering. Animals fight for survival: their
lives consist of trying to protect themselves from predators; they

move in herds, hide in their shells, or fly off when afraid. When kept in tight cages, mistreated, or about to be slaughtered, animals cry out in pain.

The natural principle that all beings long for happiness and freedom from suffering serves as the basis for generating compassion. The longing that we share with other beings makes empathy possible—it allows us to identify with their pain and their joy. According to the Buddhist view, this natural principle defines positive and negative actions by virtue of how they cause happiness and pain, rather than by morals based on ideas that are remote from our experience. The path of *bodhichitta*—the wish for others' temporal and ultimate happiness—rests upon this fundamental principle.

A CHANGE OF FOCUS

The longing for happiness and freedom from suffering expresses the great natural potential of mind, which can turn us toward our innate positivity and wisdom. Yet we may wonder why, if we have so much longing for happiness, joy is not a consistent experience. We may wonder why we feel like victims of our own minds and emotions so much of the time. Why is it we are never able to completely fulfill or meet this longing, no matter what we do?

This longing remains unfulfilled because we attempt to centralize it—to territorialize it and use it to serve only ourselves. Day in and day out we tend to the self. In countless ways we attempt to use the world to cherish and protect only ourselves: we want to be liked; we want to be loved, to feel cozy, admired, appreciated, embraced, cherished, stimulated, noticed, respected, saved, rescued. When we centralize our longing for happiness, everything that happens around us happens in relation to "me." If something good happens to someone else, it is always in relation to me. If something bad happens to someone else, it always happens in relation to me. Even when we love someone, it is all in relation to me.

If happiness could be achieved through self-cherishing, we would certainly be happy by now. But when everything is in reference to me, we naturally become victims of our own aggression, attachments, and fears. How can we succeed in living our lives according to our preferences in the face of the natural laws of change and unpredictability? Since we truly have so little control in this respect, the only logical result of focusing on me is to feel distraught, fearful, and anxious.

Happiness requires that we change our focus. Changing focus doesn't mean we have to get rid of our mind; we don't need to change the basic makeup of the mind at all. We simply need to honor the fundamental principle by including others in our wish for happiness rather than focusing solely on ourselves. Self-care is always there. When we balance self-care with care for others, we reduce our fears and anxieties. Self-service is always there; all our wants and "unwants" are always there. Expanding our thinking to include others' wants and others' freedoms, we begin to move toward a happiness that is not reliant on the conditions and preferences of self-care.

When we put others in the center, tenderness wells up from within. We feel grateful to others—witnessing their suffering brings us out of the rotten cocoon we sleep in. It makes us a little bit fearless, a little bit accepting, a little bit willing to let go of the constricted sense of self we hold on to. This kind of empathy changes the whole atmosphere of mind. It is the purest form of happiness. The sutras ask, "Where do the buddhas come from?" And the answer in the sutras is, "They come from ego." What does this mean? This means that realization comes from our ability to expand our sense of self-care and longing for happiness to include others. This is the business of a bodhisattva.

Decentralizing Self

The idea of putting others in the center sounds good but, as a practice, may feel contrived. As much as we want to expand our hearts to include others, we can't simply leap into a state of compassion and loving-kindness when, in our attempts at self-preservation, we recoil from the experience of our own pain. True happiness cannot be found through the avoidance of pain. We can't decentralize our longing for happiness when we desperately hold to our own well-being. The tendency to constrict the heart is driven by habit and motivated by fear. It is a deep-rooted and visceral experience. We can feel it in our bodies. It follows us like a shadow.

Shutting out suffering is an extremely dangerous, nondharmic act, because through our aversion, we exclude the full experience of mind. We deny impermanence and attempt to keep things in control; we ignore the truth. In short, we can't relax and let things be. In the act of abandoning the truth through rejection, we separate ourselves from everything around us. In doing so, we don't allow ourselves a bigger, expanded experience that is inclusive of our world and the other beings in it.

Ironically, we shrink from a pain that doesn't actually exist. We speak about the truth of suffering only in that we experience it. But what is suffering, really, when we stop trying to push it away? This kind of questioning needs to be the theme of our lives. We need to take delight in working with our fears. We need to study them and ask ourselves, "What am I so afraid of? Why do I need to protect myself?" We may be afraid to shed our burden because we don't know what will happen. Suffering seems to define our lives. Can we imagine a life without it?

The purpose of all practices on the Buddhist path is to decentralize this notion of a solid, independent self. This does not mean that we stop functioning as individuals, that we forget our names and wander about aimlessly like zombies. It means we stop relating to everything in a way that aims only at preserving or cherishing ourselves. When we begin to question the autonomy of me, the constricted self begins to disperse, which is another way of saying that our ignorance begins to dissolve, and we move toward wisdom. Putting others in the center is a powerful method for decentralizing the self. When the self expands to include others, exclusivity is overwhelmed by compassion in the same way that darkness disperses in sunlight.

The practice of putting others in the center is not simply a crusade to do "good." It is a practice based on the understanding that our own happiness is inextricably linked with the happiness of others. We understand that the longing we all have for happiness and freedom from suffering can be a curse or a blessing depending solely on our focus.

THE HAUNTED DOMINION OF THE MIND

In old Tibet, practitioners went to charnel grounds, springs, haunted houses, haunted trees, and so on in order to reveal how deeply their practice had cut to the core of their fears and attachments. The practice of cutting through our deepest attachments and fears to their core is called *nyensa chodpa,* which means "cutting through the haunted dominion of the mind." It is not that I am encouraging you to go to these haunted places to test yourself, but the view behind nyensa chodpa is important for all practitioners to understand, because until we are challenged, we don't know how deep our practice has gone.

We may be established practitioners. We may be comfortable with our practice and working with our mind; everything could be going smoothly. As my teacher Kyabje Dilgo Khyentse Rinpoche used to say, "Practice is easy when the sun is on your back and your belly is full." But when difficult circumstances arise and we are completely shaken from within, when we hit rock bottom, when something is haunting us and we feel completely vulnerable and exposed to all our neuroses, then it's a different story.

Challenging circumstances expose to us how much we have learned from studying and practicing the buddhadharma and how much we have learned from our meditation practice and the experience of our mind. But we don't need to place ourselves in challenging external circumstances to uncover our hidden fears and attachments. We don't need to wait for our bliss bubble to pop, for a dear one to die, or to find out we have a fatal disease. There is plenty of opportunity to practice nyensa chodpa right here in our own minds. There is plenty of opportunity because there is plenty of self-clinging.

The haunted dominion of mind is the dominion of self-clinging. It is the world of self and all the hopes and fears that come with trying to secure it. Our efforts to secure the self give rise to all the negative emotions. If we were not so concerned with cherishing and providing for the self, there would be no reason for attachment. Aggression, too, would have no reason to arise if there were no self to protect. And jealousy, which shows up whenever we think the self is lacking something, would have no impetus to eat away at our inner peace because we would be content with the natural richness and confidence of our own mind. If we had no need to shield all of the embarrassing things about the self that make us so insecure, we would have no cause for arrogance. Finally, if we were not so fixated on the self, we could rely on our innate intelligence rather than letting our stupidity escort us through the same activities that bring us so much pain time and time again.

So emotions themselves are not the cause of the problem. Yet, until we reach down to the very root of our negative emotions, they will be there, standing in line, waiting to "save" us from our fundamental insecurities. Unless we let go of grasping to the self with all its egotistical scheming, all this trying to figure out how to save the self in the usual manner, we will only continue to enforce a stronger and stronger belief in the solidity of the self. If the aim of practice is to free ourselves from our endless insecurities, then we must cut through self-clinging. Until we do, self-clinging will define our relationships with the world, whether it be the inner world of our own mind or the world outside of us.

From the perspective of the self, the world is either for us or against us. If it is for us, its purpose is to feed our infinite attachments. If it is against us, it is to be rejected and adds to our infinite paranoia. It is either our friend or our enemy, something to lure in or reject. The stronger we cling to a self, the stronger our belief grows in a solid, objective world that exists separate from us. The more we see it as solid and separate, the more the world haunts us: we are haunted by what we want from the world, and we are haunted by our struggle to protect ourselves from it.

THE MOVEMENT OF THE ENTIRE UNIVERSE

The many problems we see in the larger world today, and also encounter in our own personal lives, spring from the belief that the enemy or threat is outside of us. This split occurs when we forget how deeply connected we are to others and the world around us. This is not to say that mind and the phenomenal world are one and that everything we experience is a mere figment of our imaginations. It simply means that what we believe to be a self and what we believe to be other than self are inextricably linked and that, in truth, the self can only exist in relation to other. Seeing them as separate is really the most primitive way of viewing and engaging our lives.

To see the connectedness or interdependence of all things is to see in a big way. It reduces the artificial separation we create between the self and everything else. For instance, when we hold tightly to a self, the natural law of impermanence looms as a threat to our existence. But when we accept that we are part of this natural flow, we begin to see that the entity we cling to as a static, immutable, and independent self is just a continuous stream of experience comprised of thoughts, feelings, forms, and perceptions that change moment to moment. When we accept this, we become part of something much greater—the movement of the entire universe.

What we experience as "my life" results from the interdependent relationship between the outer world—the world of color, shape, sound, smell, taste, and touch—and our awareness. We cannot separate awareness—the knower—from that which is known. Is it possible, for instance, to see without a visual object or to hear without a sound? And how can we isolate the content of our thoughts from the information we receive from our environment, our relationships, and the imprints of our sense perceptions? How can we separate our bodies from the elements that comprise them or the food we eat to keep us alive or the causes and conditions that brought our bodies into existence?

In fact, there is little consistency in what we consider to be self and what we consider to be other. Sometimes we include our emotions as part of the self. Other times our anger or depression seems to haunt or even threaten us. Our thoughts, too, seem to define who we are as individuals, but so often they agitate or excite us as if they existed as other. Generally we identify the body with the self, yet when we fall ill, we often find ourselves saying, "My stomach is bothering me," or "My liver is giving me trouble." If we investigate carefully, we will inevitably conclude that to pinpoint where the self leaves off and the world begins is not really possible. The one thing we can observe is that everything that arises, both what we consider to be the self and what we consider to be other than self, does so through a relationship of interdependence.

The Singular Nature of Emptiness

All phenomena depend upon other in order to arise, express themselves, and fall away. There is nothing that can be found to exist on its own, independent and separate from everything else. That self and other lack clearly defined boundaries does not then mean that we are thrown into a vague state of not knowing who we are and how to relate to the world, or that we lose our discerning intelligence. It simply means that through loosening the clinging we have to our small, constricted notion of self, we begin to relax into the true nature of all phenomena: the nondual state of emptiness that transcends both self and other.

Having gone beyond dualistic mind, we can enjoy the "single unit" of our own profound *dharmakaya* nature (the empty nature of all phenomena). The singularity of emptiness is not single as opposed to many. It is a state beyond one or two, beyond subject and object, and the self and the world outside; it is the singular nature of all things. Upon recognizing the nature of emptiness, our own delusion—the false duality of subject and object—cracks apart and dissolves. This relieves us of the heaviness produced by the subtle, underlying belief that things have a separate or solid nature. At the same time, we apprehend the interconnectedness of everything, and this gives a greater vision to our lives.

CONVICTION

Cultivating a deep conviction in the view of emptiness is what the practice of nyensa chodpa is all about. *Nyensa* refers to that which haunts us; our clinging to the self and all the fears and delusion this produces. *Chodpa* means "to cut through." What is it that cuts through our clinging, fears, and delusion? It is the realization of emptiness, the realization of the truth. When the view of emptiness dawns in our experience, if even only for a moment, self-grasping naturally dissolves. This is when we begin to develop confidence in what is truly possible.

Impressed by the great Tibetan yogi Milarepa's unwavering confidence in the view of emptiness, the Ogress of the Rock, while attempting to haunt and frighten him, made this famous statement, which illustrates the view of nyensa chodpa very well. She said,

> This demon of your own tendencies arises from your mind.
> If you don't recognize the [empty] nature of your mind,
> I'm not going to leave just because you tell me to go. If you
> don't realize that your mind is empty, there are many more
> demons besides myself. But if you recognize the [empty]
> nature of your own mind, adverse circumstances will serve
> only to sustain you, and even I, Ogress of the Rock, will be
> at your bidding.

To understand emptiness conceptually is not enough. We need to understand it through direct experience, so that when we are shaken from the depth of our being, when the whole mechanism of self-clinging is challenged, we can rest in this view with confidence. When challenging circumstances arise, we cannot just conceptually patch things up with the ideas we have about emptiness. Merely thinking "Everything is empty" does little service at such times. It is like walking into a dimly lit room, seeing a rope on the ground, and mistaking it for a snake. We can tell ourselves, "It's a rope, it's a rope, it's a rope," all we want, but unless we turn on the light and see for ourselves, we will never be convinced it is not a snake, and our fear will remain. When we turn on the light, we can see through direct experience that what we mistook as a snake was actually a rope, and our fear lifts. In the same way, when we realize the empty nature of the self and the world around us, we free ourselves from the clinging and fear that comes with it. It is essential that we have conviction based upon experience, no matter how great or small that experience is.

Without this conviction we may run up against a lot of doubts about our meditation practice when difficult circumstances surface. We may wonder why our meditation isn't working. If meditation does not serve us in difficult times, what else can we do to rescue ourselves from the horror and fear we have inside? We think to ourselves, "What about all the years of practice I have done? Was I just fooling myself? Was my practice ever genuine at all?"

In times like these, we need not get discouraged about our ability to practice. Coupled with open-minded questioning, challenging circumstances can help deepen and clarify the purpose of our path because they expose how far our practice has penetrated to the core of self-clinging. Although these experiences often shock or disturb us, they bring our attention to the immediate experience of clinging and the pain it generates, and we begin to think about letting go.

We may have had the experience of letting go of our clinging and resting in the nature of emptiness many times in the past but not yet developed the trust or conviction in that experience. In the moment that our ordinary, confused perceptions collapse, we may feel some certainty. But unless we trust that experience, it will not affect the momentum of our ordinary, confused habits. Quickly we will return to believing in our experience as solid and real. However, if we are able to trust the direct experience of emptiness, we can, through hindsight, bridge that understanding with our present experience. We rely on the recollection of our direct encounter with the view to change the way we ordinarily respond to difficult situations.

On the other hand, even if we do have some conviction, it is not as if, because we have let go once, that's it—we've let go completely, and we will never cling again. Habitual mind is like a scroll of paper: When you first unroll it, it curls back up immediately. You need to continually flatten it out, and eventually it will stay. Reducing the attachment we have in the core of our mind is our constant challenge as practitioners—the true focus of our practice.

As we approach the haunted dominion with less fear, we may actually find some intelligence in the experience of being haunted. Although we continuously try to secure the self, we instinctually know that we cannot. This instinctual knowledge comes from an innate intelligence that sees the dynamic, ungraspable nature of all things. It observes things arise and fall away, both happiness and suffering, and the changes of birth, old age, sickness, and death. When we cling to self and other, our mind feels deeply conflicted and fearful because clinging is at odds with our inner intelligence. Of course, we are not clinging because we want to suffer; we are clinging because we want to avoid suffering. But clinging, by its nature, causes pain. When we let go of grasping and turn toward our innate intelligence, we begin to experience a sense of ease in our minds, and we begin to develop a new relationship with that which ordinarily haunts us.

As practitioners interested in going beyond delusion, we may find ourselves intrigued by the haunted dominion of mind. We may find that rather than trying to avoid pain, we want to move closer to that which haunts us. Emboldened by the experience of emptiness, we can question the solidity or truth of our fears—maybe things don't exist as they appear. In fact, each time we see through the haunted dominion of mind—when we see its illusory or empty nature—we experience the taste of true liberation. This is why the great yogis of the past practiced in haunted places such as charnel grounds. Places that provoke the hidden aspects of mind are full of possibilities for liberation. In this way, the haunted dominion—whether it be a charnel ground or the dominion of fear that results from our own self-clinging—serves as the very ground of our realization.

What Is Truly Possible

We don't need to cling to the self to enjoy life. Life is naturally rich and abundant. There is nothing more liberating and enjoyable than experiencing the world around us without grasping. We do not deprive ourselves of experience if we forsake our attachments. Clinging actually inhibits us from enjoying life to its fullest. We consume ourselves trying to arrange the world according to our preferences rather than delighting in the way our experience naturally unfolds.

We can find so much appreciation of life when we are free of the hopes and fears related to self-clinging; we can appreciate even all the problems we generally try to avoid and that we dread, such as old age, sickness, and death. The ability to appreciate all aspects of our mind really says something about mind's magnificent potential. It shows us that the mind is so much greater than the confusions, fears, and unrest that so often haunt us. It shows us that our personal suffering and the world of suffering outside of us are nothing more than the inner and outer world of our own delusion—samsara.

Nyensa chodpa is cutting through the mind of samsara. What could be more haunted and fearful than samsara? What could be a greater benefit than getting beyond samsara and our own self-grasping? What could be more meaningful than recognizing that samsara—that which has made us so fearful and shaken—is in essence the nondual nature of emptiness itself? If we can do the practice of nyensa chodpa in our own everyday life, it would be a wonderful way to live this life, and the work we do will measure up in the end.

Light Comes Through

When the Buddha attained enlightenment under the Bodhi tree, he found the awakened mind to be so subtle, profound, and beyond all expression that he resolved to simply rest in his realization, thinking no one could possibly understand. Aware of his accomplishment, Brahma and Indra requested the Buddha to teach and share his realization with others. Recognizing this request as an auspicious indication of beings' ability or potential to experience what he himself had discovered, the Buddha spoke to this potential, which he knew resided within all beings.

Our buddha potential, which reveals itself to us in unexpected and poignant ways—in ways we can easily identify—is an indication of who we are in our entirety. It expresses itself in our longing for happiness and freedom from suffering and in our search for meaning. We bump up against it when we know something is just not quite right—for instance, when we try so hard to hold on to permanence in the midst of our constantly changing world. It manifests as the intelligence that investigates ignorance and that knows how to distinguish positive actions from negative ones. It sees the difference between selfishness and compassion, and it exposes itself in the mind's very ability to recognize and feel touched by truthfulness. We may not directly perceive the hidden source of all this expression, and we may not know the causes and conditions that produce suffering or happiness, but the fact that we long for meaning and goodness is light coming through.

A FULLY ILLUMINATED MIND

What is this light that comes through? It is the knowing aspect of the nature of emptiness. On the path, this knowing aspect manifests as our natural intelligence and is basic to everything we experience; in its entirety, it is fully illuminated, unobstructed, pure knowing—buddhahood. But don't misunderstand; it is not a thing. It is timeless and unfindable in its emptiness. The union of pure knowing and *mahashunyata* (great emptiness) is the nature of mind and provides the power for all experience to manifest.

The nature of mind is always in its entirety. It doesn't get brighter, cleaner, or more fascinating than it already is. There is nothing to clear away or purify, there is nothing to add or improve; the nature is complete. It doesn't create phenomena, nor does it destroy them. It is the nature of all things, and its unobstructed openness functions to simply accommodate and know everything that arises.

Because the nature of mind is intrinsic to who we are—because it is always right in front of us—there is no need to pursue enlightenment or reject pain. There is no need to cling to bliss and happiness or to suppress rough, unwanted experiences. These are the activities of confused mind. The essence of all Buddhist practice aims at turning away from confusion and toward our own nature—our own potential. Practice becomes simply bringing the mind back to its source rather than fixing on an external view or fantasy. In this way, buddhahood is nothing more than a completely unobstructed experience of the nature of our own mind. Isn't it amazing we have this potential? It is present in all our experience. We just need to recognize and trust in it.

The Blue Poppy

Kathleen Willis Morton

Buddhist practice is a response to the truth of suffering—both the subtle undercurrent of unease that colors even the most pleasurable moments of our lives, and the great, undeniable sufferings of sickness, old age, and death. Times of tragedy are the true test of spiritual practice—all that comes before is just practice. Here's Kathleen Willis Morton's heartbreaking yet inspiring story of living through life's worst nightmare.

They say there is beauty in this sadness, it's true, a change will come, a change will come to you. You've got your own way of lookin' at life and its perils, got your own way of feelin' its pain, you've got your way of dealing with the trouble in mind, got your own way of knowin' how to stand in the rain. Go on and stand in the rain.
—ELANA ARIAN

Turning the corner from Hoyt Street into the hospital driveway, the rain fell, and I believe it was unusually cold for summer in Oregon. We were going for a routine weekly checkup with my midwife. At the red light just before we turned, the rain beat into a puddle in the middle of the street. The light changed. The car turned. Chris was driving. I turned my head back to that portent puddling-up, unable to take my eyes from it. Maybe I sensed something? Perhaps I wanted to stay in that moment before the turn for the worse when just the rain was falling, before the ultrasound in the midwife's office had registered a faint irregularity of heartbeat a week before my due date, before Liam got born so fast, before we learned that he wouldn't live long, burning like a shooting star through those cool midsummer days.

It was the beginning of the Something Worse summer. Every new bit of information about our baby's condition we learned seemed awful, like the worst news we could get—and then we learned worse news still. I had to learn things that summer I never wanted to know in order to take care of Liam. I also learned things I needed to know and learned that, as awful as things got, I wasn't immune to a pleasant surprise.

To feed him I learned to insert a nasogastric (NG) feeding tube into his nose. I measured it from his cheek to his stomach along his seized-up body and pinched the tube at the point where it touched just below his nose. I fumbled with one hand to plug my ears with the miniature stethoscope—the one the nurse at the neonatal intensive care unit (NICU) gave me when we decided to take our baby home—so I could listen. I didn't let go of the tube. I didn't want to lose the length I'd measured off. I flipped the tube over and began inserting it into Liam's nose and noticed that his nose looked like his father's and that his eyes were sometimes the color of sapphires. Perhaps, if things were right, they'd be blue someday. But nothing was right, there wouldn't be a someday—only that minute and my son's unblinking stare.

I learned to move slowly, to bend with the pressure.

I slowly pushed the small plastic tube into Liam's nose, feeling it hit the back of his nasal cavity. With the tiniest amount of pressure, it bent and continued down his throat. I continued feeding the tube into his nose until my fingers, pinched around the tube, were just under his nostril. Then came the important part. I had to listen to what was inside his body. I connected a large nutritional syringe, the kind that has no needle, to the end of the tube. I unwrapped Liam from the blankets and exposed his tummy. I pressed the pad of the stethoscope to his tummy, just above his navel, and got ready to listen.

I waited for the cars passing and the dogs barking outside to stop, then pushed the plunger on the syringe forcing a bit of air down the tube. I had to make sure I heard a little squeak through the stethoscope. Then I'd know that the tube was in the right place, in his stomach and not in his esophagus or windpipe. I pressed the plunger a couple of cc further and then listened for a couple of more cc if I didn't hear it.

The tiniest, almost imperceptible noise was my assurance that he wouldn't drown in mother's milk. He could've choked. He could have died right then while I was trying to feed him, if I made a mistake. I had to make sure I heard it right. I had to back the plunger up and listen again until I did. But I couldn't do it more than a couple of times, because if I filled his stomach with air, there wouldn't be room for milk, and then he'd have to wait to eat—though he wouldn't cry; he never really did. I only had a couple of shots to get it right, so I listened. I did as best as I could to listen to what was inside of him and get it right, for his sake. I learned that abnormal could feel normal since I'd never known "normal."

Once I knew the tube was placed correctly, I drew 43 cc of milk into the syringe. The doctors said formula was okay. But I pumped and gave him breast milk instead. He may have had an inadequate sucking reflex and an inefficient draw, making him unable to nurse, but at least I could give him that. "Liquid gold," my favorite NICU nurse called it. I attached the end of the syringe to the end of the feeding tube. The inattentive nurse on the night shift—not the favorite one who kept me sane and called the two-foot-by-three-foot Plexiglas box with lights and wires and warmers that held Liam "sacred ground," the other one whose pronunciation I had to correct every time she said Liam's name—she hammered down the plunger, forcing all the milk in at one blast, expanding his stomach with a quick rush of milk; three seconds and the meal was over, and she'd rush out the door of the private room in the NICU they let us sleep in with Liam while we watched over him.

I couldn't feed him like that. It made my milk seem like prescription drugs, a perfunctory chore, rather than the sweet nourishment and the normal ritual it should have been. At home, I propped Liam on my bent legs, leaned back against the hard wall, and made myself cozy on the bed. I raised the syringe above my head with my hand so the milk flowed slowly and gently into Liam's stomach. It took time for all the milk to drain. I was happy to pretend I had all the time in the world. In the meantime, I rocked Liam back and forth on my knees and sang, "You are my sunshine, my only sunshine. You make me happy when skies are gray."

I tried not to think about the copy of the do not resuscitate order that was on the coffee table on the other side of the wall in the living room. "You'll never know, dear, how much I love you. Please don't take my sunshine away."

I tried not to think about what would come next. I had no idea what and when any change would come anyway. He couldn't use an NG tube forever. The next intervention after that would be a direct gastric tube. They would have to cut his stomach and place a plastic tube in with a capped-off end that would stick out like a tire air plug. I kept singing, "The other night, dear, as I lay sleeping, I dreamed I held you in my arms." It may not come to that, the doctors said. But if it didn't, it meant that it had come to something even worse. "When I awoke, dear, I was not with you, and I hung my head and cried."

I learned I had to hold on any way I could, even knowing the end would come soon.

After some time, the last of the milk passed through the syringe into the tube. I watched the white line of the milk drain down. My arm got tired, but I held on anyway, supporting my raised elbow with my other hand when I needed to. The line slipped into his nose; the tube was cleared. I waited a couple of heartbeats more, a verse more, to make sure the milk had passed all the way into his stomach. I removed the syringe, taped off the tube, and taped it to his cheek for the next feeding. I didn't need to change it until the next day. I hoped I'd have to change it the next day, because if I didn't, it meant something even worse had happened; I'd have to do something even worse. Learn to let go.

I learned I had to make decisions I didn't want to make. My father-in-law, Jerry, arrived after flying for three days from St. Petersburg, Russia, to be with us. Chris had sent a fax to his boat, "Come now, please." Jerry was a cardiac-thoracic surgeon and head of surgery for Maine Medical Hospital, but in his transition to retirement, he took a job as a doctor on a Maine Maritime Academy ship sailing to Russia from Maine. He told us about a nurse on board who had a niece or nephew who was born Very Sick too. ("Very Sick" was hospital code for babies who were likely to die. I, unfortunately, learned that and lots of other jargon I'd rather be ignorant of: severe hypoxic ischemic encephalopathy and aortic thrombus.) That baby that the nurse told him about had an NG tube, too, for a while.

"You can make a choice," Jerry said, as we sat in my living room where the late-afternoon sun had begun to fill the room with warmth, and the butter-yellow walls had begun to glow. "People do make that decision in some extreme cases."

I took in his words but couldn't comment on them directly. "I love this glowy time of day," I said, looking down on Liam in my arms. "It's so bright and soft. I like to think of it as a golden hour."

Jerry, I think, sort of chortled and looked down. In my stupid arrogance, I thought he just liked my phrase and was pondering it. Maybe he did tell me "the golden hour" is also medical slang. But I don't think he explained it to me then. It was years later that I learned that in the ER medical community, "the golden hour" is the period of time from the onset of the injury in which, if the right remedy is applied, then the patient is likely to be saved. The physicians had just a short time, only a few chances to get it right.

I could only sit in the afternoon light holding my bright little baby and listen.

When Jerry was getting ready to leave a few days later, I was in the other room changing Liam's diaper. I hurried and brought him out and asked Jerry if he wanted to hold Liam one last time before he left. He took Liam in his arms and cried. I'd never seen Jerry cry. When he was at his car door, he turned back and said, through the wide-open space between us all, "I love you."

The decisions we had to make didn't seem like decisions; they seemed like sentences.

We had decided to sign the do not resuscitate papers a week after we brought Liam home. Chris and Liam and I sat with our hospice nurse in silence for a long time when I laid the paper down on the table after signing it. What else could we do? Hearts breaking are oppressively silent.

The end of Liam's life could come in five days, five minutes, five seconds, without warning. Another week after we signed the DNR papers, we decided to discontinue the NG tube and the seizure medication, which were the only interventions we didn't discontinue when we left the hospital. The doctors said he probably wouldn't live long enough for us to have to make that decision. Discontinuing the feeding tube felt like the most horrible thing we could do.

It was hard to imagine, it still is, that the worst thing we could think of was actually the best thing we could do to help Liam. It was an astonishing occurrence, an anguishing blessing, that Liam lived for almost four more weeks without a feeding tube, unable to nurse, and without medication. It was something that a neonatal nurse with thirty years experience had never seen happen for a baby who was so Very Sick.

I felt literally shattered. Knowing our son could die at any moment, there was an actual physical feeling that all the cells of my body were exploding and flying out from me. Every face and flower and song had more than one meaning; the universe was telling me a story, life had a narrative of its own. Every dream told me a new secret, and I was trying to take it all in to make sense of this catastrophe so utterly awful it was absurd. That obsession with interpreting the signs around me transformed everything I saw from then on; it still does. I guess I was desperate to find meaning and reason in that unreasonable situation; I sought it out and saw meaning and symbolism everywhere, obsessively.

Ordinary things in an average day that summer were different too.

I learned to make do.

I had to make sure I had a blanket with me when I went to the grocery store, not just to keep Liam warm, but because I might need it to cover him up if he died while I was in the store.

I wanted people we knew to meet him but made sure the visits were short. Only a few of our closest friends came to our house for longer than a half-hour. When other people were around, I became more aware of how different Liam's behavior was from a healthy baby's, and it hurt too much to be aware of that for too long and for anyone else to see it.

The cards and flowers that arrived when we got home from the hospital said, "Thinking of you," and offered condolences instead of congratulations for the birth of our son.

Near the end, he'd grown so thin strangers were surprised when I told them how old he was. Sometimes I lied and said yes, he was born premature. Sometimes I didn't have the strength to lie, told them the truth, and felt bad for them when the shock of it registered on their faces.

I learned ordinary days and average things were all impermanent illusions too.

Living a life, I learned, while waiting for death was like living in the space where one breath ends and the other has not yet begun; it was like sleepwalking through my worst nightmare, feeling more awake and acutely aware than I ever had been in my life; it was like drowning in thin air, like standing on a deserted shore in awe of a squall that was pulling back and gathering its force to crush me. I learned I could be, at the same time, overwhelmed with natural great love for my child who was teaching me more than I could have learned in thirty-three lifetimes without him, even though the one I gave him was rushing by quicker than most.

Liam had an equanimous presence, and was astonishingly beautiful, like a Tibetan blue poppy, a sublime and rare blossom once thought to be mythical. I am told still by the handful of people who met him that he compelled them to think in a way they never had and that he still comes to mind, even though it was a short time he was here and it's been a long time he's been gone.

The poppy's petals, an uncommon blue, evoke with its hue the cloudless sky, the vast ocean, or the true nature of the mind that abides in equanimity despite unrelenting waves of illusion and always-changing clouds of desire and attachment. In the center of the poppy's cupped petals are mustard-yellow stamens—a bright, happy contrast to the profound, solemn blue that surrounds them. In the center of that Something Worse summer, there was, despite it all, Liam. And there were some things to learn. It's natural that two aspects of one thing so different in shading, like joy and sorrow, exist side by side, one within the other. And the blue poppy's beauty is undiminished by the true, sad fact that it won't last forever, maybe not very long at all.

When Liam died, I tried to hold on to that new appreciation for accepting all aspects, the light and dark, of any situation, allowing for the joy that was the gift of his presence to take root in my life, instead of the pain and anger that his loss left. To bloom in mid-July, blue poppies require cool temperatures; they need the cold if they're going to flourish. That summer brought a cold reality of existence to life for me; I had to accept the hardship and pain with the beauty and happiness.

To see a gift amid my devastation could not have been a harder thing for me to do. But I wanted to believe it wasn't impossible. I hoped it wasn't an anathema to embrace that gift, as repugnant as it may at first seem to others to see my devastation as a teaching, a source from which to grow, and a chance to change my mind about what it means to be blessed with a rare human birth. A changed mind came to me for having known Liam. The less-awake person I was before passed away. I learned I knew how to stand—grateful—in the rain when he was with me, when I was filled up with sorrow and delight.

Razor-Wire Dharma

Calvin Malone

These days, some of the most powerful Buddhist writing is coming out of American prisons. Maybe it's the intense commitment they need to practice in prison, maybe it's the difficult psychological and moral problems many prisoners have to address. Maybe it's the danger and stress of the environment. Or maybe it's the startling contrast when a little caring and gentleness is brought into such a bad place, as in this sweet story by the prisoner Calvin Malone.

It is hard to like a man who is loud and obnoxious.

Bulldog was not only loud and obnoxious, he was big and strong as well. Few people dared to mess with him, and he knew it. His massive shoulders supported an unbelievably big head haloed by an electrified afro. When he walked toward you, the overall effect was like being in the path of an oncoming train at night without headlights. I'd never actually seen him hurt anyone, but I knew prisoners who were afraid of him and others who avoided him like bad breath.

I made sure to stay far from him as well. Not out of fear, mind you—after all, Bulldog never gave me any reason to fear him. I just don't like to be near loud, aggressive types. For years I had no real reason to associate with him on any level.

Christmas season came (as it does each year), and most inmates were not looking forward to the holiday period. Historically, there are more fights and conflicts in prison during this time than any other time of the year. Emotions run high as prisoners think of Christmases past, of families, and of times around the Christmas tree. In most prisons, there is almost nothing special done during this challenging time. In our case, there is a holiday meal: a regular old meal made "festive" by the addition of cranberry sauce and stuffing.

After the meal, we pass through a line where they give us a paper sack containing an apple, perhaps a tangerine or orange, and a banana. This fruit is bought from vendors who cannot sell the fruit because it is stunted or green or overly ripe and is unacceptable to consumers. Sometimes the sack contains a plastic ziplock bag of hard candy. Those who are inclined can go to a Christmas service at the chapel. Food items can be purchased from the inmate store. If a prisoner has money, a holiday package can be ordered through an outside vendor. These usually consist of meat and cheese. Other than that, there is little that differentiates Christmas from any other day. I believe that loneliness is the one thing that exists in abundance during the holiday season in prison. Good cheer is rare.

I had been shipped to Airway Heights Correction Center from the prison in Walla Walla, Washington, on December 19, 1995. The prison was relatively new, and only a handful of men were living in the unit I had been assigned to. My personal clothes and property were still in transit, and because of the pending holiday, I could not expect to see any of it until sometime in January or February. My inmate account could not be activated for at least two weeks, which meant I was without funds.

All of us spent the holiday time in the nearly empty unit with nothing to do and not even a Christmas card or any other traditional trapping of Christmas to mark this as a special occasion. Since the chapel had not yet been built, there was a service offered for a maximum of 120 men due to capacity limitations. I don't know what the other 1,000 men did for the holidays, but I read a book and tried not to reflect on this, the worst Christmas of my life. I vowed then and there I would not let a Christmas pass in this way again.

The next Christmas, I went to several friends and asked them to help me put on a Christmas party. By then we were all better able to contribute various types of snacks and drinks. Someone in the library where I worked discarded a thick stack of wrapping paper. I brought it back to my cell and found that half was Christmas paper. I gathered whatever I had of value, things like a jar of coffee, candy, and shampoo. These I wrapped up and numbered, later giving a number to each invited guest as they arrived. Using the donated meat and cheese from our Hickory Farms holiday package, we made platters as well as bean dips, homemade honey mustard, and fruit punch. We invited as many men as we could and, if I may say so myself, had a wonderful time. At the end of the party, everyone with a number received a correspondingly numbered, beautifully wrapped gift. Our party was the talk of the prison for a year.

Three weeks before my third Christmas here, Bulldog moved into my unit on the same side as me. It was now impossible to ignore him. He had not changed; he was still loud and aggressive. We also worked at the same industry job. At best, we were associates.

It was the time of year that everyone was gearing up for what was now billed as the "traditional Christmas party." On several occasions, Bulldog mentioned that he had heard about our parties, but I never entertained the thought of inviting him. Days before the party, I invited everyone from the previous year and several more. When I passed Bulldog's cell, something made me stop. I went back and, straight out, invited him to our party. His response was suspicious.

"Why you invite me?" he grunted from his doorway. Hoping to avoid a long conversation, I told him that it was a way for me to practice Buddhism.

"Oh, you're a Booty-hist!?" he laughed.

"Yes, something like that," I replied, as I moved away.

When they heard what I had done, two people decided that they would not attend. Others had serious reservations. I went ahead with the plans and hoped for the best.

By this time, I had invented a recipe for baking a cake using my reading lamp and the ingredients available to me through the inmate store. I blended three miniboxes of Rice Krispies with melted rocky road candy bars and pressed them into a bowl to set. Meanwhile, I melted bars of milk chocolate and added a tablespoon of strong, hot coffee. Once the Rice Krispie mixture set, I turned it out of the bowl upside down and frosted it with the melted chocolate. When that hardened, I pressed the edge of a ruler into the frosting to make indentations representing slices. On the edge of the cake and between each slice, I pressed a coffee cordial. I made a large pile of chocolate shavings from a candy bar and sprinkled these all over the cake. In the center, I pressed in a candied cherry extracted from a chocolate-covered cherry that the inmate store sold during the holidays. The overall effect was impressive and looked, if I may say so myself, as if it had been purchased at a bakery. In addition, with the help of friends, we made a variety of candy clusters and desserts.

Again, we had wrapped gifts, and everyone got something, including Bulldog. It was interesting that all those who attended were dressed in their best "civilian" clothes and made an extra effort to make this a special time for all. Throughout the party, Bulldog was quiet and nice to everyone. He got the most animated when we called out the numbers for the gifts. When he received his, he was like a child at Christmas! Later he told me that he thoroughly enjoyed himself.

Bulldog was moved to another prison after that Christmas party. Three years later, I saw him again. He was being transferred to another facility and was nearing the end of his prison term. When he saw me, he rushed up and gave me a huge hug and flashed an uncharacteristic smile. He shook his head and slapped me roughly on the back—nearly knocking me to the ground. Yelling loud enough for everyone in the next county to hear, he let me know how much that Christmas meant to him and that in all his years in prison that was his best memory. He hugged me again, which almost killed me, and took off, saying as he went that he now knew what Booty-hists were.

"Oh?" I yelled. "What are we?"

"Santa Clauses without the suit!" he shouted, then laughed and walked out of my life.

Regardless of religion or situation, Christmas can be a time of love, understanding, community, and compassion. Seeing Bulldog that last time, I really learned that each of us, no matter how unpleasant we may seem to be, needs a bit of Christmas now and again.

Mindfulness and Compassion: Tools for Transforming Suffering into Joy ⟐

Phillip Moffitt

Buddhism doesn't offer a God or anything else external to solve our spiritual problems for us. What Buddhism does offer is methods—specific, proven ways we can cut through our confusion and suffering and access our inherent wakefulness and goodness. These methods are what we generally call meditation, and the basic meditation practice common to all Buddhist schools—it's what the Buddha himself taught—is mindfulness. Here's an excellent teaching on mindfulness practice and how it can transform our lives by Phillip Moffitt.

The Buddha taught that suffering comes from ignorance. "Ignorance is the one thing with whose abandonment clear knowing arises," he said. By *ignorance,* he meant the misperceptions and delusions that your mind has about its own nature, in short, being ignorant of the Four Noble Truths. Thus, the way to free the mind from suffering is through gaining insight into what truly is. Insight is a profound level of understanding that transcends mere intellectual cognition and can only be known by experiencing it. One of the tools the Buddha taught for gaining insight is *mindfulness,* the ability to be fully aware in the moment.

Mindfulness enables you to go beneath the surface-level, moment-to-moment life experience, which is clouded with emotions, to clearly see the truth of what is happening. The untrained mind is just the opposite of mindfulness. It is often described as "monkey mind," because it is continually distracted by one thought, emotion, or body sensation after another. The monkey mind repeatedly identifies with the surface experience and gets lost in it. The insights that arise through mindfulness release the mind from getting caught in such reactivity and can even stop the cycle from beginning.

An important aspect of practicing mindfulness is *sampajanna,* which translated means "clear comprehension" —the ability to see clearly what needs to be done, what you are capable of doing, and how it relates to the larger truth of life. Obviously it is not easy to be mindful in such a manner, let alone experience the deep insights that lead to full liberation, but you can develop mindfulness through the practice of meditation.

MINDFULNESS IN DAILY LIFE

First let's look at how the insight from mindfulness might manifest in daily life. Suppose someone at work says something that upsets you, and you become angry or defensive and react by saying something you later regret. The incident ruins your day because you can't stop thinking about it. Of course you are aware of your feelings; they have registered in your brain. But this kind of ordinary awareness—simply being conscious of your emotional reaction to an experience—is not what the Buddha meant by mindfulness.

Mindfulness enables you to fully know your experience in each moment. So when your colleague upsets you, if you are being mindful, you witness that her words generate thoughts and body sensations in you that lead to a strong emotion with still more body sensations. You have the insight that these feelings are being created by a chain reaction of thoughts in your mind. While this chain reaction is going on, you acknowledge how miserable it makes you feel. But instead of reacting with harsh words when you feel the impulse to speak unskillfully, you choose not to. Your mindfulness allows you not to identify with the impulses of your strong emotions or act from them. Moreover, because you witnessed the impersonal nature of the experience, you don't get stuck in a bad mood for the rest of the day. It is an unpleasant experience, but you are not imprisoned by it. When you are being mindful, you are aware of each experience in the body and mind, and you stay with that experience, whether it is pleasant or unpleasant, such that you see what causes stress and harm to you or another and what does not.

MINDFULNESS AS A MEDITATION PRACTICE

It truly is possible to experience this wise awareness in your daily life, but you need to train yourself to do so, and mindfulness meditation is the most effective means to accomplish this. Through the practice of mindfulness meditation you develop your innate capacity to:

- collect and unify the mind (at least temporarily),
- direct your attention,
- sustain your attention,
- fully receive experience, no matter how difficult,
- investigate the nature of experience in numerous ways,
- then let go of the experience, no matter how pleasant or unpleasant it may be.

Formal meditation practice involves sitting in a chair or on a cushion in a quiet space with your eyes closed for a period of time and slowly training the mind. You can do so by simply sitting, doing nothing special, and just watching what happens, but the more common approach is to direct the mind by cultivating your power of attention. By being mindful, you train or condition your mind to be more mindful. It is not unlike training the body and mind to play the piano, dance the tango, speak a foreign language, or play a sport. You learn forms in order to train the mind in the same way that a pianist learns scales. You learn what to pay attention to in the same way a dancer learns to feel the music and to be aware of her body and her partner's.

Mindfulness meditation training begins with practicing techniques for concentrating your attention on an object, which enables you to notice how your mind is reacting to what it is experiencing. Concentration is the ability to direct your attention and to sustain it so that it becomes collected and unified. It is a skill everyone already has, but for most people it is limited to only certain specific tasks and is not within their control. When concentration and mindfulness are combined, the power of attention is transformed into a spotlight that illuminates a particular experience in the same way that a theater spotlight holds steady on a single actor until it's time to focus the audience's attention elsewhere. You learn how to direct and sustain your attention on a single experience rather than letting the mind jump from one thought or feeling to another as it usually does. In Pali, the ability to direct attention is called *vitakka,* and the ability to sustain it is called *vicara.* The Buddha referred to these skills as "factors of absorption."

Traditionally, in *vipassana,* or mindfulness, meditation, you use your breath initially as the object of concentration to collect and unify the mind. You typically stay with the experience of the breath as it touches the body in a single spot, such as the tip of the nose as it moves in and out, the rise and fall of the chest, the in-and-out movement of the belly, or the feeling of the breath in the whole body. There are many ways to follow the breath, including counting, noticing its speed, and making mental notes of what is happening, using labels such as *in* and *out,* or *rising* and *falling.* You can also learn to stay with the breath by coupling a word with each breath.

Some teachers insist on a particular method of developing concentration, while others are more flexible.

At first you won't be able to stay with the breath, but soon you will at least be able to be with one or two breaths throughout the complete cycle of inhalation and exhalation. You will also develop the ability to notice when your mind has wandered and to firmly and gently bring it back to the breath.

When your mind starts wandering, the breath becomes your anchor to which you return in order to stabilize and focus your attention. This anchor object is important because meditation is so hard to do. You may get distracted by what's worrying you or by some longing; or you may get bored, sleepy, or restless; or you may start doubting the whole process. Staying with the breath calms the mind, collects your scattered attention, and unifies the mind so that you are able to continue. It is never a mistake or a bad meditation if all you do is work on staying with the breath. Even when you constantly struggle and don't actually spend much time with the breath, it's good practice. By repeatedly returning to the breath, you are learning to just start over. Starting over is a key step in meditation. It expresses your intention to be present, and *the power of your intention is what determines your ability to be mindful in daily life.*

The manner in which you stay with the breath in meditation is called "bare attention"—you simply feel the movement of the breath and the body's response, and notice whether the breath is warm or cool, long or short. You observe the arising of a breath, its duration, and its passing. You might stay with only one of these experiences or a combination of them. In practicing bare attention, you don't judge the breath or think about how you might improve it. You simply register the experience of the breath, without reacting to the experience with mental commentary or physical action.

MOVING BEYOND THE BREATH IN MEDITATION

Once you're somewhat able to stay present with the breath, you start to open your field of attention to ever-more-subtle objects of experience that arise in the mind. This process continues until you are able to respond to all of your experiences as opportunities for mindfulness. In order to meditate in this manner, the Buddha taught what are often called the Four Foundations of Mindfulness, in which you systematically learn how to pay attention to and investigate what arises in your mind, whether the experience comes from one of your five body senses or from the mind generating thought. The four modes of investigation he prescribed are:

- knowing how any experience feels in the body (First Foundation),

- noting the pleasant, unpleasant, or neutral-feeling tone that accompanies every moment's experience (Second Foundation),

- witnessing your mental state and your emotions in the moment (Third Foundation), and finally,

- opening to the impersonal truth of life that is revealed in this moment (Fourth Foundation).

These Four Foundations of Mindfulness and all the practices associated with them are described in depth in the Buddha's *Satipatthana Sutta*. By building your awareness utilizing these four foundations, you gradually develop clear seeing (sampajanna), the ability to be mindful in the present moment. In so doing, you begin to have insight about what is true and how to respond skillfully in any situation.

When you are just beginning this practice, you serially investigate all Four Foundations of Mindfulness. For instance, if the mind is pulled away from the breath by a strong body sensation, then you temporarily abandon the breath as an object and let that body sensation become the object of your attention. When the mind gets tired of staying with the body and starts to move to other objects, return to the breath. At this stage of practice, you do not investigate your emotions or your mind states, only body sensations. The challenge is to sustain your attention on a particular body sensation in such a way that you can feel it. Is it a pulsation or a wave? Is it expanding or contracting? If it's painful, what kind of pain is it? Does it twist, stab, burn, pinch, and so forth? If it's pleasant, is it sweet, warm, tingly? In the First Foundation of Mindfulness, the attention is to be focused on the body from within the body, meaning that you are not training your mind to be a distant, indifferent observer of your body; rather, you are being with your aching back. This same method of keeping attention within the experience is used for all four Foundations of Mindfulness.

The Buddha started vipassana practice with mindfulness of the body because, for most people, it is far easier to stay present with the body than with the mind and because the body participates in all other experiences you have in ordinary consciousness. He said, "If the body is not mastered [by meditation], then the mind cannot be mastered; if the body is mastered, mind is mastered." He went on to say, "There is one thing, monks, that cultivated and regularly practiced, leads to a deep sense of urgency . . . to the Supreme Peace . . . to mindfulness and clear comprehension . . . to the attainment of right vision and knowledge . . . to happiness here and now . . . to realizing deliverance by wisdom and the fruition of Holiness: it is mindfulness of the body." Many experienced students of meditation tend to skip over the body and focus on the emotions and the mind states, thinking they are getting to the really juicy part of practice, but as the Buddha's quote indicates, this is a significant misapprehension. I encourage you to develop an almost continual awareness of your ever-changing bodily experience. I have found that cultivating this body awareness is the surest way for most students to start to impact their daily life with their mindfulness practice. Therefore, as you move from the First Foundation of Mindfulness of the Body to the Second Foundation, remember that through the practice, you use the breath as an anchor to collect and unify the mind, while expanding your mindfulness to an ever-greater range of experience.

After you develop mindfulness of the changing nature of body experience, you are ready to work with the Second Foundation— the feeling tone of your experience. You start to include the pleasant, unpleasant, or neutral flavor contained in each moment of body sensation in your field of attention. You don't try to control these sensations but simply to know them. For instance, you notice how pleasant the warm sun feels on your face on winter mornings or how an aching leg feels unpleasant from within the experience. When body sensations are neither pleasant nor unpleasant, they are neutral. Ordinarily you don't notice the neutral sensations, but with mindfulness they become part of your awareness and expand your experience of being alive. Developing awareness of pleasant, unpleasant, and neutral sensations and how they condition the mind is a critical factor in finding peace and well-being in your life.

After you have worked with body sensations, you are ready to work with the Third Foundation, mental events (your emotions, mental processes, and mind states), in your meditation. At first just take emotions as a field for investigation. Notice when your mind is pulled away from the breath by an emotion. What is the nature of the emotion? How do you feel it in the body? In my experience, all emotions are accompanied by body sensations. What is an emotion, really, when you deconstruct it? Is it not an internal image, or words, or a pleasant or unpleasant feeling accompanied by many coarse or subtle sensations? I'm not referring to what caused the emotion, which is a combination of perception, belief, intent, and response, but rather to what happens when the mind registers an emotion. Does the mind keep feeling the emotion, or does it arise and pass like a body sensation? Remember to continue to use your anchor object so that you don't get lost in your emotions.

Many times you will discover that you do not know what emotion you are feeling or that there is more than one emotion competing for attention. In these instances, just be aware of emotions; do not try to name them. Likewise, sometimes you can't name a body sensation, so it only feels like numbness; numbness then *is* the body sensation. Don't insist on specificity; just be aware that there is a body.

Now you are ready to examine your mental processes. You will quickly notice that the mind is almost always thinking and that much of this thinking is based on the past or future in the form of remembering, planning, fantasizing, and rehearsing. Observe each of these. Are they pleasant or unpleasant? What happens to them as you turn your attention on them? Do they stop or intensify? Or do you get lost in them and lose your mindfulness? What underlies your constant planning? Is it anxiety? When you bring up a fear or a worry over and over again, is it really unpleasant or does it induce a kind of reassurance? What happens if you stop? Is the constant worrying really a false reassurance? Does it actually induce a habit of anxiety? Remember to feel your mental processes from within them—the fuzziness and excitement of fantasy, the heaviness of worry and fretting, and the speed of planning. Notice what it is and how it then changes.

Finally, you are ready to experience the Buddha's insights as they manifest in your life—the life you have been examining until now, which includes your body sensations, emotions, mind states, and mental processes, and the pleasantness and unpleasantness that accompanies each of them. With the Fourth Foundation of Mindfulness, you see how each moment constantly changes and that most of what you take personally is actually impersonal and is not about you. For instance, in our earlier example, the person at the office who upset you was not really focused on you, but was reacting to her own inner turmoil, and you just happened to receive the eruption. You also notice which mind states lead to suffering and which don't, and you begin to live more wisely.

IMMEDIATE AND LONG-TERM BENEFITS OF MINDFULNESS MEDITATION

Being present or awake empowers your life. It gives you a presence that you feel and others can feel, and it opens you to the experience of being fully alive. Many people complain that something is missing in their lives, or they have some vague sense of incompleteness, dissatisfaction, or unease with life. As you wake up, such emotions start to diminish and lose their hold on you. You also begin to realize you have more choice in how you react to whatever arises, and you discover that it is genuinely possible to dance with life.

Mindfulness meditation strengthens the mind so that you can more easily be with difficult emotions or uncomfortable physical sensations that cause your mind to abandon the present moment. Mindfulness also strengthens the nervous system such that physical and mental pains don't have the same degree of "hurt," because the mind isn't contracting in anticipation of more pain in the future. For the first few years of practice, you are literally reprogramming your nervous system to free it from habitual reactivity. This alone will bring much ease and flexibility to your mind.

The most life-changing benefits of mindfulness meditation are the insights, which arise spontaneously the way a ripened apple falls from the tree of its own accord. Insight is what changes your life. Through insight you realize what brings well-being to yourself and others, as well as what brings stress, discomfort, and dissatisfaction into your life. Such insights can be small or quite dramatic. Moreover, they have a cumulative effect such that previous insights become building blocks for still more insights.

Each insight is a direct knowing, or "intuitive knowing," of the truth of your experience as contrasted with the conceptual perception that comes from your usual way of thinking. This direct knowing is what enables mindfulness meditation to have such an impact in your life—you feel the truth of your experience instead of conceptualizing it, reacting to it, or being lost in the past or the future.

During meditation, you will most often have personal insights about your life and how it has been conditioned. Such insights help you grow and understand yourself better, leading to a fuller life. For this reason, many psychotherapists teach their clients a simple form of mindfulness practice.

Less frequent, but having far greater impact when they arise, are the insights about the nature of life itself. These are universal insights about the ever-changing and impersonal nature of your life experiences. These universal insights are what constitute the Buddha's teachings of *dhamma* (in Pali) or *dharma* (in Sanskrit), which is often translated as "truth." For example, mindfulness meditation helps you realize the impersonal nature of difficult experiences, that they are just part of life. This is known as *anatta,* or "not-self," the realization that much of what you previously identified as "you" is actually "neither me nor mine." Therefore you do not take defeat or loss as personal failures, and you are much less reactive to them. You also become aware of *anicca,* the rapid and endlessly changing nature of all things in life. Not-self and the constancy of change are basic characteristics of life, but the truth of them, in the sense of being life altering, can only be known through direct insight, which comes from mindfulness.

Living in the Sacred Now

Another major benefit of mindfulness meditation practice is that it brings you into what is sometimes called the "sacred now." This is a state of being fully present such that you are both "in time" and "not in time." Mystics in most contemplative traditions throughout the ages have extolled this as an exalted state but have seldom given instructions for how to achieve it. What most people discover once they start meditating is that they ordinarily spend much of their time not in the present, but lost in thoughts about the past and the future, whether planning, daydreaming, anticipating, remembering, or just spacing out. Your life isn't in the past or the future, because in this moment you are not there to live it; both are just mental constructs based on the mind's ability to remember, conceptualize, and imagine. When you are stuck in either past or future thinking, you create suffering for yourself and miss much of the actual experience of the gift of having embodied consciousness. For instance, you go for a hike and see a beautiful sunset. At first you feel really alive and fully present as you watch the sky change colors, but then your mind starts judging and planning. You say to yourself, "I don't do this enough. I'm too lazy, I've got to be more disciplined and take time for myself. Now, if I would just do this once a month.

I remember taking this hike a year ago and saying I would do this more. I really need to . . ." On and on the mind goes. Meanwhile, you're not actually experiencing the beauty that initially enthralled you. You have lost this moment to pointless judging, reminiscing, and fantasizing.

As shocking as it may be to realize, you spend most of your time some distance removed from what is actually happening in the present moment. You are lost in past associations or future planning, or caught in judging yourself or another. Or you've split from the experience and distanced yourself by conceptualizing it, constantly moving your attention, or daydreaming. This is true for body sensations, whether they're pleasant or unpleasant, as well as all the other senses and your thoughts themselves. Most of the time you do not stay with the music or even the friend you are listening to; you don't even stay present for your own thoughts and certainly not your emotions. By developing mindfulness, however, you gain the power to be more fully present for your life and to have keen insight about it.

It is not that evaluating, planning, and remembering are un-skillful activities—they are useful and are all part of a rich experience of life—but you obsess or get lost in them at the expense of being present for your own life. Mindfulness meditation establishes this capacity for being present. It retrains the mind and breaks it of its old, unskillful habit of tuning out.

T. S. Eliot describes the power of being present in the sacred now in this manner in *Four Quartets*:

You can receive this:
"On whatever sphere of being
The mind of a man may be intent
At the time of death"—that is the one action
(And the time of death is every moment)
Which shall fructify in the lives of others:
And do not think of the fruit of action.

Eliot is saying that there is only *this* moment in your life, and each moment is a death and rebirth. You only exist as a string of moments, and you are new and different in each moment. It is only when you are present in a moment that you are capable of affecting your life or another's. You fail to notice this truth because life is constantly changing and because of the power of memory and association.

When Eliot cautions not to think of the fruit of your actions, he is echoing the Buddha's teaching of nonattachment. To be nonattached is to care and to not care simultaneously, which can only be realized as an insight, not as a concept. Through meditation practice, you slowly come to understand this paradoxical wisdom, which is the way to dance with life.

What Is This? ﹚﹚

Martine Batchelor

All Buddhist meditation combines two elements: concentration and insight.
In the Zen tradition, the object of concentration can be a question, story,
or paradox, known as a koan, and the insight may come in a flash, when
the koan is "answered" by a sudden transcendence of conventional mind.
In thinking about life, we've all wondered, "What is this?" and Martine
Batchelor teaches us how to take this as our koan.

In sixth-century China, the Buddhist schools were quite scholastic
and focused on the scriptures. To move away from this academic
direction and toward the Buddha's original teaching of practicing
meditation and realizing awakening in this very life, the Zen school
developed its koan practice, in which stories of monks' awakenings
became a starting point for meditative inquiry. By asking and focusing on a single question as a meditative method, Zen practitioners
aimed to develop a rich, experiential wisdom.

In the Korean Zen tradition, one generally meditates on the
koan "What is this?" This question derives from an encounter between the Sixth Patriarch, Huineng (638–713 C.E.), and a young
monk, Huaijang, who became one of his foremost disciples:

> Huaijang entered the room and bowed to Huineng. Hui-
> neng asked, "Where do you come from?"

"I came from Mount Sung," replied Huaijang.

"What is this, and how did it get here?" demanded Hui-neng.

Huaijang could not answer and remained speechless. He practiced for many years until he understood. He went to see Huineng to tell him about his breakthrough.

Huineng asked, "What is this?"

Huaijang replied, "To say it is like something is not to the point. But still it can be cultivated."

The whole story is considered the koan, and the question itself, "What is this?" is the central point—*hwadu* in Korean, or *huatouin* in Chinese. The practice is very simple. Whether you are walking, standing, sitting, or lying down, you ask repeatedly, "What is this? What is this?" You have to be careful not to slip into intellectual inquiry, for you are not looking for an intellectual answer. You are turning the light of inquiry back onto yourself and your whole experience in this moment. You are not asking, "What is this thought, sound, sensation, or external object?" If you need to put it in a meaningful context, you are asking, "What is it that is hearing, feeling, thinking?" You are not asking, "What is the taste of the tea or the tea itself?" You are asking, "What is it that tastes the tea? What is it before you even taste the tea?"

My own teacher, Master Kusan (1909–1983), used to try to help us by pointing out that the answer to the question was not an object, because you could not describe it as long or short, this or that color. It was not empty space either, because empty space cannot speak. It was not the Buddha, because you have not yet awakened to your buddhanature. It was not the master of the body, the source of consciousness, or any other designation, because those are mere words and not the actual experience of it. So you are left with questioning. You ask, "What is this?" because you do not know.

We are not speculating with our mind. We are trying to become one with the question. The most important part of the question is not the meaning of the words themselves but the question mark. We are asking unconditionally, "What is this?" without looking for an answer, without expecting an answer. We are questioning for questioning's own sake. This is a practice of questioning, not of answering. We are trying to develop a sensation of openness, of wonderment. As we throw out the question "What is this?" we are opening ourselves to the moment. There is no place we can rest. We are letting go of our need for knowledge and security, and our body and mind themselves become a question.

You are giving yourself over entirely to the question. It's like diving into a pool: the whole body is engaged in the act, and the whole body and mind are refreshed. You are trying to develop a sensation of questioning and an inquiry that brings about the sense of bewilderment you feel when you have lost something. You are going somewhere; you put your hand in your pocket to grab your car keys. They are not there. You check this corner and that corner of the pocket again and again, and there is nothing. For a moment before you try to remember where you've left them, you are totally perplexed; you have no idea what might have happened. This is very similar to the sensation you are trying to develop in Zen questioning.

Concentration and inquiry are brought together with this technique. Concentration is developed as you come back again and again to the words of the question, back to the present moment. The question is the anchor of your meditation, the fixed point. By cultivating concentration, you allow for a certain calmness and spaciousness to develop. The process of inquiry is vivid, because you are not repeating the words like a mantra—the words themselves are not sacred, nor do they have a special resonance. They are just the diving board from which you dive into the pool of questioning. By repeatedly questioning with the energy and interest of someone who has just discovered she has lost something, you evoke a brightness in your whole being. This questioning gives you energy, because there is no place to rest, and it allows for more possibilities and less certainty. It is a kind of wonderment similar to a young child's when he discovers and marvels at the world around him—very immediate, not lost in the future or in the past. This practice is just being with the moment and looking deeply, asking, "What is this?" and being open to this as it happens to be.

If you meditate in this way, your mind will become more flexible, and you will start to see that actually you have more choices in your actions and behavior than you thought possible. This seeing will allow you to respond creatively to thoughts by knowing what you are thinking and realizing when you come into contact with a new thought. Normally, a thought emerges so fast that you are not even aware of its arising. You just think it and act impulsively or habitually. When you meditate, sitting quietly, trying to focus on the question "What is this?" you start to notice what takes you away from your focus. Generally it is a thought of one kind or another. The meditation is intended not to stop you from thinking but to help you discover what and how you think.

There are different practical ways to meditate with this method. The easiest way is to ask the question in combination with the breath. You breathe in, and as you breathe out, you ask, "What is this?" Master Kusan used to suggest asking the question by making it like a circle. You start with "What is this?" and as soon as you end one question, you start another "What is this?" Another way is to just ask the question once and remain for a while with the sensation of questioning. As soon as it fades away, you ask it once more, staying with the pregnant sense of questioning until it dissipates again. You have to be very careful not to ask the question with too tight a mental focus. Usually it is recommended that you ask the question as if it were coming from the belly or even the toes. You need to bring the energy down and not tighten it like a knot in the mind. If the question makes you feel agitated, speculative, or confused, just come back to a simple and calming breath practice for a while before returning to the question.

Keep in mind that you are not trying to force yourself to find an answer. You are giving yourself wholeheartedly to the act of questioning. The answer is in the questioning itself. It is like a child who has never seen snow. You tell him it is white and cold. He thinks it is like a piece of white paper in the fridge. You take him near a mountain and show him the top. He says that it looks like coconut ice cream. It is only when he touches the snow, feels it, plays with it, and tastes it that he really knows what snow is. It is the same with the question, and the tasting is in the questioning itself. Master Kusan was reputed to have had three awakenings—break-throughs in understanding confirmed by his teacher—and still he continued to ask the question. A Western monk asked him why he continued questioning. After three awakenings, surely he must have found the answer. Master Kusan told him it did not work that way. As you meditated with this question, the practice developed in its own way and slowly evolved. So of course we asked him how he did the questioning at that point. He would not answer. He said that we had to find this out by ourselves. Any descriptions of his would give us misconceptions.

The most important part of the practice is for the question to remain alive and for your whole body and mind to become a ques-tion. In Zen they say that you have to ask with the pores of your skin and the marrow of your bones. A Zen saying points out: Great ques-tioning, great awakening; little questioning, little awakening; no questioning, no awakening.

Guided Meditation: What Is This?

- Sit in a quiet and secluded place. Keep your back straight. Remain poised, at ease, and attentive. With your eyes half-closed, gently gaze in front of you.

- With the first few breaths, connect the question to the out-breath. As you breathe out, ask, "What is this?"

- You are not repeating the question like a mantra; you are cultivating a sensation of perplexity, asking unconditionally, "What is this?"

- This is not an intellectual inquiry. You are not trying to solve this question with speculation or logic.

- Do not keep the question in your head. Try to ask it from your belly.

- With the whole of your being, you are asking, "What is this? What is this?"

- The answer is not found in the Buddha, or in a thing, or in empty space, or a designation.

- You are asking, "What is this?" because you do not know.

- If you become distracted, come back to the question again and again.

- The question "What is this?" is an antidote to distracted thoughts. It is as sharp as a sword. Nothing can remain on the tip of its sharp blade.

- By asking this question deeply, you are opening yourself to the whole of your experience with a deep sense of wonderment and awe.

- When the session is finished, move your shoulder, back, and legs, and gently get up with a fresh and quiet awareness.

Koans for Troubled Times))

Joan Sutherland

Because reality is ultimately beyond concept, rationality is a necessary but not sufficient means to understand it. All our quandaries—including social, political, and economic problems—are ultimately koans because they can't be fully understood by the rational mind. The American Zen teacher Joan Sutherland says the Buddhist masters of ancient China searched for new ways to deal with difficult times, just as we are searching today.

Several years ago, in the face of a creeping despair about the state of the world, I began to reread my favorite twentieth-century Russian and Eastern European writers. Those folks knew how to keep small embers alive in a fierce wind: Anna Akhmatova, who turned love into a revolutionary act, and Adam Zagajewski, reassuring us that the good always returns, though at the maddening pace of an old gent on a bicycle, the day *after* the catastrophe.

People are worried, and we're looking for ways to climb onto our bicycles and pedal out to see what we might do to help. Recently, I've been exploring what my own Zen koan tradition has to say about unending conflict, environmental disaster, the starvation of millions, and the small figure in the corner of the painting, tipping her head back to take it all in.

It turns out that the koan tradition was born at a similarly urgent moment in Chinese history. Twelve hundred years ago, a few Chan (Japanese: Zen) innovators had a fierce desire to leap out of the usual ways of doing things and into new territory—not to escape the catastrophe looming around them, but to meet it more fully. If they were going to be helpful, they had to develop—and quickly—flexibility of mind, an easy relationship with the unknown, and a robust willingness to engage with life as they found it. Perhaps most importantly, they needed a really big view. For them, Chan practice wasn't about getting free of the world; it was about being free in the world. The first koans are field notes from their experiment in the getting of this kind of freedom.

In the eighth century, Chinese culture was flourishing. It was an age of art and philosophy, prosperity and trade. At the same time, the strains of empire were beginning to show. A huge country with an imperial foreign policy has a long border to defend; the constant warfare took a lot of money to pay for and many soldiers to fight. The people were being taxed into poverty, and able-bodied men were on the borders making war rather than on the farms making food. Authority outside the capital began to break down, and life was growing harsher and more capricious.

Eventually the Tang government had to bring in mercenary armies from as far away as Asia Minor. For a while, it worked just well enough: the mercenaries would come in and crush the latest incursion or rebellion, the government would pay them for their services, and they would head back home. But at midcentury this precarious status quo crumbled when one of the foreign armies refused to leave. They set up a rebel stronghold in the ancient capital of Changan, the City of Everlasting Peace.

This An Lushan Rebellion ushered in a decade of civil war, famine, and disease so devastating that two out of three Chinese died. *Two out of three.* And it happened in the blink of an eye. China went from being one of the greatest empires the world had ever seen to a nation devastated by conflict and starvation, and its population had shrunk by two-thirds in about ten years. A kind of order was eventually restored, but it would be centuries before the country fully recovered.

The great poet Du Fu was trapped in Changan during the An Lushan Rebellion, and he wrote a poem about it called "The View This Spring." The poem contains two spare lines that sum it all up:

The nation is destroyed,
mountains and rivers remain.

Some Chan practitioners saw what Du Fu saw, from their own perspective: In our world things are always getting broken and mended and broken again, and there is also something that never breaks. Everything rises and falls, and yet in exactly the same moment things are eternal and go nowhere at all. How do we see with a kind of binocular vision, one eye aware of how things are coming and going all the time, the other aware of how they've never moved at all? How do we experience this not as two separate ways of seeing, but as one seamless field of vision?

Mazu (Ma) Daoyi and Shitou Xiqian, who became Chan teachers around the time of the An Lushan Rebellion, pushed these questions further. They asked, "What does it mean for each of us to be wholeheartedly part of this world? How do we fall willingly into the frightened, blasted, beautiful, tender world, just as it is?" Because, as Peter Hershock formulates it in his wonderful study, *Chan Buddhism*, "It's not enough to see what buddhanature is; you have to realize what buddhanature does."

Perhaps it's significant that these two creative geniuses came from the margins of Chinese society; in unprecedented times, no one is an expert yet, and anyone might become one. Both lived long lives that spanned the eighth century, and both had connections to Huineng, the sixth Chinese ancestor; from Ma's heirs came the Linji (Japanese: Rinzai) school, while some of Shitou's descendants formed the Caodong (Japanese: Soto) line. They never met but had great respect for each other; in their day it was said that you didn't really know Chan until you had studied with both of them. They had a sometimes spooky connection that had unsettling effects on the students who passed between them. Here's a typical story: Once a monk went to see Shitou. The monk had carefully prepared for all the challenges he could anticipate, but Shitou caught him off guard by crying, "Alas! Alas!" as soon as he saw him. Unable to respond, the monk consulted Ma, who slyly suggested that the next time Shitou cried, "Alas! Alas!" the monk should puff twice. The monk went back to see Shitou, but before he could say anything, Shitou puffed twice.

In middle age, Shitou settled down on South Mountain in Hunan province. At first he built a meditation hut on top of a large, flat rock, which is where he got his name—Shitou, or Stone Head. When the Buddhist temple next door invited him to live there, he refused, preferring the independent life of a mountain recluse. "Better to drown at the bottom of the sea for eternity than to seek liberation by following the wise," he once remarked.

Shitou might have been a hermit, but he was a hermit in a lively neighborhood. South Mountain was one of the Five Holy Mountains of Chinese Buddhism and also the home of Taoist temples and a Confucian academy. Hundreds of recluses lived and practiced in the area, and Shitou also attracted many students over the years. Open-minded and curious, he was deeply influenced by Taoism and Huayan Buddhism, and the An Lushan Rebellion apparently only deepened his conviction that sectarianism causes nothing but suffering. He had seen where grand schemes and big ambitions could lead, and while differences between people were natural, he taught that when we start attaching values to the differences, we open the door to heartache. "In the Way, there are no Northern or Southern ancestors," he said; there are only ancestors common to us all. No red states and blue states, he would say today, just Kansas and California and Georgia, in all their complexity.

Mazu Daoyi was born in the far west of China near the border with Tibet, the son of the town garbageman. He began studying

Chan when he was still young, and his studies eventually brought him to central China. For more than twenty years, during the time of the An Lushan Rebellion and its aftermath, Ma walked from one temple to another through the devastated countryside. Eventually he settled down in Jiangxi province, and his monastery became the great Chan training center of the age. Chan teachers usually take their name from the place they live and teach; Ma is the only one who is known by his family surname (Ma) and an honorific usually translated as "Great Master" (Zu).

Ma's teaching style was direct, uncompromising, and often physical. It was clearly influenced by what he saw on his long walk through a devastated land. In those days, people came to the monasteries for a lot of reasons, from spiritual turmoil to the promise of steady food. But anyone who was looking for escape at Ma's monastery was in for a shock. When he was once asked about the essence of his school, he replied, "Oh, it's just the place where you let go of your body and your life." That was quite a statement during a time when everyone knew people who had lost both. From Ma's perspective, the situation was so urgent, and the need was so great, that there wasn't time for people to despair or lack confidence or run away. It was as if he were saying, "We need you to get clear *right now* about your own nature and the nature of life, so that you can roll up your sleeves and start doing something about it."

Shitou and his descendants tended to emphasize reconciliation and the restoration of peace and stability in times of chaos. Ma's line valued Chan's independence from the mainstream, which allowed it to offer both a critique of the status quo and an alternative to it. Neither thought he had the one true way or tried to impose his view on the other. Ma and Shitou had different temperaments and ways of teaching, but they shared something fundamental: both were deeply affected by the sorrows of their age, and as a result, both were determined to reimagine what Chan Buddhism was for.

Until then, Chan was largely an introspective meditation practice; you looked inward to find your true self. Huineng, for example, described meditation as "clearly seeing your original nature inside yourself." Shitou and Ma raised the eyes of Chan to the horizon. In Shitou's words, "What meets the eye is the Way." This true self you are looking for, they said, is not just here, in your own heart/mind, but everywhere. Everything you see is buddhanature; everything shines with that light. Everything you see is you—and this at a time when what you saw included blighted fields, refugees starving by the roadside, deserted towns, parents mourning their children killed in the wars. There's something moving about the large and generous spirit of these two men who responded to the devastation around them by saying, "This is all me, this is all you." They showed that the way to come to terms with life's pains is not by turning away from them, but by moving deeper into life and encouraging as many others as possible to join you. They embraced the great matter of their time: what do we do now, we one in three who survive?

Before Ma and Shitou, formal Chan teaching had consisted largely of lectures given to groups of students. The heart of Shitou's and particularly Ma's teaching was something new: an intimate meeting of two people, either alone or in front of a group. Awakening, they saw, happens in relationship. We meditate together and talk together. We hear birds calling and cars laboring up a hill. We tend a feverish child and recite the words of the ancestors. As Ma and Shitou did with each other, we find a deep communion with someone we've never met.

We spend a lot of time in the company of our thoughts and feelings, and sometimes we are a companion to silence. Even a hermit sits in a web of connections with things visible and invisible. Our meditation is made not just of the vastness and the deep engine of concentration; it is also made of these relationships. And then one day, for no apparent reason, something in particular comes to fetch us: the cook coughs or the morning star rises, and we fall open. A particular intimate meeting with a particular other opens us to an intimate relationship with life itself.

Practice is about making us fetchable. It helps us to recognize what gets in the way of our being fetched, and then it gives us a method to deconstruct the obstacle. Most people find this difficult to do on their own, and for Ma and Shitou, that's where the power of intimate meetings comes in.

The earliest koans are records of Ma's encounters with his students—encounters that could be mild, probing, or literally upending, but are never about winning an argument or making someone feel stupid. Over and over again—tirelessly, relentlessly—they are an invitation to freedom. In a time of crisis, talking about freedom or even modeling a free life wasn't enough; these intimate meetings allowed people to experience freedom for themselves.

When Shitou was helping his questioners recognize and dismantle what stood between them and freedom, he tended to ring variations on "Are you sure about that?" His method was to take nothing for granted and to question everything, especially someone's most cherished beliefs.

"What about liberation?" asked a monk.

"Who binds you?" countered Shitou.

"What about the Pure Land?"

"Who corrupts you?"

"What about nirvana?"

"Who keeps you in the cycle of birth and death?"

Ma, on the other hand, startled people out of their habitual thoughts and into another territory entirely, where the thoughts just didn't exist anymore—the method of a high-risk demolitions expert, compared to Shitou's plank-by-plank approach. Once, when a questioner named Shuiliao asked Ma the meaning of Chan, Ma kicked him in the chest, knocking him down. This awakened Shuiliao, and he stood up grinning and clapping. Later he said, "Since the day Ma kicked me, I haven't stopped laughing."

Neither Ma nor Shitou allowed his questioners to remain for a moment in the position of someone who doesn't get it. But they weren't interested in replacing that position with a better one: "I didn't used to get it, but now I do." Their project was more radical: "What's it like to have no position at all?" Shitou would challenge his questioner's self-doubt, which is often the unacknowledged basis of a position.

Someone asked Shitou, "What am I supposed to do?"

"Why are you asking me?"

"Where else can I find what I'm looking for?"

"Are you sure you lost it?"

Shitou's responses aren't dismissals; he really means what he's asking. "Why do you assume that you need to ask me, and what's it like when you do? What is your deepest longing, and what if you realized that you already have what you long for?"

In a similar way, Ma would challenge the assumption that if you don't understand something, that's a problem to be fixed. Someone once told Ma that he didn't understand one of Ma's famous sayings, that mind is Buddha. Ma replied, "The mind that doesn't understand is exactly it. There's nothing else."

When we think there's something wrong with not getting it, when the mind makes up commentaries about what it means not to get it— well, that's mind being Buddha, but it's usually hard to see it. To be wholehearteedly unsure, to sincerely take up a question like "What does it mean that mind is Buddha, I wonder?" without veering off into commentary—that, Ma found, was a much more direct way for people to experience for themselves the mind that is Buddha.

But even that was sometimes too much chitchat for Ma's taste. When someone froze because they didn't know how to respond to his question, or tried to present the answer they thought displayed their accomplishment or would please him, Ma was likely to hit or kick or brusquely send them away. He'd put his hand over someone's mouth just as they were about to speak. He tweaked noses and shouted so loud it deafened people for days. This style of teaching later became a menace and a cliché, but originally it arose from the urgency of the times.

Ma knew the power of our habits of bondage, and he also knew the power of being free of them, if only for a moment. He pulled the rug out with the hope of surprising us into free fall. The art critic Peter Schjeldahl, in his *Notes on Beauty*, described the encounter with beauty in a way that Ma would entirely recognize: Beauty stops you in your tracks, so that it's suddenly impossible to continue in the direction that a moment before seemed inevitable. Something pleasurable or attractive (like replacing old, flawed positions with new and improved ones) enhances the feelings you already have ("Now I've got it"). On the other hand, genuine beauty, like suddenly having no position at all, stops the flow of your feelings ("Nothing I thought applies anymore"), and when they resume they're moving in a different direction entirely.

Behind the shock tactics, Ma's perspective was deeply optimistic and encouraging. Right here and right now, he invited, find your footing as a realized human being. Meet me eye to eye, as an equal. Drop the notion that there's something to get. You already have it; let's see it. In the language of his descendent Linji, let us be true persons without rank together, and let us see what becomes possible when we do.

Once we've done some serious deconstruction and experienced falling freely, we have to do something with that experience. A monk who carefully observed Ma's method wrote about the time Ma kicked Shuiliao in the chest: "Emptiness, that idle land, is shattered. The iron boat sails straight onto the Ocean of the Infinite."

Even the purity of emptiness, in which nothing ever happens, has to be left behind. There is a boat to build and sail, a vast sea to navigate. There are refugees to feed and orphans to rear, art to rescue from the bonfire, and songs to write so people won't forget. Ma was passionate that responding to our time is an essential part of realization. He once said that from the point of view of the bodhisattva, burying oneself in emptiness and not knowing how to get out is like suffering the torments of hell. As our hearts and minds open in meditation, it is actually painful not to open our hands as well. For Ma, hell wasn't the trouble he saw all around him; hell was turning away from it, trying to escape into a separate peace.

Why is it an unfloatable iron boat that we have to sail? In Chan, iron boats take their place next to flutes without holes and stone women who get up to dance, representing the moment-by-moment miracle that emptiness appears as all the things of the universe—as redwood trees and freeway overpasses and the dark matter we can't even see. We're participating in the same miracle when, having experienced the free fall of emptiness, we step back into the thick of life to turn our awakening into matter.

How do we do that? Well, Shitou and Ma didn't think it was by way of a practice that requires all kinds of special conditions to do it correctly. This may be the place where you lose your body and your life, but there's nothing special about it, and certainly nothing that you can control through fear and fussiness. Ma maintained that "a person bathing in the great ocean uses all the waters that empty into it." We launch that iron boat by truly understanding that wherever we find ourselves, whatever we're faced with, that's the Way. There are no detours from the Way; we can't lose our Way. To engage and entangle ourselves with whomever and whatever we meet, to care about them, to throw our lot in with them—that is the Way. Every moment, every circumstance, is another chance to experience things as they are rather than as we wish or fear them to be.

We turn the same warmth and curiosity toward our own heart/ mind. Ma famously said that ordinary mind is the Way. We don't reject our own thoughts and feelings; even in a desperate time, the grieving, the rage, the flashes of bravery and generosity in ourselves and in others—all of that is the Way too. Even, maybe especially, the mind that doesn't understand is exactly it. In our own time, anyone who claims to have an explanation for what's going on probably doesn't, whether it's from a political or metaphysical or conspiratorial or any other perspective. It's a good time to be asking questions, to appreciate the grounding of the ordinary mind in its impulses to make a warm breakfast on a cold day, and to research what it would take to become carbon-neutral. In other words, there is a unity between our inner lives and the outer world, a continuum that only appears to be separated into pieces that are sometimes in conflict. Turn too far toward your own heart/mind and you become self-obsessed; turn too far in the other direction and you burn out. Bring an attitude of warmth and curiosity to both, and the Way begins to open on its own. This is what Ma called living a natural life according to the times. Be part of what's going on around you, and "just

wear clothes, eat food, always uphold the way of the bodhisattva."
We might chuckle and think, "Oh sure, clothes, food, way of the
bodhisattva—nothing to it, right?" Just so, according to Shitou:
"Your essential mind is absolutely still and completely whole, and its
ability to respond to circumstances is limitless."

This fundamental wholeness and responsiveness is what Ma
urged people to experience for themselves; it's where Shitou invited
us to rest. It's the freedom of having no position; there's no running
around in circles waving our hands, no updating the inventories of
everything that's missing, and no illusion that what we're capable of
is determined solely by our will. Put all that down and things get big
and alive. Our essential mind isn't bounded by our skull, and our
capacity to respond isn't either. This aspect of realization also has
everything to do with relationship: we feel whole and at peace and
able to respond because we know we're part of something very large.
Remembering this even some of the time can make a huge difference; it can make us bold.

The World We Have

Thich Nhat Hanh

*Only when we combine our concern for the planet with spiritual practice
will we be able to make the profound personal changes necessary to address
the environmental crisis the world is facing. In his important book* The
World We Have, *Thich Nhat Hanh offers us the guiding principles for a
new ecospirituality of mindful living.*

We are like sleepwalkers, not knowing what we are doing or where
we are heading. Whether we can wake up or not depends on whether
we can walk mindfully on our Mother Earth. The future of all life,
including our own, depends on our mindful steps. We have to hear
the bells of mindfulness that are sounding all across our planet. We
have to start learning how to live in a way so that a future will be possible for our children and our grandchildren.

I have sat with the Buddha for a long time and consulted him
about the issue of global warming, and the teaching of the Buddha is
very clear. If we continue to live as we have been living, consuming
without a thought to the future, destroying our forests and emitting
greenhouse gases, then devastating climate change is inevitable. Much
of our ecosystem will be destroyed. Sea levels will rise and coastal cities will be inundated, forcing hundreds of millions of refugees from
their homes, creating wars and outbreaks of infectious disease.

We need a kind of collective awakening. There are among us men and women who are awakened, but it's not enough; the masses are still sleeping. They cannot hear the ringing of the bells. We have built a system we cannot control. This system imposes itself on us, and we have become its slaves and victims. Most of us, in order to have a house, a car, a refrigerator, a TV, and so on, must sacrifice our time and our lives in exchange. We are constantly under the pressure of time. In former times, we could afford three hours for one cup of tea, enjoying the company of our friends in a serene and spiritual atmosphere. We could organize a party to celebrate the blossoming of one orchid in our garden. But today we can no longer afford these things. We say that time is money. We have created a society in which the rich become richer and the poor become poorer, and in which we are so caught up in our own immediate problems that we cannot afford to be aware of what is going on with the rest of the human family or our planet Earth. In my mind I see a group of chickens in a cage disputing over some seeds of grain, unaware that in a few hours they will be killed.

The Chinese, the Indians, and the Vietnamese are still dreaming the "American dream," as if that dream were the ultimate goal of mankind—everyone has to have a car of their own, a bank account, a cell phone, a television set. In twenty-five years the population of China will be 1.5 billion people, and if each of them wants to drive their own private car, China will need 99 million barrels of oil every day. But world production today is only 84 million barrels per day, so the American dream is not possible for the Chinese nor the Indians nor the Vietnamese. The American dream is no longer possible for the Americans. We cannot continue to live like this. It is not a sustainable economy.

We have to have another dream: the dream of brotherhood and sisterhood, of loving-kindness and compassion, and that dream is possible right here and now. We have the dharma; we have the means; we have enough wisdom to be able to live this dream. Mindfulness is at the heart of awakening, of enlightenment. We practice breathing to be able to be there in the present moment, so that we can recognize what is happening in us and around us. If what's happening inside us is despair, we have to recognize that and act right away. We may not want to confront that mental formation, but it is a reality, and we have to recognize it in order to transform it.

We do not have to sink into despair about global warming; we can act. If we just sign a petition and forget about it, obviously nothing is going to change. Urgent action must be taken at the individual and the collective levels. We all have a great desire to be able to live in peace and environmental sustainability. What most of us don't yet have are concrete ways of making our commitment to sustainable living a reality in our daily lives. We haven't organized ourselves. We can hardly blame our leaders for the chemicals that pollute our drinking water, for the violence in our neighborhoods, for the wars that destroy so many lives. It is time for each of us to wake up and take action in our own lives.

Violence, corruption, abuse of power, and self-destruction are happening all around us, even in the community of leaders, both spiritual and social. We all know that the laws of our country don't have enough strength to manage corruption, superstition, and cruelty. Only faith, determination, awakening, and a big dream can create an energy strong enough to help our society rise above and go to the shore of peace and hope.

Buddhism is the strongest form of humanism we have. It came to life so we could learn to live with responsibility, compassion, and loving-kindness. Every Buddhist practitioner should be a protector of the environment. We have the power to decide the destiny of our planet. If we awaken to our true situation, there will be a collective change in our consciousness. We have to do something to wake people up. We have to help the Buddha wake up the people who are living in a dream.

Yet everything, even the Buddha, is always changing and evolving. Thanks to our practice of looking deeply, we realize that the sufferings of our time are different from those of the time of Siddhartha, and so the methods of practice should also be different. That is why the Buddha inside of us also should evolve in many ways, so that the Buddha can be relevant to our time.

The Buddha of our time can use a telephone, even a cell phone, but he is free from that cell phone. The Buddha of our time knows how to help prevent ecological damage and global warming; he will not destroy the beauty of the planet or make us waste all our time competing with each other. The Buddha of our time wants to offer the world a global ethic, so that everyone can agree on a good path to follow. He wants to restore harmony, cultivate brotherhood and sisterhood, protect all of the species of the planet, prevent deforestation, and reduce the emission of greenhouse gases.

As you are the continuation of the Buddha, you should help him offer the world a path that can prevent the destruction of the ecosystem, one that can reduce the amount of violence and despair. It would be very kind of you to help the Buddha continue to realize what he began twenty-six hundred years ago.

Our planet Earth has a variety of life, and each species depends on other species in order to be able to manifest and to continue. We are not only outside of each other but we are inside of each other. It is very important to hold the Earth in our arms, in our heart, to preserve the beautiful planet and to protect all species. The *Lotus Sutra* mentions the name of a special bodhisattva: Dharanimdhara, or Earth Holder, someone who preserves and protects the Earth.

Earth Holder is the energy that is holding us together as an organism. She is a kind of engineer or architect whose task is to create space for us to live in, to build bridges for us to cross from one side to the other, to construct roads so that we can go to the people we love. Her task is to further communication between human beings and other species and to protect the Earth and the environment. It is said that when the Buddha tried to visit his mother, Mahamaya, it was Dharanimdhara who built the road on which the Buddha traveled. Although the Earth Holder bodhisattva is mentioned in the *Lotus Sutra*, there is not a chapter devoted entirely to her. We should recognize this bodhisattva in order to collaborate with her. We should all help to create a new chapter for her, because Earth Holder is so desperately needed in this era of globalization.

When you contemplate an orange, you see that everything in the orange participates in making up the orange. Not only the sections of the orange belong to the orange; the skin and the seeds of the orange are also parts of the orange. This is what we call the universal aspect of the orange. Everything in the orange is the orange, but the skin remains the skin, the seed remains the seed, the section of the orange remains the section of the orange. The same is true with our globe. Although we become a world community, the French continue to be French, the Japanese remain Japanese, the Buddhists remain Buddhists, and the Christians remain Christians. The skin of the orange continues to be the skin, and the sections in the orange continue to be the sections; the sections do not have to be transformed into the skin in order for there to be harmony.

Harmony, however, is impossible if we do not have a global ethic, and the global ethic that the Buddha devised is the Five Mindfulness Trainings. The Five Mindfulness Trainings are the path we should follow in this era of global crisis, because they are the practice of sisterhood and brotherhood, understanding and love, the practice of protecting ourselves and protecting the planet. The mindfulness trainings are concrete realizations of mindfulness. They are nonsectarian. They do not bear the mark of any religion, particular race, or ideology; their nature is universal.

When you practice the Five Mindfulness Trainings, you become a bodhisattva helping to create harmony, protect the environment, safeguard peace, and cultivate brotherhood and sisterhood. Not only do you safeguard the beauties of your own culture, but those of other cultures as well, and all the beauties on Earth. With the Five Mindfulness Trainings in your heart, you are already on the path of transformation and healing.

In the First Training we vow to cherish all life on Earth and not support any acts of killing. In the Second Training we pledge to practice generosity and not support social injustice and oppression. In the Third Training we make a commitment to behave responsibly in our relationships and not engage in sexual misconduct. The Fourth Training asks us to practice loving speech and deep listening in order to relieve others of suffering.

The practice of mindful consumption and mindful eating is the object of the Fifth Mindfulness Training:

> Aware of the suffering caused by unmindful consumption, I vow to cultivate good health, both physical and mental, for myself, my family, and my society by practicing mindful eating, drinking, and consuming. I vow to ingest only items that preserve peace, well-being, and joy in my body, in my consciousness, and in the collective body and consciousness of my family and society. I am determined not to use alcohol or any other intoxicant or to ingest foods or other items that contain toxins, such as certain TV programs, magazines, books, films, and conversations. I am aware that to damage my body and my consciousness with these poisons is to betray my ancestors, my parents, my society, and future generations. I will work to transform violence, fear, anger, and confusion in myself and in society by practicing a diet for myself and for society. I understand that a proper diet is crucial for self-transformation and the transformation of society.

The Fifth Mindfulness Training is the way out of the difficult situation our world is in. When we practice the Fifth Training, we recognize exactly what to consume and what to refuse in order to keep our bodies, our minds, and the Earth healthy, and not to cause suffering for ourselves and for others. Mindful consumption is the way to heal us and to heal the world. As a spiritual family and a human family, we can all help avert global warming by following this practice. We should become aware of the presence of bodhisattva Earth Holder in every one of us. We should become the hand, the arms of the Earth Holder in order to be able to act quickly.

You may have heard that God is in us, Buddha is in us. But we still have a vague notion of what Buddha is in us and God is in us. In the Buddhist tradition it is very clear. Buddha resides inside us as energy—the energy of mindfulness, the energy of concentration, and the energy of insight—that will bring about compassion, love, joy, togetherness, nondiscrimination. Our friends in the Christian tradition speak about the Holy Ghost or the Holy Spirit as the energy of the Buddha. Wherever the Holy Spirit is, there is healing and love. We can speak in the same way of mindfulness, concentration, and insight. The energy of mindfulness, concentration, and insight gives rise to compassion, forgiveness, joy, transformation, and healing. That is the energy of a buddha. If you are inhabited by that energy, you are a buddha. And that energy can be cultivated and can manifest fully in you.

It's wonderful to realize that we are all in a family, we are all children of the Earth. We should take care of each other, and we should take care of our environment, and this is possible with the practice of togetherness. A positive change in individual awareness will bring about a positive change in the collective awareness. Protecting the planet must be given the first priority. I hope you will take the time to sit down with each other, have tea with your friends and your families, and discuss these things. Invite bodhisattva Earth Holder to sit and collaborate with you. Make your decision, and then act to save our beautiful planet Earth. Changing your way of living will bring you a lot of joy right away. Then the healing can begin.

Cranes in the DMZ ⟩⟩⟩

Alan Weisman

In his introductory essay to Thich Nhat Hanh's The World We Have, *Alan Weisman, author of* The World Without Us, *meditates on the connection between impermanence and caring for the world. Paradoxically, both lead to great peace.*

A few years ago, while researching my book, *The World Without Us,* I visited a tribe in Ecuador whose remaining shred of once bountiful Amazon forest was so depleted that they'd resorted to hunting spider monkeys. This was especially grim because they believed themselves to be descended from those very primates. In essence, they'd been reduced to eating their ancestors.

In Thich Nhat Hanh's book *The World We Have,* there is a remarkable corollary, called the *Sutra of the Son's Flesh.* Its moral is that if we don't consume with mindfulness and compassion, we will, in effect, be eating our children.

In *The World Without Us,* I imagined how our planet might respond if humans were suddenly extracted. How long would it take the rest of nature to obliterate our deep tracks, undo our damage, replenish our empty niche, subdue our toxins, soften our scars? As my research revealed, many of our monumental works and seemingly invincible structures would succumb surprisingly quickly.

Other matters that we've set in motion, however, such as all the carbon we've exhumed and redeposited in the atmosphere, would take nature much longer to reabsorb.

And yet, nature has all the time in the world. Scientists, materials engineers, and the Buddha concur: nothing we do is permanent.

In fact, our world has been through far greater losses than the one we're currently perpetrating. Periodically, volcanic eruptions that lasted up to a million years and cataclysmic asteroid strikes have so devastated this planet that nearly everything alive was extinguished. Nevertheless, life, so awesomely resilient, is continually reborn in some unexpected and fertile incarnation—filling the Earth in one era with colossal reptiles, in another with magnificent mammals. This mysterious, wondrous life has recycled before and will again.

Just as no person lives forever, no species escapes eventual extinction, and ours is no exception. Yet to be alive, as Thich Nhat Hanh so eloquently reminds us, is both a blessing and an honor to uphold. To realize that we are part of a grand, changing, living pageant—one that, no matter how deep a wound it sustains, will always be renewed—brings great peace. But this grand perspective doesn't relieve us of the responsibility of living and acting at the highest possible level of awareness while we are here now. On the contrary, in one of those illuminating paradoxes that a Buddhist like Thich Nhat Hanh handles so deftly, the way to achieve enlightened freedom from the confines of the physical realm emerges directly from how consciously we engage with it.

One bright, cold afternoon in November 2003, I stood with five admirably engaged and dedicated fellow humans at the edge of a deep valley. We were north of Ch'orwon in South Korea's Kangwon-do province, staring at one of the most beautiful and terrifying places on Earth. Below us was the demilitarized zone (DMZ): a buffer four kilometers wide that bisects the entire Korean peninsula. For fifty years it had kept two of the world's largest and most hostile armies from murdering each other.

Even so, each could still clearly see the other's hillside bunkers, bristling with weapons that neither would hesitate to fire if provoked.

Compounding this tragedy was the sad irony that these mortal enemies shared the same history, language, and blood.

But they also shared a miracle. After a half-century, the abandoned no-man's-land between them had reverted from rice paddies and villages to wilderness. Inadvertently, it had become one of the most important nature refuges in Asia. Among the imperiled species that depend on it was one revered throughout the Orient: the red-crowned crane. The second rarest on Earth after the whooping crane, it is repeatedly depicted in paintings and silks as a symbol of longevity and as a manifestation of the noble virtues of Confucian scholars and Buddhist monks. Many, if not most, of these fabulous birds now winter in the DMZ.

My hosts were scientists and staff from the Korean Federation for Environmental Movement. Together, we watched as eleven red-crowned cranes—cherry caps, black extremities, but otherwise as pure and white as innocence itself—silently glided between the seething North and South Korean forces. Placidly, they settled in the bulrushes to feed. Because only fifteen hundred of these creatures remain, it was thrilling to see juveniles among them.

Privileged as we were to witness this, it was impossible to forget—and even harder to reconcile—that this auspicious setting owed its existence to an unresolved war. If peace were ever restored, developers of suburbs to the south and industrial parks to the north had plans for this place that didn't include wildlife. The reunification of Korea could mean a habitat loss that might shrink the red-crowned cranes' gene pool critically enough to doom the entire species.

Unless, that is, Korean leaders realized that amid the sorrow of this divided land lay a great opportunity. A growing alliance of world scientists, including my hosts, have proposed that the DMZ be declared an international peace park. It would be a gift of life to our Earth, protecting this haven to scores of precious creatures. By preserving the common ground between them, the two Koreas would not only save many irreplaceable species, but also earn immense international goodwill.

I asked my companions if they thought this would happen.

"We'll never stop trying."

But three days later I realized the challenge they faced, when one of them took me to a Buddhist temple in the mountains north of Seoul. This was one of the oldest Zen monasteries in Korea, a site that monks and environmentalists alike were fighting to exclude from a plan to ring the swelling capital city with new eight-lane highways—one of which would tunnel directly under this ancient sacred ground.

Outrageous, surely. And yet, I asked the head monk, did their struggle to save this sanctuary conflict with Buddhist principles of nonattachment to material things? For that matter, might the ethos of an environmental activist like my companion, clinging for dear life to the planet he courageously defended, actually be an impediment to his spiritual progress? If Buddhism teaches impermanence, is the impulse to preserve the environment—or anything, for that matter—therefore pointless?

It is true, the monk replied, that our world is impermanent. Yet, he added, just as we need to keep our bodies healthy and pure as we seek enlightenment, while we dwell on this planet, we have a duty to cherish and protect it.

I sensed an intricate lesson in this paradox. Before leaving, I had another question for the monk. In a large hall below his quarters where we sat drinking tea, disciples seated on a wooden floor were chanting. I'd glanced in when we arrived: it was adorned with carved dragons and gilded bodhisattvas. For a while, I'd lingered and listened, not understanding, yet something within me stirred.

"What are they singing?" I asked.

"That is the *Diamond Sutra*."

"What does it mean?"

He explained that what appears as form is really emptiness, but that emptiness also has form.

I didn't quite understand.

"Perhaps you need to listen more."

Thich Nhat Hanh defines the *Diamond Sutra* as the essence of ecology, a description of how nothing exists as an isolated self, because it is dependent upon and connected to everything else. No more than a flower can exist apart from the sun that energizes it, or from the soil that nourishes it, or from the creatures that pollinate it, or from the rain that waters it, we have no existence separate from all else. The *Diamond Sutra,* Nhat Hanh explains, teaches that to see ourselves only as humans is a sad limitation of our true essence. We descend not just from our human ancestors, but from animal and plant ancestors, and even from the stuff of the Earth itself: its mineral components are our own.

Thich Nhat Hanh reminds us that we have been rocks, clouds, and trees: "We humans are a young species. . . . We have to remember our past existences and be humble."

The humility he describes is an admonition to respect not just human intelligence, but an orchid's knowledge of how to produce mesmerizing blossoms or a snail's ability to make a flawless shell. To respect, however, means not merely to bow before the butterfly and the magnolia or to serenely meditate on an oak's marvels. Just as two warring Koreas have an opportunity in the flowering ground between them not only to give the world a gift but to draw closer to each other, so in the epic crisis that threatens to choke our entire planet do we have a chance to join in a common cause greater than all our imagined differences.

The environment unites every human of every nation and creed. If we fail to save it, we all perish. If we rise to meet the need, we and all to which ecology binds us—other humans, other species, other everything—survive together. And that will be peace.

The Living Soil: The Ground of Beginner's Mind

Wendy Johnson

"In the beginner's mind there are many possibilities, but in the expert's mind there are few," said Shunryu Suzuki Roshi in his classic Zen Mind, Beginner's Mind. *Green Gulch Farm Zen Center, in Marin County, California, was one of the practice communities established by this Zen pioneer, and its extensive gardens still supply both the center and the famed Greens vegetarian restaurant in San Francisco. One of the garden's founders was Wendy Johnson, longtime Zen student and gardening columnist for* Tricycle *magazine. Here she discusses bringing the open, curious mind of the beginner to the vocation of gardening.*

The soil is dark, the wind is red, and my dreams are snake green with long white roots. At the back of my mouth, way behind memory and longing, is the taste of the ground I garden every day, grit that lingers on my tongue and tells me who I am. Gardens come up out of the ground, surfacing from fissured rock, blank air, and moving water, all teeming with indivisible life. Every garden is stamped with the indelible and evolving signature of its home soil.

The Zen tradition speaks of cultivating an empty field. This is the field of our whole life, full of every possibility and empty only of a permanent, unchangeable identity, of one absolute way to be. It takes true grit to cultivate this empty field that, from the beginning, is vast and complete unto itself. This field includes all beings, animate and inanimate, in the fold of its ground.

Gardening unfolds from this empty field and from engaging with your home soil and getting to know it in every way. Even if your garden is composed of earth trucked in from miles away, as soon as this soil is deposited on your land and you put your hands into it, your work begins. You are cultivating your life as well as your garden.

The word *cultivate* comes from the Latin *colere*, "to culture, to worship, to respect, to till, and to take care of," from the still older root *kwel*, which means "to revolve around a center."

The ground that is cultivated in the garden is common ground, shared by many and host to multitudes. Every particle of soil, every atom of earth, is alive with mystery and potential all stirred up together. Every soil is a long, winding story told in the voices of water and inhaled and exhaled air; of the stone-slow cycles of rock itself becoming soil; and in the voices of the swarming masses of microorganisms feeding, breeding, and dying on fertile dust, creating new life out of their own bodies made from exploded stone.

One of my favorite sights in the summer garden is the California quail taking leisurely dust baths in the endlessly cycling soil on the dry margins of our irrigated fields. They bob and coo and hunker down, making nests of soft dust and cleaning themselves with dirt. Sometimes after a long day of work in the garden, I have a mind to put down my digging spade and join the quail for a long, slow dust bath in the bottomless soil of our garden. After all these years of working the land, I am made of the soil and water of my home place. I have become these elements and they have become me. I may pretend that my work is growing red currants, long-stemmed noisette roses, and Greek oregano, but I know better. My real work is getting to know, inside out, my home ground.

Every garden is based on affinity for and knowledge of the ground, on true intimacy and kinship with your home soil that comes not only from cultivating the garden, but also from sitting completely still on the earth that you garden and walking aimlessly and mindfully about on this same ground. These practices are rooted in listening to your soil and in following your garden down to its source. Begin by sitting still and doing absolutely nothing. Make yourself very comfortable on the ground, and then don't move at all. Give your full attention to what is happening around you. Watch the shadows of the black mulberry leaves move like cirrus clouds across the face of your garden. Be ordered by the beat of the ruby-throated hummingbird pulling red nectar out of full-blown salvias. Sink down to earth and sit deep in the saddle of your home garden. Settle yourself on yourself, and let the flower of your life force bloom.

In the first years of Green Gulch Farm, whenever a new Zen student came to work in the garden, he or she was sent out alone to spend the day sitting in meditation somewhere in the garden. When you slow down like this, the real garden is uncovered. And so is the real gardener. You unfold together. This takes time and a willingness to sit still past the moment when you get bored, or past the moment when you think of at least thirty worthy garden tasks that you need to accomplish immediately. Instead, give yourself all the time in the world, and don't move, even if by the clock you only have half an hour to be in the garden. This is radical cultivation, for out of this stillness, the real nature of your garden soil is exposed. The digger ants near the spot where you are sitting show you how to cultivate dry land. You learn tilling from the blue earthworms pulling rotted straw down into the subsoil around the quince tree. Pay attention to the jay pecking into the first apples and to what she shows you about the ripening sequence of your fruit and about the soil that grows good fruit. But beyond any particular lesson, sitting still on the earth restores you to yourself and to the freshness of the whole garden.

Sitting still is also risky business. In your core, you begin to "un-know" your garden. The unknown garden, the secret garden, waits inside the garden where you sit. Whenever I let myself sit down and get really quiet in the garden, I think of Shakyamuni Buddha finding his place more than twenty-five hundred years ago under a massive ficus tree in northeastern India. Frustrated in all his striving for enlightenment, he sat down and vowed not to move until he understood how to relieve suffering. Shakyamuni was challenged by Mara, the Great Tempter, who tried to unseat him by sending spooks, goblins, and violent storms, and when all that failed to dislodge him, Mara sent seductive beauties to lure the Buddha into moving off the ground at the center of his life. Resolute, the Buddha sat still under the tree of life. Finally, Mara sought to undermine Buddha's confidence and determination by challenging his right to be sitting on the ground. "Look at you," he said. "Who do you think you are sitting there? Countless beings have attempted this task and failed. By what authority do you take this seat?" In response, Buddha extended his right hand and touched the earth, and the earth confirmed his presence with a great, resounding cry of affirmation. In the oldest of iconographic representations, the spirit of earth is pictured swimming up through channels of dark soil to hold her hand just beneath Buddha's hand as he sat absolutely still and fully awake.

The best gardeners I know continue to find time both to sit still and to walk the margins of their land. This walking is not to arrive anywhere in particular, and certainly not to plan what needs to be done in the garden. It is the walk of a mangy coyote exploring soft edges, the boundary line where garden and wilderness meet. This kind of margin-line walking is a matter of finding your true pace, your breath coordinated with your steps in mindful ease.

The most important thing is to relax and move through your garden in mindfulness, without trying to control your walking or your breathing. Let the earth carry you forward. Some days I walk really slowly, especially when I know there is a lot of work to be done. Breathing in, I take a step; breathing out, another step, moving slowly and steadily, like sugar maple sap rising in early spring sunshine. Other days I move a little faster—maybe three or four steps on the inhalation, four or five as I exhale. Often, when I walk this way, I feel the ground rising up to meet the sole of my foot. I know that this world and the garden are breathing all around me and that they are larger than I know. Walking in mindfulness settles me on this truth. So I open my eyes and really look at the world as I walk.

When I slow down sufficiently to actually arrive in the garden, I see that everything around me is constantly changing. My gardening mentor, Alan Chadwick, inspired by Heraclitus, pointed out that you never step into the same garden twice. And when I really slow down, I see that garden and gardener are changing too, ripening and decaying with every breath.

If I paid attention to what work needed to be done on these garden walks, I would go deaf from the shouting demands of all the plants. Plus, I would never return. I'd be eaten by the unpruned cherry tree and belched out next year as a tiny, dried pit. Walking in mindfulness, however, has no aim except to meet and know the life of the garden, the garden that is changing in every moment.

When Suzuki Roshi came to San Francisco, he decided to stay on because he found that American Zen students were able to kindle the fire of beginner's mind in their practice, the mind that notices everything and questions without preconceptions and without fear. This is the mind that looks with confidence into the unknown and takes responsibility and action for what is difficult. Beginner's mind suffuses the mind of the gardener unafraid to come down to earth, to sit absolutely still on the ground, to walk without searching for a path, and moment by moment, to know the unknowable life of the soil.

Waking Up to Your World))

Pema Chödrön

Throughout our day, we can pause, take a break from our usual thoughts, and wake up to the magic and vastness of the world around us. The outstanding American Buddhist teacher Pema Chödrön says this easy and spacious type of mindfulness practice is the most important thing we can do with our lives.

One of my favorite subjects of contemplation is this question: "Since death is certain, but the time of death is uncertain, what is the most important thing?" You know you will die, but you really don't know how long you have to wake up from the cocoon of your habitual patterns. You don't know how much time you have left to fulfill the potential of your precious human birth. Given this, what is the most important thing?

Every day of your life, every morning of your life, you could ask yourself, "As I go into this day, what is the most important thing? What is the best use of this day?" At my age, it's kind of scary when I go to bed at night and I look back at the day, and it seems like it passed in the snap of a finger. That was a whole day? What did I do with it? Did I move any closer to being more compassionate, loving, and caring—to being fully awake? Is my mind more open? What did I actually do? I feel how little time there is and how important it is how we spend our time.

What is the best use of each day of our lives? In one very short day, each of us could become more sane, more compassionate, more tender, more in touch with the dreamlike quality of reality. Or we could bury all these qualities more deeply and get more in touch with solid mind, retreating more into our own cocoon.

Every time a habitual pattern gets strong, every time we feel caught up or on automatic pilot, we could see it as an opportunity to burn up negative karma. Rather than seeing it as a problem, we could see it as our karma ripening, which gives us an opportunity to burn up karma or at least weaken our karmic propensities. But that's hard to do. When we realize that we are hooked, that we're on automatic pilot, what do we do next? That is a central question for the practitioner.

One of the most effective means for working with that moment when we see the gathering storm of our habitual tendencies is the practice of pausing, or creating a gap. We can stop and take three conscious breaths, and the world has a chance to open up to us in that gap. We can allow space into our state of mind.

Before I talk more about consciously pausing or creating a gap, it might be helpful to appreciate the gap that already exists in our environment. Awakened mind exists in our surroundings—in the air and the wind, in the sea, in the land, in the animals—but how often are we actually touching in with it? Are we poking our heads out of our cocoons long enough to actually taste it, experience it, let it shift something in us, let it penetrate our conventional way of looking at things?

If you take some time to formally practice meditation, perhaps in the early morning, there is a lot of silence and space. Meditation practice itself is a way to create gaps. Every time you realize you are thinking and you let your thoughts go, you are creating a gap. Every time the breath goes out, you are creating a gap. You may not always experience it that way, but the basic meditation instruction is designed to be full of gaps. If you don't fill up your practice time with your discursive mind, with your worrying and obsessing and all that kind of thing, you have time to experience the blessing of your surroundings. You can just sit there quietly. Then maybe silence will dawn on you, and the sacredness of the space will penetrate.

Or maybe not. Maybe you are already caught up in the work you have to do that day, the projects you haven't finished from the day before. Maybe you worry about something that has to be done or hasn't been done, or a letter that you just received. Maybe you are caught up in busy mind, caught up in hesitation or fear, depression or discouragement. In other words, you've gone into your cocoon.

For all of us, the experience of our entanglement differs from day to day. Nevertheless, if you connect with the blessings of your surroundings—the stillness, the magic, and the power—maybe that feeling can stay with you, and you can go into your day with it. Whatever it is you are doing, the magic, the sacredness, the expansiveness, the stillness, stays with you. When you are in touch with that larger environment, it can cut through your cocoon mentality.

On the other hand, I know from personal experience how strong the habitual mind is. The discursive mind, the busy, worried, caught-up, spaced-out mind, is powerful. That's all the more reason to do the most important thing—to realize what a strong opportunity every day is and how easy it is to waste it. If you don't allow your mind to open and to connect with where you are, with the immediacy of your experience, you could easily become completely submerged. You could be completely caught up and distracted by the details of your life from the moment you get up in the morning until you fall asleep at night.

You get so caught up in the content of your life, the minutiae that make up a day, so self-absorbed in the big project you have to do, that the blessings, the magic, the stillness, and the vastness escape you. You never emerge from your cocoon, except for when there's a noise that's so loud you can't help but notice it, or something shocks you or captures your eye. Then for a moment you stick your head out and realize, "Wow! Look at that sky! Look at that squirrel! Look at that person!"

The great fourteenth-century Tibetan teacher Longchenpa talked about our useless and meaningless focus on the details, getting so caught up that we don't see what is in front of our nose. He said that this useless focus extends moment by moment into a continuum, and days, months, and even whole lives go by. Do you spend your whole time just thinking about things, distracting yourself with your own mind, completely lost in thought? I know this habit so well myself. It is the human predicament. It is what the Buddha recognized and what all the living teachers since then have recognized. This is what we are up against.

"Yes, but . . ." we say. Yes, but I have a job to do, there is a deadline, there is an endless amount of e-mail I have to deal with, I have cooking and cleaning and errands. How are we supposed to juggle all that we have to do in a day, in a week, in a month, without missing our precious opportunity to experience who we really are? Not only do we have a precious human life, but that precious human life is made up of precious human days, and those precious human days are made up of precious human moments. How we spend them is really important. Yes, we do have jobs to do; we don't just sit around meditating all day, even at a retreat center. We have the real nitty-gritty of relationships—how we live together, how we rub up against each other. Going off by ourselves, getting away from the people we think are distracting us, won't solve everything. Part of our karma, part of our dilemma, is learning to work with the feelings that relationships bring up. They provide opportunities to do the most important thing too.

If you have spent the morning lost in thought, worrying about what you have to do in the afternoon, already working on it in every little gap you can find, you have wasted a lot of opportunities, and it's not even lunchtime yet. But if the morning has been characterized by at least some spaciousness, some openness in your mind and heart, some gap in your usual way of getting caught up, sooner or later that is going to start to permeate the rest of your day.

If you haven't become accustomed to the experience of openness, if you haven't got any taste of it, then there is no way the afternoon is going to be influenced by it. On the other hand, if you've given openness a chance, it doesn't matter whether you are meditating, working at the computer, or fixing a meal, the magic will be there for you, permeating your life.

As I said, our habits are strong, so a certain discipline is required to step outside our cocoon and receive the magic of our surroundings. The pause practice—the practice of taking three conscious breaths at any moment when we notice that we are stuck—is a simple but powerful practice that each of us can do at any given moment.

Pause practice can transform each day of your life. It creates an open doorway to the sacredness of the place in which you find yourself. The vastness, stillness, and magic of the place will dawn upon you if you let your mind relax and drop for just a few breaths the story line you are working so hard to maintain. If you pause just long enough, you can reconnect with exactly where you are, with the immediacy of your experience.

When you are waking up in the morning and you aren't even out of bed yet, even if you are running late, you could just look out and drop the story line and take three conscious breaths. Just be where you are! When you are washing up, or making your coffee or tea, or brushing your teeth, just create a gap in your discursive mind. Take three conscious breaths. Just pause. Let it be a contrast to being all caught up. Let it be like popping a bubble. Let it be just a moment in time, and then go on.

You are on your way to whatever you need to do for the day. Maybe you are in your car or on the bus or standing in line. But you can still create that gap by taking three conscious breaths and being right there with the immediacy of your experience, right there with whatever you are seeing, with whatever you are doing, with whatever you are feeling.

• • •

Another powerful way to do pause practice is simply to listen for a moment. Instead of sight being the predominant sense perception, let sound, hearing, be the predominant sense perception. It's a very powerful way to cut through our conventional way of looking at the world. In any moment, you can just stop and listen intently. It doesn't matter what particular sound you hear; you create a gap simply by listening intently.

In any moment, you could just listen. In any moment, you could put your full attention on the immediacy of your experience. You could look at your hand resting on your leg or feel your bottom sitting on the cushion or on the chair. You could just be here. Instead of being not here, instead of being absorbed in thinking, planning, and worrying, instead of being caught up in the cocoon, cut off from your sense perceptions, cut off from the power and magic of the moment, you could be here. When you go out for a walk, pause frequently—stop and listen. Stop and take three conscious breaths. How precisely you create the gap doesn't really matter. Just find a way to punctuate your life with these thought-free moments. They don't even have to be thought-free *minutes*, they can be no more than one breath, one second. Punctuate, create gaps. As soon as you do, you realize how big the sky is, how big your mind is.

When you are working, it's so easy to become consumed, particularly by computers. They have a way of hypnotizing you, but you could have a timer on your computer that reminds you to create a gap. No matter how engrossing your work is, no matter how much it is sweeping you up, just keep pausing, keep allowing for a gap. When you get hooked by your habit patterns, don't see it as a big problem; allow for a gap.

When you are completely wound up about something and you pause, your natural intelligence clicks in, and you have a sense of the right thing to do. This is part of the magic: our own natural intelligence is always there to inform us as long as we allow a gap. As long as we are on automatic pilot, dictated to by our minds and our emotions, there is no intelligence. It is a rat race. Whether we are at a retreat center or on Wall Street, it becomes the busiest, most entangled place in the world.

Pause, connect with the immediacy of your experience, connect with the blessings; liberate yourself from the cocoon of self-involvement, talking to yourself all of the time, completely obsessing. Allow a gap, gap, gap. Just do it over and over and over; allow yourself the space to realize where you are. Realize how big your mind is; realize how big the space is, that it has never gone away, but that you have been ignoring it.

Find a way to slow down. Find a way to relax. Find a way to relax your mind and do it often, very, very often, continuously throughout the day, not just when you are hooked, but all the time. At its root, being caught up in discursive thought, continually self-involved with discursive plans, worries, and so forth, is attachment to ourselves. It is the surface manifestation of ego-clinging.

So, what is the most important thing to do with each day? With each morning, each afternoon, each evening? It is to leave a gap. It doesn't matter whether you are practicing meditation or working, there is an underlying continuity. These gaps, these punctuations, are like poking holes in the clouds, poking holes in the cocoon. And these gaps can extend so that they can permeate your entire life, so that the continuity is no longer the continuity of discursive thought but rather one continual gap.

But before we get carried away by the idea of continual gap, let's be realistic about where we actually are. We must first remind ourselves what the most important thing is. Then we have to learn how to balance that with the fact that we have jobs to do, which can cause us to become submerged in the details of our lives and caught in the cocoon of our patterns all day long. So find ways to create the gap frequently, often, continuously. In that way, you allow yourself the space to connect with the sky and the ocean and the birds and the land and with the blessing of the sacred world. Give yourself the chance to come out of your cocoon.

The Majesty of Your Loving: A Couple's Journey Through Alzheimer's

Olivia Ames Hoblitzelle

Of all the ways we identify who we are, our mind is probably the most important. There are so many things we could lose and still know who we are, but who are we, our loved ones, any of us, when the mind no longer perceives, thinks, and expresses itself as it used to? Olivia Ames Hoblitzelle and her beloved husband, Harrison (known as Hob), were longtime practitioners of Insight Meditation who faced this terrible question when Hob was diagnosed with Alzheimer's at the age of seventy-two. Whatever happened, they were determined to live it with courage, love, and awareness.

The diagnosis of any life-threatening illness thrusts us into a new dimension. I was intensely aware that we now lived with a third presence—Alzheimer's disease. There was no way to know how it would unfold, for everyone's experience of the disease is unique. For the spouse or family member, there will be a parallel but utterly

different experience. I knew that this was going to be a formative—
and formidable—journey for both of us. Maybe it was denial, but
we had discussions about what attitudes to bring to the disease.
Wishing not to accept the usual pathological approach, we would
see if we could remain open and curious about an unpredictable
journey. Besides surviving, I was determined to reap the benefits,
teachings, even perhaps the graces of the disease. And I trusted that
our many years of meditation practice would help to sustain us.

After the landmark morning at the diagnostic clinic, I also recognized that we were living with another dimension of time. Something in our midst felt different; we lived with a heightened awareness
of what the Greeks called *kairos*, or "vertical time," entirely different
from *chronos* time, which is linear and familiar. In that verticality,
there was a sense of timelessness, sad and sweet. Whether it was the
cardinal's arrival at the bird feeder, the palette of a twilight sky, or
the tenderness in Hob's eyes, the littlest moments shimmered with
clarity. Life sometimes seemed unbearably precious and precarious.

Then, of course, I would forget. In the early stages—the first
couple of years—our lives went on as before. I was teaching, coun-
seling, and writing. Hob was still teaching his classes in Buddhist
meditation, although he was more preoccupied over preparing for
them than he used to be. He was also still driving and, for the most
part, managing his affairs. But there was an accelerating succession
of little indicators: the names forgotten, the errant word, the lost
keys, the touching exchange. Life may be woven of ordinary moments, yet increasingly, poignancy or grief or humor intensified the
quality of our life together.

Hob had always had a penchant for playing with words. He had
majored in English, received a PhD in comparative literature, and
taught most of his life. His love of language was a continual source
of delight and wit for him and everyone around him. Hard as it was
to watch his "word hoard," as he called it, growing smaller, his play-
fulness with language was to be a blessing. He often transformed the
frustration of the moment into a funny expression, a game with
words, or a pun.

"I get betrayed by colors!" he would say, laughing as he tried to find something. He'd refer to "the wily trickster of the physical plane," his expression for describing his increasingly perilous relationship with the material world. Things disappeared. Familiar objects weren't in drawers. Carefully crafted lists dematerialized off his desk. "I'm always being tricked by things. Grab on to whatever stick of kindling you can when you're going down with the Titanic," he declared with a laugh.

He turned to humor and poetry as lifelines to a fading world. One early morning during the winter after his diagnosis, he stood by the bedroom window looking out at the stately elm beside the house, now covered with several inches of newly fallen snow. The morning was dark with the heavy cloud cover of the departing storm. For someone who was almost unfailingly cheerful first thing in the morning, he seemed as somber as the weather. He turned toward me with a furrowed expression.

"I can't get it. Just fragments are there. Here, sit with me on the bed until I can find the rest," he said, as we sat down together in the half-light.

"Can you remember anything about what the subject is?" I asked. "Something that happened yesterday or . . ."

"I'm not sure it's articulable," he began and then paused. "It's inarticulable. It's a poem, part of a sonnet that Milton wrote to his recently departed wife. Like the feel of this morning, all in a few lines. I remember that much. It drives me crazy not to be able to come up with something I know so well. It's about his dream. He could only see her in his dream.

"'So happy but I waked'—There's one line. . . . I think it's coming back."

Another long silence while I slipped into the familiar practice of waiting. I could feel his struggle to remember something treasured that was now irretrievable. It seemed so urgent. With every loss, one more symbolic sinking. These slow, attenuated exchanges had become more frequent. I felt a surge of impatience, then realized that the problem wasn't a need to hurry but my own grief at his growing disability. Impatience was easier to deal with than feeling the depth of my grief.

Then Hob began to squeeze my hand in rhythm with the lines as he recited them.

> I dreamed I saw my late departed wife,
> So happy but I waked, she fled,
> And day brought back my night

"There, that's it!" he exclaimed, as if he'd just discovered a lost treasure. "You can't imagine what this is like," he continued. "Those words express something I could never say as well, but they elude me. I get consternated. I'm sorry." He turned to me, his expression forlorn again.

"I actually had the chutzpah to think I could beat the rat—beat this diagnosis—but this morning it doesn't look that way," he said. "Now it's about finding out how many fire escapes there are in a building. I don't know where to find the help I need. It's like being condemned to death by hanging and then going around looking for someone who fixes sore throats."

Heavy as the subject was, he began to laugh at his own image.

"Now that's a good one! Don't know where that came from." And he turned to hug me as if to celebrate that some great weight had been lifted from his shoulders.

The exchange that morning epitomized how life with Hob had taken on a precipitous, even vertiginous quality. I never knew what the next loss or shock might be. I was stunned by the fluctuations in his states. At times, he was so articulate. I'd forget that anything was wrong. Other times, his faltering words reverberated between us, leaving a vacuum. Parts of him seemed to have disappeared. One minute almost his old self; the next an old man, dreamy and disconnected, moving slowly as if under water. I felt caught between the two realities. There was the enduring sense of the person I'd always known—vivid, engaged, and amusing—but then the new reality would break over me in waves. Sometimes the waves were small and mildly breath-catching; other times they threatened to tumble me into a chaos of overwhelming feelings.

Most of us, most of the time, rest complacently in the illusion that our lives have some measure of stability. In reality, we all live on the edge of the unknown. "Maybe even on the edge of an abyss," an older friend once remarked to me wryly. Something about the nature of Hob's illness finally drove home that stark truth.

More frequently now, his expression collapsed into flatness. His eyes were dull, his demeanor almost that of a dead man walking. Where was his former spark of life? The animation? The connection? Who was he now? A succession of questions gathered on the edge of my awareness.

As a result of never knowing where he might be on this dramatic continuum, I discovered a new dimension of mindfulness: gentle vigilance. Mindfulness—also described as moment-to-moment awareness—is a simple but powerful approach to life that lies at the heart of Buddhist practice. I purposefully invoked openness and flexibility. I cultivated equanimity. In this new, unpredictable world where I often felt as if I were walking into gale force winds, I leaned into the moment, fiercely awake, ready for anything.

After a series of unnerving episodes, I evolved a ritual for coming home, even if I'd been away for only a few hours. I thought of it as my "pathway practice," not something I'd heard in a dharma talk (a Buddhist teaching talk) or read in a book, but spontaneous practice that arose in response to a difficult situation. Each time I arrived home, in those moments between leaving the car, stepping onto the old brick walk, and entering the house, I shifted into mindfulness practice: walking and breathing mindfully, aware of each step, each breath. Just before the door, I repeated a simple *metta,* or loving-kindness prayer. That was how I steadied myself in preparation for the inevitable—the latest crisis waiting for me on the other side of the door.

"I can't find my date book, and I think I have an appointment now."

"Someone's urgently trying to reach you, but I can't find my note for you."

"When you're gone, I feel this melancholy creeping over me, and I have catastrophic fantasies that something's happened to you."

I'd feel the chains of responsibility tightening. How could I leave the house every day? How could I sustain my own life, apart from this caretaking? How would I survive the intensity of his feelings—the urgency, even desperation, behind his questions?

I wondered about the ruthlessness of his swings. Did he experience them too, or was he protected by some diminishment in awareness? What did he experience when the blankness descended? One of my Buddhist teachers asked me during a meditation retreat if I could simply observe what happened to Hob's awareness in the course of the disease. I knew from his compassionate inquiry that he was also declaring himself an ally in our journey, a support for me. He had once spoken of his own fears of dementia, a fear which probably every one of us carries.

Because of my passionate wish to understand what Hob was experiencing, I questioned him frequently. "Where are you?" or "What's going on?" or "Can you tell me what you're experiencing right now?" His answers were usually vague.

"Oh, just dreaming." Or because he sensed my concern, he would pull up some practical response, such as, "Just thinking the gutters need to be cleaned."

Was it hard for him? Or was he blessedly suspended in some *bardo*-like state, some in-between moment, like a sailboat in irons adrift because, momentarily, there is no wind in its sails? (In the Tibetan tradition, the term *bardo* refers to any in-between moment, especially passing from life into death and beyond.) Determined to remain steady, I responded to each latest crisis. I soldiered on as if nothing had changed from the last thirty-four years of our lives together. Yet I knew in my heart that more often he was drifting away into inaccessible realms. Like sound disappearing into the distance, his vibrant, engaged self was vanishing, ever more diffuse, ever more remote.

When we first learned of Hob's diagnosis, we discussed how our years of Buddhist practice could help us navigate whatever lay ahead.

We saw that Buddhist teachings were a container to hold the shifting realities of disease, that they could offer a helpful perspective as well as inspiration. All of us know, at some level, that we will face aging, dying, and death, but our youth-oriented culture is steeped in denial and phobic about these topics. Hob and I refused to collude in this denial. Rather, we were determined to face directly into what was happening. We talked about it regularly. And he was unusual both in his openness about having the disease and in his attitude toward death.

"Fools! Would you live forever?" he would declare with theatrical flair, quoting the words of some general exhorting his troops to go fearlessly into battle, fearless even to death.

For me, there was an added incentive to face this challenge. In the case of my mother, our family's experience, and surely hers, was complicated by lack of knowledge about Alzheimer's, as well as by her inability to speak about it.

I was determined to do everything I could to enable Hob to live his last years with more ease than my mother had. Part of that decision was to seek new perspectives wherever I could find them.

One of my fist steps was to call upon Tulku Thondup, a Tibetan teacher whom I had met years earlier when I first began looking for a meditation teacher. As I was then very new to Buddhist teachings, it was a memorable meeting. Tulku Thondup, also known as T.T., had talked about the law of impermanence in a quiet, compelling way. His words about this core teaching of the Buddha stayed with me, like a wisdom treasure to which I could turn whenever I remembered. Periodically, I would call upon him, especially when I was going through difficult times and needed a more spacious perspective. He became a spiritual friend—a *kalyana-mitta*—that beautiful term from the Buddhist tradition that describes a special relationship with someone who supports and inspires one's inner life.

One brilliant, windy October morning, I was on my way once again to meet with T.T. He lived on a quiet side street in my neighborhood, and as I walked, watching leaves dance along the pavement, I was preoccupied with the increasing challenges of Hob's disease. I wanted to ask him how Tibetans look upon dementia, how they care for their elders, and what approaches from the Buddhist teachings might help us.

He welcomed me to his small apartment and brought out green tea in blue and white mugs that had little lids to keep the tea warm.

He settled into his wingback chair. Like many Tibetans, he seemed ageless, his presence both gentle and strong. As I spoke, he listened, his expression serene, the hint of a smile softening his face. Then he began to speak in a stream of observations that seemed to flow effortlessly from a deep source.

"You and Hob have common karma," he told me. "Take it as a blessing. Any situation can be a source of growth. This is difficult, but it is teaching, a training, a blessing. And so you should try to use it as much as you can. You should feel very fortunate for what you have; feel gratitude for all the blessings of your life. See them. Feel them. Then this whole situation becomes a healing process. Why worry? Whatever we do for each other and for others will be an improvement, will be a healing of this life.

"Taking care of him will become a meditation for you, a practice. Meditation, as you know, creates many good merits. It may not be visible to others, but our helping each other is a merit-making process. If you need to help him, you will be practicing the six perfections [patience, generosity, discipline, diligence, contemplation, and wisdom]. This is the most important practice. Even giving a mouthful of food could include all these perfections. Maybe some hardship will be involved, but then you cultivate patience."

I realized that he was explaining how the simplest activity of helping can be a practice, a way to reframe difficulties and cultivate helpful qualities.

He went on, "Whatever you do to help, do it with total concentration. The wisdom in this case would be the wisdom of nonself, giving as a dedication, as a service to others, with no attachment or grasping. Do whatever you do joyfully, because discipline—the true meaning of the word—is characterized by doing something with joy. Even the little things: see them as an opportunity, a blessing, a meditation, as spiritual practice. Then, even if it's difficult, it will be good. If you use hardships in a proper way, they can even bring inner peace."

"What about in Tibet?" I asked. "How do people regard dementia there? How do families handle it?"

"Of course, many older people get dementia, but it's not seen as something so unusual, like here," T.T. said. "Families usually live in villages or in some community where there are many people in the extended family to help. Someone can wander around and it's okay. If it's a lama or someone who has done a lot of practice, they assume that they are in high states even if they seem crazy or in strange mind states."

I was struck by his last point. In his culture the dissembling of the mind is looked upon as a natural process, like the dissembling of the body. Both are in the natural order of things. Because community and extended family remain strong forces in society, the elders remain in community. Caregiving is shared by many more family and friends than we have in our nuclear models of living.

"Remember," T.T. continued, " we can reframe our attitude toward pain. It can even be good, because whenever you are in pain, you know you are burning past bad karmas. When problems come to you, try not to see them as negative. They are a part of life, like day and night, day and night. It's not day, day, day. Use negative situations positively, and they can all become a helpful source of benefit—even if they are painful. Pain is the most powerful tool of meditation. In the human plane there is so much turmoil, and that means this is a place for practice. Use the problems in your life as incentives for growth; then they become a blessing, not a curse.

"Human life is so blessed," he continued. "We are blessed because we know of so many ways to deal with these challenges. Our experiences are always teaching us. You can be tortured or worshipped or peaceful—all in one life."

I assumed he was referring to the pervasive suffering that the Tibetans have endured since the Chinese invasions. I knew that he had fled the country, lost family members, suffered as an exile, his earlier life destroyed.

He continued, "So problems remind us to practice. And the most important thing is to prepare for our death. All of our practices, especially meditation, are a preparation for death. So you end up turning life into practice—that is what we want to do. With meditation, you develop peace and strength. They are the same, like synonyms: if you're peaceful, you have strength; if you have strength, you have peace. True strength is when someone is calm, peaceful, without worries.

"Acknowledge the peacefulness in yourself—see it, feel it, believe in it. By cultivating a positive quality like peace, compassion, or any other quality, you use the power of belief to enhance that quality in you. These positive qualities are always present. You realize them by recollection, by remembering, by waking up."

He paused, and then said, "Remember also that the wise ones are a source of protection and blessings which you can call on. At night when you prepare to sleep, bring the visualization of them into your heart, and you will receive protection and blessings through the night."

His perspective, born of his culture and training, created space around the difficulties of my life. His quiet assurance made anything seem possible. I felt supported in my determination to approach Hob's dementia with the wisdom of the dharma, the classic teachings. They would help us to meet whatever lay ahead.

Compassion Is the Root of All Practices ⟫

His Holiness the Seventeenth Karmapa

The essence of Buddhism is selflessness, in both the philosophical and moral senses. But while much is made of the Buddhist doctrine of emptiness, or lack of inherent self, Buddhist teachers actually point to the other, more ordinary meaning—the selflessness of putting other people first—as the true definition of Buddhist practice. His Holiness the Seventeenth Karmapa, a young Tibetan lineage figure destined to be one of the major Buddhist teachers of the twenty-first century, says that what we need to cultivate is compassion for others' suffering, that is so strong that we can hardly stand it.

All of the Buddha's teachings are based on refraining from harming others and engaging in helping others. It is therefore of great importance for Buddhists to have these two principles as the ground of their practice. The roots of Buddhist practice are the attitudes of altruism and nonharm. In other words, the roots of Buddhist practice are loving-kindness and compassion.

From among these two qualities, I think that compassion is foremost: in general, we develop loving-kindness by relying on compassion. In the beginning, therefore, compassion is in a sense more important. Our compassion must have a broad focus, not only including ourselves, but including all sentient beings.

Why must it include all sentient beings? Because all sentient beings, oneself and others, want to be happy and free of suffering. This basic desire is the same for everyone. Nevertheless, most of the sentient beings we see at present experience only suffering; they cannot obtain happiness. Just as we have a desire to clear away the suffering in our own experience and to enjoy happiness, through meditating on compassion we come to see that all other beings have this desire as well. So other beings are not only worthy of our compassion, they are also the cause for our meditation on compassion to become possible.

According to the Mahayana teachings, all sentient beings are "our parents of the past, present, and future." This means that, of all sentient beings, some have been our parents in the past, some are our current parents, and some will be our parents in the future: there are no beings who are not, in the end, our parents. For this reason, all sentient beings have a connection of affection toward us. They have a connection of kindness toward us. These affectionate and kind parents are trapped in a state of suffering, unable to actualize their desire for happiness. It is crucial for us to begin meditating on compassion for them, in this very moment. I think that this explains clearly why it is necessary to include not only the benefit of ourselves but the benefit of others as well in the purpose of our meditation on compassion.

When we practice the meditations on compassion, it is not enough for us simply to feel a compassionate sensation in our minds. We must bring our meditation on compassion to the deepest level possible. In order to make our compassion as deep as possible, we reflect on the suffering of sentient beings in all six realms of samsara. These sentient beings who are undergoing such intense suffering are the same beings who are our kind parents of the past, present, and future. In short, all of these sentient beings are individuals with whom we are connected.

Therefore, since we are connected to all of these beings, it is possible for us to further our connection to them by bringing them benefit. The most excellent connection we could possibly make would be to cultivate the heart of compassion for them and to think of ways we can reduce their suffering. Reflecting on our connection to these beings, we must engender a compassion that cannot bear their suffering to endure any longer. This great, unbearable compassion is extremely important. Without it, we might be able to feel a compassionate sensation in our minds from time to time, but this sensation will not bring forth the full power of compassion. It cannot form the basis of a comprehensive practice.

On the other hand, once unbearable compassion takes birth in our hearts, we will immediately be compelled to altruistic action. We will automatically start thinking about how we can free sentient beings from suffering. Therefore, the way to develop altruism is through meditating on compassion. When our compassion becomes genuine and deep, our actions for the benefit of others will be effortless and free from doubt. That is why it is so crucial for us to deepen our practice of compassion until our compassion becomes unbearable.

Unlike our usual approach to compassion, where we meditate here and there on the general notion that sentient beings experience suffering, unbearable compassion penetrates and moves our heart. If we were to see someone trapped in a raging fire, we would not postpone our assistance to that person. Right then and there, we would immediately begin thinking of and engaging in ways to extract him or her from the fire. Similarly, with unbearable compassion, we witness the suffering of all sentient beings of the six realms and immediately seek out ways to free them from that suffering. Not only do we genuinely try to free them from suffering, we are also completely willing to endure any obstacles we may encounter on our path to freeing them. We are unfazed by complications and doubts.

All sentient beings have basic compassion. Even people we would generally consider ill-tempered have compassion; they simply have not brought their basic compassion to a refined level. If ill-tempered people did not have any compassion at all, it would be impossible for them to *develop* their compassion by practicing on the path. All beings have compassion, but their door to the mastery of compassion has thus far been locked. So even though it may seem that some people have no compassion whatsoever, everyone has at least a small seed of compassion. That small seed can grow into great compassion; the potential we all have for great compassion can be made manifest.

Though the great, noble beings can let the full extent of their potential for compassion shine through, we ordinary beings cannot. Though we have the seed of compassion, we do not have the compassion we want: precisely when we need compassion the most, we cannot access it; the door of our compassion is closed.

To make our compassion strong and to make our seed of compassion ripen, we need the path. When we enter the path of compassion, we begin to connect with the compassion that we need in order to help others, and we begin to develop the compassion we need in order to attain enlightenment. We already have compassion, *bodhichitta*, wisdom, and many other positive qualities, yet our mental afflictions are far stronger than all of these most of the time. It is as if the afflictions have locked all of our positive qualities away in a box.

One day, when we open that box and all of our good qualities spring forth, we will not have to go looking for our compassion. It is not available for purchase anywhere. We will discover that compassion is present in our minds spontaneously. A wealth of excellent qualities will become available to us.

The Wooden Puppet and Iron Man: Selfless Compassion, Radical Optimism ⏵⏵

Joan Halifax

Since Buddhism is all about suffering, it's natural that one of its greatest contributions in the West has been new ways to work with dying and death. The Buddhist approach (to this and pretty much everything else) is that the most important thing we bring to the dying process, both our own and others', is our own state of mind. One of the leaders of the contemplative care movement is the Zen teacher Joan Halifax. Here she shows us how we can approach death with a mind of fearlessness, compassion, and nonattachment to outcome.

Over the years people have asked me questions like, "How can you touch someone whose body is covered with lesions?" "Isn't it difficult to be around so much pain and suffering?" "Don't you feel worn out from giving so much?" "What kind of gratification is there in doing this kind of work when the outcome is death?" "Don't people's emotions overwhelm you?" "Isn't it frightening to be around dying all the time?" "Don't you get numb from facing loss and sorrow so often?"

In the beginning it wasn't easy. It did not come naturally or instinctively. Working so closely with death often scared me; I was afraid I might get what the dying person had. When I recognized, however, that I already have what dying people have—mortality—I stopped being afraid of catching it.

Recognizing this very interconnectedness is the ground of giving no fear and the beginning of compassion. Patient and caregiver are one and the same, connected by life and death as by suffering and joy. When we manage to step through fear by reconnecting with each other, real compassion arises.

Zen uses the images of the iron man and the wooden puppet to describe giving no fear. The iron man—or iron woman—embodies compassion through unshakable strength and equanimity. He exemplifies the three qualities of resoluteness, resilience, and durability. He's not attached to outcome and has absolutely no interest in offering consolation—he expresses love without pity. With his deep equanimity, the iron man works from a pivot of intention that allows him to be fully present and immovable in this very moment. He puts himself in a difficult position and is strengthened by it as he offers strength to it. This is the very heart of our work with being with dying, this ongoing practice of sublime defeat, like a tempered sword, defeated by the fire and pounded to become strong.

My father was an iron man as he faced his death. A friend with AIDS was an iron man as he lay in my arms and accepted his death as a gift to all those who suffered like him. One caregiver friend showed an iron woman's strength as she sat quietly by her mother's bedside, bearing witness to four days of unrelenting, wild anger that finally resolved into bliss at the moment of her mother's death.

The other Buddhist image for giving no fear is the wooden puppet, a very different kind of symbol for compassion. The puppet simply responds to the world as it is. There is no self; there is no other. Someone is hungry; food is given. Someone is thirsty; drink is offered. Someone is sleepy; a bed is made. For the wooden puppet, the world is the puppeteer to which she seamlessly responds without strategy, motivation, or thought of outcome. She can always be counted on because her front is soft and open; to be a wooden puppet is to bear witness and respond to suffering with a tenderness that knows no bounds.

The wooden puppet and the iron man both practice what I call "radical optimism." They don't have expectations about a specific outcome—about dying a good death or being a perfect caregiver. And because they don't have these ideas or expectations, they can really practice optimism. This kind of optimism arises directly out of not-knowing. It's free of time and space, self and other—yet it's embedded in the very stuff of our daily lives.

This might sound cryptic, but it has real meaning in being with dying. When I sit with a dying person or with prisoners in maximum security at the local penitentiary, if I allow one single thought of outcome to rear its head, the truth of the moment dies. I've stopped being with what is, and I've started to have ideas about the way I think it should be.

People often ask me about having a "good death." But in the view of the radical optimist, there is no good or bad death. Being with dying is simply being with dying; each being does it his or her way. With no gaining idea, no attachment to outcome, the radically optimistic caregiver bears witness and gives no fear. An old Zen saying offers another way of putting it: "fishing with a straight hook," meaning don't look for results. Whether at the beginning, in the middle, or at the end, just exist in the right-now.

A friend of mine with AIDS struggled long and hard in his dying. But he finally came to a place where, after a lot of pain, he decided that he was suffering for all men who had Kaposi's sarcoma. In this way he brought himself into peace. As he felt his connection with all those whose bodies bloomed with purple lesions, his self-absorption left him, and he was flooded with love. He told me one day that he could see why Christ's suffering was a model for ours. "When you suffer, you suffer along with everyone else," he said. In his pain, he knew he was not alone.

As he spoke, I saw a tear of relief slide slowly down his cheek. His fingers reached out to mine. There was nothing to say. We simply let our fingers touch and intertwine. He then asked me to hold him and sing. As I held him, he looked like a small, emaciated child, purple blooms covering his body. He sighed in tune with the simple song he had requested. For a time, he was completely relaxed and seemed to be free of pain. And I relaxed too. He had given both of us a deep reason to live and to let go.

A spiritual life is not about being self-conscious or wearing a button that says "I'm a bodhisattva!" It is about doing what you have to do with no attachment to outcome. True compassion just does what needs to be done because it's the only thing to do—just because it's natural and ordinary, like smoothing your pillow at night. Sometimes the outcome can seem to be a happy one. And often enough we are faced with so-called failure. And thus it is.

There's a famous Zen story about compassion that consists of a dialogue between two brothers, Tao Wu and Yun Yen. It goes like this:

Yun Yen asked Tao Wu, "What does the Bodhisattva of Great Compassion use so many hands and eyes for?"

Wu said, "It's like someone reaching back, groping for a pillow in the middle of the night."

Yen said, "I understand."

Wu said, "How do you understand it?"

Yen said, "All over the body are hands and eyes."

Wu said, "You have said quite a bit there, but you've only said 80 percent of it."

Yen said, "What do you say, Elder Brother?"

Wu said, "Throughout the body are hands and eyes."

This conversation seems kind of mysterious until we think about what a bodhisattva really is—a Buddhist archetype of compassion and fearlessness, an awakened being who has vowed to come back lifetime after lifetime in order to save others from suffering. Bodhisattvas could leave our world of pain and suffering behind forever, but they deliberately choose to be reborn into the terrible and beautiful wilderness of life to practice compassion.

Earthly bodhisattvas are those men and women, those wooden

puppets and iron men, who have dedicated their lives to awakening these qualities—whether caregivers or those receiving care. In the metaphor Yun Yen uses, they're covered with eyes that see others' needs and hands that reach out to help.

So this exchange between the two brothers teaches us that true compassion, with its myriad hands and eyes, is every bit as natural and ordinary as pulling the pillow toward your head in the darkness of night. Then Tao Wu goes further: he observes that compassion is like the blood in our body, like the nerves running through our fingers—it *is* our whole being.

In total compassion, Tao Wu suggests, throughout the whole body, we feel and give no fear. My friend Susanna, an anthropologist, lived with Huichol Indians in northwestern Mexico when she was a young woman. One day she met a large Huichol family as they visited the remote mountain village where she lived. The mother held a baby in her arms, an infant who looked ill and neglected. When Susanna asked what was wrong with the baby, the mother told her the little one was dying. Horrified, Susanna wanted to know why they weren't doing anything, but the mother simply repeated that the baby was going to die.

Bewildered by what was happening, she asked the family if they would let her take care of it. She took the little one, washed and fed her, wrapped her snugly in a thick blanket, curled up around her, and fell asleep. When she woke in the morning, the baby was dead. The parents reminded her that they had already told her the child would die. As she related this incident to me twenty years later, she said very simply that she would still do nothing different.

Death is inescapable. All beings, you and me, are heading straight into its mouth. What kind of optimism can be born from such a raw truth? "Learn to cooperate with the inevitable," Jonas Salk once advised me. In the bright light of the inevitable, how do we sustain buoyancy, optimism, and the heart to help others?

Simple, but not necessarily easy: we abandon our fixed ideas of outcome. If there is even one wish for a certain kind of result, then we aren't being with what's actually happening. The radical optimist is not investing in the future, but in the present moment, free of design. Only a radical optimist can bear to bear witness. When I sit across from the man on death row who raped and killed an eleven-year-old girl, his eyes stare into mine through the food port in his narrow cell door; any thought of "saving his soul" would destroy the truth of that moment. I watch ideas about what I want for him arise, and I let them go with a breath. When I touch the hand of an old woman as the breath rattles out of her body, wanting to make her dying easier would only be an obstacle to my being there with her. Can we hold such moments without a sense of tragedy, frustration, or fear? I, for one, don't find it easy—I have a basic intolerance of suffering. But I give it my close attention, while holding myself as open as possible.

Years ago, a student of mine contracted kidney cancer while still a young man. One day as I was visiting him, he complained about his useless life of the past. Only now was he having a taste of what he thought was really important to him, a life that was not about making deals and making money, but a life that might be of help to others, a life where suffering was teaching him about humility and kindness, a life that was without hope, in the best sense of the word. In spite of pain after surgery and with an undetermined prognosis, his spirits were high and he felt an unusual optimism.

As it turned out, my friend's cancer went into remission. During this period, he was grateful beyond words for what had happened to him. He was free of cancer, and his enthusiasm for life and his love of others was like a fresh lake after rain. He valued most especially the insight that he could now live a different kind of life if he wanted to. At the same time, he also expressed concern that he might forget and fall back into his old ways.

Robert Aitken Roshi once said that he was not so interested in the day you attained enlightenment—he was interested in the day after! As my friend feared, after a year went by, he forgot his commitment to his inner life as his old priorities again took hold of him. He went about his everyday living rarely giving thought to the fact that he had recently recovered from cancer. He went back into doing business, and we saw little of each other. When we did meet, he spoke only about money and women.

Several years later, when we met again, slightly wiser for his misery, he wondered aloud what had happened. He saw that the habit of materialism was so strong in him that not even the threat of dying of cancer had been enough to keep him on the path for long. He felt that he was living a lie and denying the gift of insight that had been given to him as a result of his illness. He felt deeply dissatisfied.

Another year went by, and my friend increasingly felt that life was meaningless. He found himself in another catastrophe, but this one was psychological: he was suffering from severe depression. He felt angry with himself and at the world, and helpless in the face of his habits of mind. As I sat with him, listening to him pour out his unhappiness and failure to find anything worthwhile in his life, I tried to let go of my expectations of a good outcome for my young friend. My only job was to bear witness to his suffering and, at the same time, to see his good heart steadily beating underneath all of his misery.

One day, he said to me, "You seem to see something that I don't." I asked him what it was that he thought I saw. He paused and then replied, "I think you see who I really am." I asked him what that was, and he said, "I don't know, but when you see it, I can feel it." At that moment, we both relaxed and smiled together for the first time in five years. Although he had lost sight of the gifts suffering had brought him, he regained his vision. I felt glad that I'd borne witness to both his suffering and his true nature, so that he too could glimpse his own fundamental goodness.

Tibetan teacher Chögyam Trungpa Rinpoche often talked about "spiritual materialism," meaning our desire to "get" enlightenment and even our noble-seeming aspirations to help others. Aspiring to awaken or to benefit others can be useful—it often helps with our priorities, just as having the goal of a sane and conscious death can help us to appreciate and relish this present moment. But if practice becomes a means to a "greater" end, then it becomes an investment—and we start expecting a profit. How can we be at one with a particular moment if we're expecting something? How can we die freely if we're fettered with the expectation of a so-called good death? And how can we really serve others if we're attached to our particular altruistic outcome? When we first start to practice, and for a long time thereafter, altruism can give our practice body and depth. The commitment engendered by kindness helps us to remain steadfast when practice gets difficult. So the vow of the bodhisattva can be a skillful strategy at first, helping us to move away from our self-centeredness. Practicing for the well-being of others, we take a step away from the local, small self and move toward the realization of our boundless interconnectedness.

But ultimately, the radical optimist realizes that there is no self, no other—no one helping, no one being helped. The radical optimist becomes like a wooden puppet responding to the world, her limbs pulled by strings connected to the world's suffering. With time and experience we may develop a way of working with suffering rooted in raw and honest self-observation, and a view of reality that actualizes our awareness, equanimity, and compassion in seamless responsiveness to the world.

A person practicing in this way tries to exclude nothing from his heart. This often takes effort. It may take effort to mourn deeply or to sit for hours doing nothing by the bedside of a dying child or a spouse dying of Alzheimer's. It may take effort to help others and not expect something in return. It may take effort to return our mind to practice. And it usually takes effort to bring energy and commitment to everything we do. Effort at its very core means letting go of fear. It is the courage and stamina to stay stripped to the bone and come face-to-face with what is. It is also manifesting wholeheartedness in the midst of the tight knot of suffering.

Effort gives our practice depth, character, strength, and resiliency. Can we hang in there when the situation is hopeless? Can we return again and again to our intention in doing this work? Can we be disciplined about self-care when the world around us seems to be crying out for attention? Can we be wholehearted in the midst of a heartless world?

Some years ago, walking across the Himalayas, I realized I would never make it over those mountains unless I let go of everything extra. That meant I had to lighten up my mind as well as my overloaded day pack. It all came down to one simple sentence: *Nothing extra!* Just as these two legs carried me across mountains, those same words carry me through complicated days. They always remind me to let go. They also remind me of the weightlessness and ease of a whole and dedicated heart.

Like souls in Dante's Purgatory, we carry the load of living and dying not simply to suffer but to learn to bear burdens lightly. The stones of hidden and silent wisdom become our teachers and companions along the way. They slow us down, ground us, and teach us about the weightiness and lightness of being. They ask us to stop and bend down low, touch the earth, and lift that which seems impossible to bear. Finally, making our backs strong, we open our eyes and discover that the stones are also beautiful.

When the Zen teacher Suzuki Roshi was dying, one of his students went to say good-bye. Standing at his bedside, the student asked his beloved teacher, "Where shall we meet?" The old dying man made a small bow from his bed, and then the gesture of a circle with his hand. I think he was telling his student they were meeting right then and there, in form and in emptiness as well. Past and future were in that moment, and at the same time, the past and the future did not exist—and there was no place to meet that could be greater than the openness and intimacy of that very moment.

The radical optimist follows that intimate path, the path of impermanence through the great ocean of change. She is one with the tides of transition, unresisting. A true bodhisattva, she surfs on the waves of birth and death, with no destination in mind as she rides along, no other shore to head for. Having realized unconditional acceptance and cast aside her expectations, she coasts on the crest of the wildest waves with effortlessness and total involvement. Choice has disappeared in her world. She is thoroughly alive, and she gives no fear.

Sailing Home ◎⟫

Norman Fischer

Poet, Zen teacher, essayist, and business consultant, Norman Fischer is American Buddhism's renaissance man, shining his erudite, Zen-trained mind on many subjects. In his book Sailing Home, *he uses Homer's* Odyssey *to reflect on the spiritual path as a journey of return to who we really are. Crucial to that journey is a return to the body, so vulnerable, ever changing, and magnificent, because it is the vehicle of enlightenment.*

Note that the basis of the Buddha's forbearance, and the basis of ours as well, is the body. When things get tough in our meditation practice, we hold on with the body, paying close attention to the body in sitting, walking, breathing, and so on. Staying with the body brings calm and gives us a concrete, definite way to be with our experience without running away.

In the Abhidharma, the Buddhist psychological teachings, the body is called "the soil in which understanding grows." This is, of course, true: the body calms and grounds the mind and heart, and a stable mind and heart produce wisdom and happiness. And yet (another paradox!), the trustworthy body is also, like the heart, radically vulnerable. In fact, this is its very nature. The Abhidharma's definition of the body is "that which can be molested." In other words, the nature of the body—and of everything that is material, physical—is that it can be broken, squashed, scraped, scratched, burned, and worn away. Thoughts and feelings may be pleasant or unpleasant, but they cannot be broken, squashed, burned, or worn away. How is it that this fundamentally breakable body is the basis of truth, enlightenment, redemption?

When I look in the mirror, I see a familiar image I call "myself." Once the image of an infant, then a child, then an adolescent, it now reflects a grown adult. Is it accurate to think of this series of images as one evolving person? Or, since science tells me that not a single cell that existed in my body at infancy exists in it now, is it more accurate to see this present image as someone new?

The human body is not an object in the world. It is a magnificent process, a ceaseless flow, a journey in itself. Without my intending or thinking about it, my heart beats, my lungs expand and contract, blood surges through many thousands of miles of capillaries, arteries, and veins, nourishing muscles and organs. When the sense organs receive stimulation, a world springs into view as chemical and electrical reactions in the brain and nervous system give rise to thoughts, emotions, intentions, experiences. Without making any complicated or belabored effort, I can naturally desire, move, act in this world.

I eat a meal, but I don't digest—the body does this on its own, whether I want it to or not, taking meat and bread, eggs, fish, and carrots, and transforming them into energy and waste, into meaning, purpose, dilemmas, love. They're transformed into life, the ongoing flow of life that expresses itself through the body I call "me," as if I owned it, as if I knew what it was, as if I were in charge of it and could direct it according to my will. What is my will exactly? In what part of my body does it reside?

I can tell my body to walk or sit or stand or jump, and it will. But I cannot order my body not to age or not to bleed if my finger is cut. If I become ill, I can tell my body to get well, but I do not know if it will obey. My body will fight the illness whether I tell it to or not, and most of the time my body will eliminate the illness, restoring itself to health, because no matter how sick my body becomes, there is always more right with it than wrong. The body is a vehicle for life's flow; it is ruled by life, determined by life, much more than it is ruled and determined by me.

I did not design or engineer this body, nor did I choose it, ordering it from a selection of floor models. Somehow the body appeared without the application of volition on my part, and then later on, little by little, "I" began to inhabit the body, although I am not sure I can say that "I" am something other than the body. I can't imagine what "I" would be without the body, yet I can think of myself as other than the body, as thought, as feeling, as a vague sense of subjectivity I take quite for granted, though I can neither define nor completely confirm its existence. All my desire, intention, will, effort, emotion, and intelligence are very small and crude compared to the body's skills— the mystery, power, and subtlety of the body's ongoing flow.

The body does not persist endlessly on its course. When the flow of life, having passed through the body for just the right amount of time, moves on, the body becomes inanimate, a mere physical presence, uncanny still, but in a different way. Like all physical objects, the inanimate body dissolves gradually into the elements that make it up. What will I be when that happens? But even after the body dissolves into air, water, fire, earth, and light, life will still flow on. My thinking, my desire, my language, my sense of vulnerability, my conditioning sees the breakup of the body as my tragic problem. But the body does not have this problem. For all I know, the body might see its final dissolution as an exciting journey of return, a liberation, a homecoming, a release, a frolic through time, space, and beyond.

The living body breathes. This is one of its most salient features. Air enters through the nostrils or mouth, fills the lungs, enriches the blood that flows through the heart and from the heart throughout the body, renewing life. Then, easily and naturally—without any decision or intention on my part—spent air goes out through the mouth or nostrils, carrying with it what the body no longer needs, releasing the body's past, its used-up moments, out into the world from which they came. Moment after moment the body does this:

renewing life, letting go of life, with each breath in and out. Breathing is another version of the journey of return.

A sudden breath is the first thing that happens when the tiny mammalian body leaves its watery home inside its mother and enters the harsh, cold light of the outer, wider world. The first breath in, rush of cold air—what a shock! How unexpected, how unwelcome. The first breath must feel sharp, aggressive, like the world forcing us to participate whether we want to or not, causing us to gasp, as we will continue to gasp for the rest of our lives in the face of life's relentless aggression. We cry out, though none of us remembers this. And at the end of a life, when the final moment comes, the moment when the body returns home to earth, its elements seeking their original places of repose ("Ashes to ashes, dust to dust"), the lungs let go, and there is one last breath out. And there is peace, rest, rejoining.

Human life in the world always begins with an inhalation and always ends with an exhalation. And between those two decisive breaths there is always breathing going on. We say, "We breathe," but it would be better to say, "We are breathed." Twenty-four hours a day, 365 days a year, year after year, decade after decade, there is no end, no pause, to breathing. If, out of disgust for life or out of sheer weariness, we wanted to stop breathing, we could not. All our will-power, all our despair, fear, or loathing, would not be sufficient to carry out the intention "from now on I will not breathe."

There is only so much air on the planet, and we must share it with all other breathing creatures. Now and since the beginning of breathing, we have all been breathing the same air, taking it into our bodies, transforming it and being transformed by it, using it to move through time, moment by moment, to be what we are. This is intimacy: we take into our bodies the very air that others have breathed. Molecules of air that Buddha breathed, that Jesus breathed, that Plato, Hitler, Napoleon, Einstein, Shakespeare, the pope, the heavyweight champion of the world breathed; air breathed by men, women, and children, by heroes and murderers, by animals, plants, and insects, throughout time on earth—some of these same molecules have been inside of us.

In the Bible's great story of creation, God creates the mountains, the sky, the sea, and all that dwells within them by pronouncing words. But the human being is created when God breathes a breath into him. One of the Hebrew words for "soul," *nefesh* (and also the Greek word *pneuma* and the Latin word *spiritus*), means "breath." Soul, spirit is breath.

For some years before his enlightenment night, Buddha tried all sorts of extreme practices. He meditated on bliss, peace, and happiness. When this did not produce the lasting change he sought, he meditated on spaciousness, consciousness, nothingness, and on a state called neither-perception-nor-nonperception. When none of these profound trances helped, he tried ascetic practices. He stood on one foot in a lake with water up to his neck for days at a time. He tried cow practice and dog practice—not speaking or bathing, and eating, sleeping, behaving, and vocalizing as if he were a cow or a dog. Next he tried hardly eating at all, till gradually he got down to one sesame seed a day. When none of these worked, he gave them up too.

On the point of despair, the Buddha suddenly remembered a simple, natural meditation that he'd fallen into when he was a child sitting under an apple tree at a festival, just quietly breathing, just being aware. So he decided to trust the feeling of his childhood and to return to this simple practice, which, as he sat under the enlightenment tree, finally won him through to awakening. Zen meditation is just this simple, childish practice. Just sitting, just breathing, being with whatever arises, but then letting go and coming back to just sitting and breathing, trusting that being alive in the body, the breath, the mind, and the heart is enough. Being content not to know but simply to be present with life as it appears.

Meditation is not what we think it is: it is not peacefulness or bliss or even a technique for insight or enlightenment. In its widest sense, meditation is an open and creative way of returning home to ourselves, a way in which the mystery that we actually are can have its full expression. Meditation is not limited to a particular technique or posture; any open-ended spiritual or creative exercise can be a form of meditation.

Formal sitting meditation practice, as done in Zen or other schools of Buddhism (and in other traditions too), is a powerful way to foster this open, creative engagement with ourselves. In formal sitting we practice the journey of return in a literal way, returning awareness to the breath, to the body, to the present moment, whenever it strays away. Most simply understood, formal sitting meditation is the effort to return to the concrete feeling of being alive, a feeling that is always with us but that we almost never notice, so preoccupied are we with our problems and issues.

Meditation in general, and formal sitting meditation in particular, is radically simple. There's almost nothing to it. Letting go, coming back—that's all. The only difference between meditation and nonmeditation is that when we meditate we are not grasping anything or trying to do anything; instead, we are releasing ourselves to our lives, with trust that our lives are all we need. A monk once asked Zen Master Zhaozho what meditation is. "It's nonmeditation," he answered. "How can meditation be nonmeditation?" the monk asked. "It's alive!" was Zhaozho's response.

Here is a simple, formal meditation practice I often teach. Like all meditation techniques, it is provisional, which is to say it is not crucial that you do it precisely or correctly or that you take it too seriously. The point of it is to help you in your effort to return to the present, which can sometimes be difficult without something concrete to focus on.

First, sit down in a quiet spot. Whether you sit on a chair or a cushion, sit up straight, with your spine extended, your upper body open. Fold your hands in your lap; put them on your knees; or use the Zen hand position of left palm on top of right, with the palms gently curved, making an oval, thumb tips just barely touching. Cast your eyes downward (you can close them if you like, but watch out not to get too dreamy or sleepy) and begin by sweeping your awareness lightly through the body: forehead, eyes, cheeks, jaw, neck, shoulders, arms, and so on. The point is to arrive in the body, to be aware of the body as sensation and process, to ground yourself in the body as basis so that thought and emotion don't fly too far afield.

Once you are actually sitting there, all of you, mind and body in one place, begin to turn your attention to the breath. Breathe in and out gently through the nose, paying attention to the breath in the abdomen area. Begin with counting the breath, saying the numbers one to ten silently with each exhale. If you lose count, go back to one and begin again, as much as possible without blame or dismay. Once you can count fairly well or get bored with counting, next just follow the breath in the belly, feeling it there, in, out, in, out, and so on (you can say these words or, better, just be with the sensation or, still better, be the sensation).

If this begins to make you sleepy, or if you would just like to move on, see the whole breath more brightly and fully: become aware of the beginning, middle, and end of the inhalation; the beginning, middle, and end of the exhalation; the odd and almost imperceptible places where inhalation ends and exhalation begins, or exhalation ends and inhalation (after a nonbreathing gap) begins. Every breath is a whole life; see if you can feel that life and live it fully, from one end of it to the other.

If you can and would like to move on, then make the breath vivid and alive, brighter and brighter, as if you were turning up a rheostat to make the light in your room gradually brighter. Now you don't need to count, follow, or see the whole breath—just make it alive, breath after breath, until it is full of interest and passion. If you can get that far, then you will be able to let go of the breath altogether and just sit with an open awareness, open to sounds, thoughts, feelings, the whole universe that swirls around you and inside you.

To summarize the process: establish awareness of the body, count, follow, discriminate the whole breath, make it alive, jump off. These are the steps, but it is not necessary to do them all or to do them in this order. Be flexible with your practice and figure out for yourself what is most natural, what will work to give you a grounding strong enough to bring you back to the present moment of your being alive right here where you are. Also, remember to stay engaged with the feeling of the body the whole time, which you will find that you can do, even while you are paying attention to the breath. After twenty to thirty (or more!) minutes of meditation, if you have time, you may find it worthwhile to spend another fifteen minutes doing some spiritual reading or some prayer, chanting, or other exercise or form of worship.

Repetition is the soul of spiritual practice. In any tradition I know of, there are daily practices like this one and a sense of faithfulness to a daily routine. This takes some gentle self-discipline encouraged by some support from others within whatever spiritual community you can find to belong to. Doing the same thing over and over again may seem dull, but the more you immerse yourself in spiritual practice, diving into it day after day like jumping into the bracing ocean with its sunlit wave tips, the more wonderful it becomes.

Life's like that too. We might seek novelty, but even where there seems to be novelty, what's really going on underneath the surface is pattern repetition. Whether we are in Hawaii on vacation, sick in the hospital, or absorbed in our workweek, there is always going to sleep, waking up, eating, going to the toilet, walking, standing, sitting, reclining, seeing, hearing, tasting, touching, smelling, feeling, thinking. Every day goes this way. The sun rises, the sun sets. Life comes, goes, and comes back again. You could see this as boring. Or you could realize that life's archetypal repetition is a form of the journey of return, the deep joy of moment-by-moment renewal, with each breath and heartbeat. The daily routine of spiritual practices brings this reality home to us. Gertrude Stein, the great genius of repetition, once said, "The question of repetition is very important. It is important because there is no such thing as repetition." Each moment in the ever-repeated pattern is, by virtue of the repetition, always new; whatever comes back around again in the great cycle of things is always fresh.

Spiritual practice in all its manifestations is the practice of coming home. The journey of return is profound, but it is also vague and dark. It is, to a great extent, hidden from us. And yet we know about it. The world's religious and imaginative literature gives us many hints and pointers, and we ourselves have inklings and flashes of it at the center of our experience and sometimes at the edges. So we know it is real and we know how much it matters. The journey of return involves not only our so-called spiritual lives but the whole of our lives, work, relationships, creative expression, dreams, sickness, wellness, and dying. Meditation practice is at the center of the journey of return, fueling and inspiring us.

Intimate Relationship as a Spiritual Crucible

John Welwood

Living with someone we love, with all its joys and challenges, is one of the best—and some say fastest—ways to grow spiritually. But real awakening only happens, says the psychologist John Welwood, in the charnel ground where we are willing to acknowledge and work with our wounds, fears, and illusions.

While most people would like to have healthy, satisfying relationships in their lives, the truth is that everyone has a hard time with intimate partnerships. The poet Rainer Maria Rilke understood just how challenging they could be when he penned his classic statement, "For one person to love another, this is the most difficult of all our tasks."

Rilke isn't suggesting it's hard to love or to have loving-kindness. Rather, he is speaking about how hard it is to *keep* loving someone we live with day by day, year after year. After numerous hardships and failures, many people have given up on intimate relationship, regarding the relational terrain as so fraught with romantic illusion and emotional hazards that it is no longer worth the energy.

Although modern relationships are particularly challenging,

their very difficulty presents a special arena for personal and spiritual growth. To develop more conscious relationships requires becoming conversant with how three different dimensions of human existence play out within them: ego, person, and being.

Every close relationship involves these three levels of interaction that two partners cycle through—ego to ego, person to person, and being to being. While one moment two people may be connecting being to being in pure openness, the next moment their two egos may fall into deadly combat. When our partner treats us nicely, we open— "Ah, you're so great." But when they say or do something threatening, it's "How did I wind up with you?" Since it can be terribly confusing or devastating when the love of our life suddenly turns into our deadliest enemy, it's important to hold a larger vision that allows us to understand what is happening here.

RELATIONSHIP AS ALCHEMY

When we fall in love, this usually ushers in a special period, one with its own distinctive glow and magic. Glimpsing another person's beauty and feeling, our heart opening in response provides a taste of absolute love, a pure blend of openness and warmth. This being-to-being connection reveals the pure gold at the heart of our nature, qualities like beauty, delight, awe, deep passion and kindness, generosity, tenderness, and joy.

Yet opening to another also flushes to the surface all kinds of conditioned patterns and obstacles that tend to shut this connection down: our deepest wounds, our grasping and desperation, our worst fears, our mistrust, our rawest emotional trigger points. As a relationship develops, we often find that we don't have full access to the gold of our nature, for it remains embedded in the ore of our conditioned patterns. And so we continually fall from grace.

It's important to recognize that all the emotional and psychological wounds we carry with us from the past are relational in nature: they have to do with not feeling fully loved. And this happened in our earliest relationships—with our caretakers—when our brain and body were totally soft and impressionable. As a result, the ego's relational patterns largely developed as protection schemes to insulate us from the vulnerable openness that love entails. In relationship, the ego acts as a survival mechanism for getting needs met while fending off the threat of being hurt, manipulated, controlled, rejected, or abandoned in the ways we were as a child. This is normal and totally understandable. Yet if this is the main tenor of a relationship, it keeps us locked in complex strategies of defensiveness and control that undermine the possibility of deeper connection.

Thus, to gain greater access to the gold of our nature in relationship, a certain alchemy is required: the refining of our conditioned defensive patterns. The good news is that this alchemy generated *between* two people also furthers a larger alchemy *within* each of them. The opportunity here is to join and integrate the twin poles of human existence: *heaven*—the vast space of perfect, unconditional openness—and *earth*—our imperfect, limited human form shaped by worldly causes and conditions. As the defensive/controlling ego cooks and melts down in the heat of love's influence, a beautiful evolutionary development starts to emerge—the genuine person, who embodies a quality of very human relational presence that is transparent to open-hearted being, right in the midst of the dense confines of worldly conditioning.

RELATIONSHIP AS CHARNEL GROUND

To clarify the workings of this alchemy, a more gritty metaphor is useful, one that comes from the tantric traditions of Buddhism and Hinduism: relationship as charnel ground. In some traditional Asian societies, the charnel ground was where people would bring dead bodies to be eaten by vultures and jackals. From the tantric yogi's perspective, this is an ideal place to practice, because it is right at the crossroads of life, where birth and death, fear and fearlessness, impermanence and awakening unfold right next to each other. Some things are dying and decaying, others are feeding and being fed, while still others are being born out of the decay. The charnel ground is an ideal place to practice because it is right at the crossroads of life, where one cannot help but feel the rawness of human existence.

Chögyam Trungpa Rinpoche described the charnel ground as "that great graveyard, in which the complexities of samsara and nirvana lie buried." Samsara is the conditioned mind that clouds our true nature, while nirvana is the direct seeing of this nature. As Trungpa Rinpoche described this daunting crossroads in one of his early seminars,

> It's a place to die and be born, equally, at the same time. It's simply our raw and rugged nature, the ground where we constantly puke and fall down, constantly make a mess. We are constantly dying, we are constantly giving birth. We are eating in the charnel ground, sitting in it, sleeping on it, having nightmares on it. . . . Yet it does not try to hide its truth about reality. There are corpses lying all over the place, loose arms, loose hands, loose internal organs, and flowing hairs all over the place, jackals and vultures are roaming about, each one devising its own scheme for getting the best piece of flesh.

Many of us have a cartoonlike notion of relational bliss, that it should provide a steady state of security or solace that will save us from having to face the gritty, painful, difficult areas of life. We imagine that finding or marrying the right person will spare us from having to deal with such things as loneliness, disappointment, despair, terror, or disintegration. Yet anyone who has been married for a long time probably has some knowledge of the charnel-ground quality of relationship—corpses all over the place, and jackals and vultures roaming about looking for the best piece of flesh. Trungpa Rinpoche suggests that if we can work with the "raw and rugged situation" of the charnel ground, "then some spark or sympathy or compassion, some giving in or opening can begin to take place. The chaos that takes place in your neurosis is the only home ground that you can build the mandala of awakening on." This last sentence is a powerful one, for it suggests that awakening happens only through facing the chaos of our neurotic patterns. Yet this is often the last thing we want to deal with in relationships.

Trungpa Rinpoche suggests that our neurosis is built on the fact that

> large areas of our life have been devoted to trying to avoid discovering our own experience. Now [in the charnel ground, in our relationships] we have a chance to explore that large area which exists in our being, which we've been trying to avoid. That seems to be the first message, which may be very grim, but also very exciting. We're not trying to get away from the charnel ground, we don't want to build a Hilton hotel in the middle of it. Building the mandala of awakening actually happens on the charnel ground. What is happening on the charnel ground is constant personal exploration, and beyond that, just giving, opening, extending yourself completely to the situation that's available to you. Being fantastically exposed, and the sense that you could give birth to another world.

This also describes the spiritual potential of intimate involvement with another human being.

Another quote with a similar feeling comes from Swami Rudrananda (known as Rudi, a German teacher who was a student of the Indian saint Swami Nityananda), further describing how to work with neurosis in this way:

> Don't look for perfection in me. I want to acknowledge my own imperfection, I want to understand that that is part of the endlessness of my growth. It's absolutely useless at this stage in your life, with all of the shit piled up in your closet, to walk around and try to kid yourself about your perfection.

Out of the raw material you break down [here he is also speaking of the charnel ground] you grow and absorb the energy. You work yourself from inside out, tearing out, destroying, and finding a sense of nothingness. That nothingness allows God to come in. But this somethingness—ego and prejudices and limitations—is your raw material. If you process and refine it all, you can open consciously. Otherwise, you will never come to anything that represents yourself. . . . The only thing that can create a oneness inside you is the ability to see more of yourself as you work every day to open deeper and say, "Fine, I'm short-tempered," or "Fine, I'm aggressive," or "Fine, I love to make money," or "I have no feeling for anybody else." Once you recognize you're all of these things, you'll finally be able to take a breath and allow these things to open.

Rudi suggests that we have to acknowledge and embrace our imperfections *as* spiritual path; therefore, grand spiritual pretensions miss the point. In his words, "A man who thinks he has a spiritual life is really an idiot." The same is true of relationships: beware of thinking you have a "spiritual relationship." While loving connection provides a glimpse of the gold that lies within, we continually corrupt it by turning it into a commodity, a magical charm to make us feel okay. All the delusions of romantic love follow from there. Focusing on relationship as a spiritual or emotional "fix" actually destroys the possibility of finding deep joy, true ease, or honest connection with another.

Sooner or later relationship brings us to our knees, forcing us to confront the raw and rugged mess of our mental and emotional life. George Orwell points to this devastating quality of human love in a sentence that also has a charnel-ground flavor to it: "The essence of being human is that one does not seek perfection, and that one is prepared, in the end, to be defeated, and broken up by life, which is the inevitable price of fastening one's love upon other human individuals."

This then is the meaning of the charnel ground: we have to be willing to come apart at the seams, to be dismantled, to let our old ego structures fall apart before we can begin to embody sparks of the essential perfection at the core of our nature. To evolve spiritually, we have to allow these unworked, hidden, messy parts of ourselves to come to the surface. It's not that the strategic, controlling ego is something bad or some unnecessary, horrible mistake. Rather, it provides the indispensable grist that makes alchemical transformation possible.

This is not a pessimistic view, because some kind of breakdown is usually necessary before there is any significant breakthrough into new ways of living not so encumbered by past conditioning. Charnel ground, then, is a metaphor for this breakdown/breakthrough process that is an essential part of human growth and evolution, and one of the gifts of a deep, intimate connection is that it naturally sets this process in motion. Yet no one *wants* to be dismantled. So there are two main ways that people try to abort this process: running away and spiritual bypassing.

The problem with running away when a relationship becomes difficult is that we are also turning away from ourselves and our potential breakthroughs. Fleeing the raw, wounded places in ourselves because we don't think we can handle them is a form of self-rejection and self-abandonment that turns our feeling body into an abandoned, haunted house. The more we flee our shadowy places, the more they fester in the dark and the more haunted this house becomes. And the more haunted it becomes, the more it terrifies us. This is a vicious circle that keeps us cut off from and afraid of ourselves.

One of the scariest places we encounter in relationship is a deep inner sense of unlove, where we don't know that we're truly lovable just for being who we are, where we feel deficient and don't know our value. This is the raw wound of the heart, where we're disconnected from our true nature, our inner perfection. Naturally we want to do everything we can to avoid this place, fix it, or neutralize it, so we'll never have to experience such pain again.

A second way to flee from the challenges of relationship is

through spiritual bypassing—using spiritual ideas or practices to avoid or prematurely transcend relative human needs, feelings, personal issues, and developmental tasks. For example, a certain segment of the contemporary spiritual scene has become infected with a facile brand of "advaita-speak," a one-sided transcendentalism that uses nondual terms and ideas to bypass the challenging work of personal transformation.

Advaita-speak can be very tricky, for it uses absolute truth to disparage relative truth, emptiness to devalue form, and oneness to belittle individuality. The following quotes from two popular contemporary teachers illustrate this tendency: "Know that what appears to be love for another is really love of Self, because other doesn't exist," and "The other's 'otherness' stands revealed as an illusion pertaining to the purely human realm, the realm of form." Notice the devaluation of form and the human realm in the latter statement. By suggesting that only absolute love or being-to-being union is real, these teachers equate the person-to-person element necessary for a transformative love bond with mere ego or illusion.

Yet personal intimacy is a spark flashing out across the divide between self and other. It depends on strong individuals making warm, personal contact, mutually sparking and enriching each other with complementary qualities and energies. This is the meeting of I and Thou, which Martin Buber understood not as an impersonal spiritual union but as a personal communion rooted in deep appreciation of the other's otherness.

A deep, intimate connection inevitably brings up all our love wounds from the past. This is why many spiritual practitioners try to remain above the fray and impersonal in their relationships—so as not to face and deal with their own unhealed relational wounds. But this keeps the wounding unconscious, causing it to emerge as compulsive, shadowy behavior or to dry up passion and juice. Intimate personal connecting cannot evolve unless the old love wounds that block it are faced, acknowledged, and freed up.

As wonderful as moments of being-to-being union can be, the alchemical play of joining heaven and earth in a relationship involves a more subtle and beautiful dance: *not losing our twoness in the oneness, while not losing our oneness in the twoness*. Personal intimacy evolves out of the dancing-ground of dualities: personal and transpersonal, known and unknown, death and birth, openness and karmic limitation, clarity and chaos, hellish clashes and heavenly bliss. The clash and interplay of these polarities, with all their shocks and surprises, provide a ferment that allows for deep transformation through forcing us to keep waking up, dropping preconceptions, expanding our sense of who we are, and learning to work with all the different elements of our humanity.

When we're in the midst of this ferment, it may seem like some kind of fiendish plot. We finally find someone we really love, and then the most difficult things start emerging: fear, distrust, unlove, disillusion, resentment, blame, confusion. Yet the fact that it brings our wounds and defenses forward into the light is a form of love's grace. For love can only heal what presents itself to be healed. If our woundedness remains hidden, it cannot be healed; the best in us cannot come out unless the worst comes out as well.

So instead of constructing a fancy hotel in the charnel ground, we must be willing to come down and relate to the mess on the ground. We need to regard the wounded heart as a place of spiritual practice. This kind of practice means engaging with our relational fears and vulnerabilities in a deliberate, conscious way, like the yogis of old who faced down the goblins and demons of the charnel grounds.

The only way to be free of our conditioned patterns is through a full, conscious experience of them. This might be called "ripening our karma," what the Indian teacher Swami Prajnanpad described as *bhoga,* meaning "deliberate, conscious experience." He said, "You can only dissolve karma through the bhoga of this karma." We become free of what we're stuck in only through meeting and experiencing it directly. Having the bhoga of your karma allows you to digest unresolved, undigested elements of your emotional experience from the past that are still affecting you: how you were hurt or overwhelmed, how you defended yourself against that by shutting down, how you constructed walls to keep people out.

Another term for directly engaging our karma might be "conscious suffering." This involves saying yes to our pain, opening ourselves to it, as it is. This kind of yes doesn't mean, "I like it; I'm glad it's like this." It just means, "Yes, this is what's happening." Whatever comes up, you are willing to meet it and have a direct experience of it. For example, if you're hard-hearted, you have a full experience of that. Then you see how acknowledging this affects you and what comes from doing that.

Bhoga involves learning to ride the waves of our feelings rather than becoming submerged in them. This requires mindfulness of where we are in the cycle of emotional experience. A skilled surfer is aware of exactly where he is on a wave, whereas an unskilled surfer winds up getting creamed. By their very nature, waves are rising 50 percent of the time and falling the other 50 percent. Instead of fighting the down cycles of our emotional life, we need to learn to keep our seat on the surfboard and have a full, conscious experience of going down. Especially in a culture that is addicted to "up," we especially need our yes when the down cycles unfold—to be willing to fall apart, retreat, slow down, be patient, let go. For it's often at the bottom of a down cycle, when everything looks totally bleak and miserable, that we finally receive a flash of insight that lets us see the hidden contours of some huge ego fixation in which we've been stuck all our life. Having a full, conscious experience of the down cycle as it's occurring, instead of fighting or transcending it, lets us be available for these moments of illumination.

While the highlands of absolute love are most beautiful, few but the saints can spend all their time there. Relative human love is not a peak experience nor a steady state. It wavers, fluctuates, waxes and wanes, changes shape and intensity, soars and crashes. "This is the exalted melancholy of our fate," writes Buber, describing how moments of I/Thou communion cannot last very long. Yet though relationships participate fully in the law of impermanence, the good news is that this allows new surprises and revelations to keep arising endlessly.

RELATIONSHIP AS KOAN

Relating to the full spectrum of our experience in the relational charnel ground leads to a self-acceptance that expands our capacity to embrace and accept others as well. Usually our view of our partners is colored by what they do for us—how they make us look or feel good, or not—and shaped by our internal movie about what we want them to be. This, of course, makes it hard to see them for who they are in their own right.

Beyond our movie of the other is a much larger field of personal and spiritual possibilities, what Walt Whitman referred to when he said, "I contain multitudes." These multitudes are what keep a relationship fresh and interesting, but they can only do that if we can accept the ways that those we love are different from us—in their background, values, perspectives, qualities, sensitivities, preferences, ways of doing things, and, finally, their destiny. In the words of Swami Prajnanpad, standing advaita-speak on its head, "To see fully that the other is not you is the way to realizing oneness. . . . Nothing is separate, everything is different. . . . Love is the appreciation of difference."

Two partners not holding themselves separate, while remaining totally distinct—"not two, not one"—may seem like an impossible challenge in a relationship. Bernard Phillips, an early student of East/West psychology, likens this impossibility of relationship to a Zen koan, a riddle that cannot be solved with the conceptual mind. After continually trying and failing to figure out the answer, Zen students arrive at a genuine solution only in the moment of finally giving up and giving in. In Phillips' words,

> Every human being with whom we seek relatedness is a koan, that is to say, an impossibility. There is no formula for getting along with a human being. No technique will achieve relatedness. I am impossible to get along with; so is each one of you; all our friends are impossible; the members of our

families are impossible. How then shall we get along with them? . . . If you are seeking a real encounter, then you must confront the koan represented by the other person. The koan is an invitation to enter into reality.

In the end, to love another requires dropping all our narcissistic agendas, movies, hopes, and fears, so that we may look freshly and see "the raw other, the sacred other," just as he or she is. This involves a surrender, or perhaps defeat, as in George Orwell's words about being "defeated and broken up by life." What is defeated here, of course, is the ego and its strategies, clearing the way for the genuine person to emerge, the person who is capable of real, full-spectrum contact. The nobility of this kind of defeat is portrayed by Rilke in four powerful lines describing Jacob's wrestling match with the angel:

Winning does not tempt that man
For this is how he grows:
By being defeated, decisively,
By constantly greater beings.

In relationship, it is two partners' greater beings, gradually freeing themselves from the prison of conditioned patterns, that bring about this decisive defeat. And as this starts reverberating through their relationship, old expectations finally give way, old movies stop running, and a much larger acceptance than they believed possible can start opening up between them. As they become willing to face and embrace whatever stands between them—old relational wounds from the past, personal pathologies, difficulties hearing and understanding each other, different values and sensitivities—all in the name of loving and letting be, they are invited to "enter into reality." Then it becomes possible to start encountering each other nakedly, in the open field of nowness, fresh and unfabricated, the field of love forever vibrating with unimagined possibilities.

Love's Garden ⟫

Peggy Rowe-Ward and Larry Ward

Loving-kindness, compassion, joy, and equanimity—these four summarize the Buddha's teachings on love. They are called "the dwelling place of Brahma," because if they suffuse our lives, we truly dwell in heaven. Peggy Rowe-Ward and Larry Ward, a married couple, are ordained Buddhist teachers and students of Thich Nhat Hanh. In their guide to mindful relationships, they offer stories, meditations, and exercises that invite us to experience love in a new and deeper way.

> Shall we compare our hearts to a garden—with beautiful blooms, straggling weeds, swooping birds and sunshine and rain—and most importantly, seeds?
> —GREG LIVINGTON

Picture the lotus flower. In Buddhist art, the Buddha is often depicted sitting on a lotus-flower throne. The lotus represents our own peace and happiness and our innate yearning for the peace and happiness of others. Compassion resides in each of us naturally, but we need to create space in our heart and mind for it to be nurtured and to allow it to flower. Benefiting others brings us joy, and our mind and heart become bigger when we care for, think about, and act in the interest of others.

The teachings on true love offered by the Buddha are called the four brahmaviharas. *Vihara* means "abode" or "dwelling place," and *brahmavihara* means "dwelling place of the god Brahma." These teachings are also referred to as the four immeasurables: loving-kindness (*maitri*), compassion (*karuna*), joy (*mudita*), and equanimity (*upeksha*). They are referred to as immeasurables because if you practice them, the love in your heart will grow so much it cannot be measured.

True Love

Maitri is the first aspect of true love, the intention and the capacity to offer joy and happiness. Listening and looking deeply help us to develop this capacity so that we can be a good friend to ourselves and to others. Some Buddhist teachers define *maitri* as "loving-kindness," because they believe the word *love* has become tarnished in our popular language. Thich Nhat Hanh uses the phrase "true love," encouraging us to restore love to its true meaning.

The second aspect of true love is karuna, the intention and capacity to lighten sorrow and relieve and transform suffering. *Karuna* is generally translated as "compassion." To develop compassion in ourselves, we need to practice mindful breathing, deep listening, and deep looking. Looking deeply and listening carefully, you understand the suffering of the other person. You accept him or her, and naturally your love and compassion flow freely. This is the most beautiful practice and the most powerful method of bringing about transformation and healing. Happiness is made of one substance—compassion—and compassion is made of understanding. If you don't have compassion in your heart, you cannot be happy. Cultivating compassion for others, you create happiness for yourself and for the world.

Someone recently asked us the difference between love and compassion. Love is the practice of nonharming in our thinking, in our speech, and in our actions. Compassion is the practice of helping relieve the suffering of others with our own thoughts, actions, and speech.

The third aspect of true love is mudita, or joy. True love always brings joy to the ones we love, as well as to ourselves. In this way we can tell if our love is true or not. Is our love increasing the joy of those we love, or is it stifling them or making them miserable? If the love we offer does not bring joy to both ourselves and our beloved, then it's not true love.

Joy is filled with peace and contentment. It is settled, solid, and light at the same time. We delight in the happiness of others. There is no jealousy, and we can feel this happiness in our own being.

The fourth element of true love is upeksha, which means equanimity and nonattachment. *Upa* means "over," and *iksh* means "to look." With upeksha, we can see our whole garden. We don't favor one flower over the other or only take care of one patch while leaving the rest to wither and wilt. If our love has clinging, attachment, prejudice, or discrimination, it is not true love.

Upeksha is the wisdom of letting go. Without upeksha, our love can become possessive. If you say you love someone but don't understand his or her aspirations, needs, and challenges, then your love is a prison. True love allows us to preserve the freedom of our beloved along with our own freedom.

Until we're able to embrace ourselves with love and care, our capacity to offer true love to others remains very limited. One day the Buddha gave a teaching about the Earth's capacity to receive, embrace, and transform. He said we should learn to be like the Earth, because no matter what people pour on the Earth, whether milk, perfume, flowers, jewels, urine, excrement, or mucus, the Earth receives them all without discrimination. This is because the Earth is immense, so it has the capacity to receive, embrace, and transform. If you cultivate your heart so that it is open, you become immense like the Earth and can embrace anyone or anything without suffering.

If you put a handful of salt in a bowl of water and stir it, the water becomes undrinkable. But if you put that salt in a river, it's not affected because the river is so great. If your heart is large like the river, you won't suffer because of small problems. Our practice is to cultivate the four aspects of true love—loving-kindness, compassion, joy, and equanimity—that have the capacity to receive, embrace, and transform everything.

A True Friendship

The best thing you can do for your relationship is to begin to learn to fully love yourself. This self-love will not make you more inward or selfish. Rather, it is only the person who truly loves him- or herself who is able to offer that love outward. There is a Buddhist sutra called the *Raja* (King). In this teaching story, the Buddha states that no being is more precious to us than our own self. King Pasenadi of Koshala asks his queen, Mallika, who is the one in the world who is the most dear to her. He expects her answer to be that it is he, her husband. But she answers that it is she herself who is most dear to her. The king realizes that the same is true for him, that no one is as dear to him as he is himself. The king and queen go to ask the Buddha about this, and he confirms their discovery with this teaching:

> I visited all quarters with my mind
> nor found I any dearer than myself;
> self is likewise to every other dear;
> who loves himself may never harm another.

According to the Buddha, every creature holds itself most dear of all; every being wants to live and thrive. Our recognition of this is the basis of our compassion for ourselves and others: "who loves himself may never harm another." Through the practice of loving and understanding we will feel our heart grow to include more people and beings.

A good friend accepts us just as we are. We can tell when someone wants to change us; it doesn't feel good. The same is true when we critique ourselves. To be able to love our partner and others in the world, we need to first practice being that good friend to ourselves and accepting ourselves completely. This requires looking deeply at ourselves without flinching and accepting the whole of what we discover. If we say, "I'll love you when you lose ten pounds," or "You must do this or that before I can love you," then we aren't being a true friend.

Once we realize we're the closest and most precious person on Earth to ourselves, we'll stop treating ourselves as an enemy. The conditions for happiness are present and available to us right now, without us having to improve ourselves. As we grow in acceptance of ourselves, we become a safer, kinder, gentler place to inhabit for ourselves and for others.

Several years ago, we had the good fortune of joining Thich Nhat Hanh and monks, nuns, and other laypeople on a tour of China. An elderly monk with a wide grin and gentle gait was our tour guide at a monastery in the south. We stepped into a large meditation room. The only object in the room was a large oval mirror placed in the center of the room. The monk turned to us with an engaging grin, pointed to the mirror, and said, "Advanced practice."

METTA PRACTICE

How do you talk to yourself? Whose voice is it? Is the voice critical or loving? Are you in touch with a sacred voice that you hear within? This constant inner conversation is the basis of the love relationship that we have with ourselves.

Metta is a practice of uncovering the brilliance of light and love that rests in each of us. This radiance is often covered up with ignorance, fear, anger, and the wounds from life experience, but it is there. *Metta* comes from the Sanskrit word *mitra*, which means "friend." We begin by befriending ourselves, learning to talk kindly and sweetly to ourselves, learning to offer ourselves a blessing instead of a curse or a complaint. Actively being a loving friend to your own self is the foundation of the practice.

The practice is simple. We gently repeat phrases that are meaningful in terms of what we wish for ourselves and, eventually, for others.

We begin by offering metta to ourselves. There are four phrases used in classic Buddhist teachings:

> May I be free from danger.
> May I have mental happiness.
> May I have physical happiness.
> May I have ease of well-being.

May I be free from danger. With this prayer, we are touching the wish that all beings have for protection, safety, and a place of refuge. We have the aspiration that all beings may be free from accidents, external strife, and external violence. Our heart's desire is that everyone can have a place of safe haven. Other phrases for this meditation might include "May I be safe and free from injury," "May I have safety," or "May I have a safe place."

May I have mental happiness. Even in the best of circumstances, we can make ourselves suffer with our own mind. Mental happiness is a mind that is free from anger, affliction, fear, and anxiety. Mental happiness arises through looking at ourselves with the eyes of understanding and love. Then we practice by recognizing and touching the seeds of joy and happiness in ourselves. We also learn to identify and see the sources of anger, craving, and delusion in ourselves. Other phrases people sometimes use are "May I be happy," "May I be peaceful," or "May I be liberated."

May I have physical happiness. With this we are wishing ourselves a healthy and happy body. We touch the deep aspiration that all beings experience a life without physical pain. We're in touch with our desire that no one experience ill health and physical suffering. Other phrases might be "May I be healthy," "May I embody vibrant health," or "May I be healed."

May I have ease of well-being. With this phrase, we are addressing our everyday life. We are touching the wish that our lives be filled with the energies of grace and harmony rather than struggle and conflict. We aspire to live in a way that we experience solidity, freshness, and freedom. We pray for well-being, peace, lightness, and to be spared from strife. Other phrases could be "May I dwell in peace," "May I experience ease," or "May I live in harmony."

LOVING-KINDNESS

When we practice being a good friend to ourselves, we are practicing the art of loving-kindness. Loving-kindness can be described as our ability to bring joy to ourselves and others. The basis of loving-kindness is understanding and acceptance. We practice it first with ourselves, looking deeply at our own self and accepting what we find. With practice, love will arise more and more often. We will feel a natural desire to go in the direction of what is good, true, and beautiful.

You may feel rusty about how to treat yourself with loving-kindness. To begin, it may be helpful for you to recall a time when you were moved by the loving-kindness of another person. When we reflect on goodness, we think of small acts of kindness, like saying good morning, offering a cup of tea, giving a welcoming smile or a warm hug, or scratching Larry's dog's ears. Here is Peggy's memory of goodness:

> I remember driving home several days after my husband Steve's passing. As I stepped out of my car, I noticed something colorful on the front porch. Walking up the steps, I realized that it was a pile of toys and games. There were a number of dolls, a fire truck, and a board game. I picked up a small, bright blue plush toy that had black-and-white eyes, and it made me smile, something that I hadn't done in days. That evening, I received calls from two of my friends. They told me that when their children learned of Steve's death, they insisted that they be driven to my house, where they left their favorite toys and games. The mothers insisted that it was the idea of the children.

Larry remembers his first golf lesson with Peggy's mother:

My feet are slipping on the practice green, slipping in my
nongolf shoes. I notice the sign in this backcountry golf
course that says No Cowboy Boots, No High Heels, and I
know I am far from the 'hood. I recall my father's stories of
not being allowed to play golf due to policies of racial discrimination. Something in me quickens as I realize that I
am here for my father too. I am also frustrated. How could
something that looks so easy be so challenging? Peggy's
mother says, "Oh, Larry, what a lovely day. I'm so happy to
be here," and I am awakened to the presence of beauty, the
soft breeze from the Idaho mountains, and the gift of friendship. "Here, let me help you," she says as she stretches her
short arms around my belly. I can feel her heart beat next to
mine. She positions the club in my hands. What am I doing
on a golf course in Idaho? I am with my friend, and I soften
into this offering of love. We practiced for hours, and all I
remember is her kindness and gentle coaching.

The practice of true love encourages us to live our life directed by
the energy of goodness. At first it helps to be more intentional and to
make this a conscious process. We might wake up and actively welcome
the day by stating our intention to move in the direction of love, goodness, and happiness. We then can use our own experiences of the day as
a teaching device. What does goodness feel like, smell like, taste like,
and sound like? What embodies goodness? What are the faces of goodness? Can I sense it in me and around me?

Practicing in this way, goodness develops into a feedback system, a sensor. It is a kind of homing device that supports us in moving in the direction of goodness. We will have more and more
experiences when we feel transported by the energy of goodness itself. We will not need to think. We will feel moved, called, propelled
by that which is good, true, and beautiful. This will happen all on its
own. We know that you have had this experience.

A LOVING-KINDNESS MEDITATION

How do you love and talk to yourself? The inner conversation we conduct at all hours is the basis of the love relationship that we have with ourselves. Whose voice is it that loves or chides you? Is the voice critical or loving? Is there a sacred voice that you hear within?

Loving-kindness meditation practice is designed to uncover the brilliance of light and love that dwells in each of us. This radiance is just covered up with ignorance, fear, anger, and the red dust of life. But it is there. We begin by befriending ourselves, learning to talk kindly and sweetly, learning to offer ourselves a blessing instead of a curse or a complaint. This is the foundation of the practice of true love, of actively being a loving friend to ourselves.

The practice is simple. We kindly and gently repeat the phrases that are referred to as the heavenly abodes in classic Buddhist teachings. The phrases are:

> May I be free from danger.
> May I have mental happiness.
> May I have physical happiness.
> May I have ease of well-being.

The practice of loving-kindness meditation begins by extending these aspirations to our own self. We send these thoughts as a blessing and a prayer. We connect with our aspiration and our heartfelt desire that we experience safety, happiness, good health, and well-being. We connect with these sentiments as energy of light and of love.

The Kindness Handbook: Communication ꩜

Sharon Salzberg

Passion, aggression, and ignorance—Buddhism calls these the three poisons. In our relationships, the three poisons manifest in our classification of people as either friends, enemies, or those to whom we are indifferent. Sharon Salzberg shows us how we can transcend these labels, whose only reality is our own self-interest, and connect to people as they really are, free of the usual ways we judge them.

A friend once told me about repeated fights he had with his wife early on in their marriage. Much of their conflict centered on how to have dinner. He liked to eat hurriedly, standing up in the kitchen, getting it over with as quickly as possible. She liked to set the table elegantly, sit down, and eat leisurely together. Many nights they fought instead of eating. Finally they sought the help of a marriage counselor.

As they examined the layers of meaning hidden in the simple and familiar word *dinner*, they each discovered how many associations, and how many people, they were actually bringing to that table. He talked about his father, a brutal man who was often only at home at dinnertime, which became a nightmarish experience to be escaped from as quickly as possible. She spoke of her fractured family and her mentally ill brother who consumed her mother with worry. It was mainly at dinner that her family made an effort to talk to *her,* to find out about her day—where she felt she indeed belonged to a family.

For each of them dinner was rarely just dinner, and their partner was often not the person standing in front of them, but an "other" made of an amalgam of past hurts and long-held dreams and tentative new yearnings.

Can we ever actually see another person? If we create an other out of our projections and associations and ready interpretations, we have made an object of a person; we have taken away their humanity. We have stripped from our consciousness their own sensitivity to pain, their likely wish to feel at home in their bodies and minds, their complexity and intricacy and mutability.

If we have lost any recognition of the truth of change in someone and have fixed them in our minds as "good" or "bad" or "indifferent," we've lost touch with the living essence of that person. We are dwelling in a world of stylized prototypes and distant caricatures, reified images, and often very great loneliness.

Meditation practice is like a skills training in stepping back, in getting a broader perspective and a deeper understanding of what's happening. Mindfulness, one of the tools at the core of meditation, helps us not be lost in habitual biases that distort how we interpret our feelings. Without mindfulness, our perception is easily shaped by barely conscious thoughts, such as "I'm shaking, and my stomach is roiling with what seems to be fear, but I can never allow myself to admit that. I'll pretend it never came up." If we do that, it is a great struggle to be kind. There is no ready access to kindness without awareness.

Mindfulness also helps us to see through our prejudices about another person. For example, a person might think, "All older women are fuzzy thinkers, so she can't possibly be as sharp as she is pretending to be." Mindfulness helps us to see by showing us that a conclusion such as that one is simply a thought in our own mind.

Mindfulness enables us to cultivate a different quality of attention, one where we relate to what we see before us, not just as an echo of the past or a foreshadowing of the future, but more as it is right now. Here too we find the power of kindness, because we can connect to things as they are.

Making the effort to truly see someone doesn't mean we never respond or react. We can and do attempt to restore a failing marriage or protest at loud cell phones in public places or try with everything in us to rectify injustice. But we can do it from a place that allows people to be as textured as they are, that admits our feelings to be as varied and flowing as they are, that is open to surprises—a place that listens, that lets the world come alive.

One essential step in learning to see each other more genuinely is to bother to look. If someone yells at us or annoys us or dazzles us with a gift, we do pay attention to them. Our challenge then is to see them as they are, not as we project or assume them to be. But if they don't make much of an impression on us, we have a different challenge: it is all too easy to look right through them.

In particular, the meditation exercise of offering loving-kindness (*metta*) to a neutral person confronts our tendency to look through people we do not know. We choose a person whom we don't strongly like or dislike; we feel, indeed, rather neutral or indifferent toward them. Very often it helps to select a near-stranger or someone who plays a certain role or function in our lives—the checkout person in the grocery store, for example, or the UPS delivery person. We may not know much about them, not even their name.

When we send a neutral person loving-kindness, we are consciously changing a pattern of overlooking them or talking around them to one of paying attention to them. The experiment in attention we are making through these benevolent wishes asks of us whether we can practice loving "thy neighbor as thyself" when we don't know the facts about someone's dependent, elderly parent, or at-risk teenager, and so our heartstrings have not been tugged.

When we think of our neutral person, we haven't learned the story of their suspicious mole or empty evenings. We have no knowledge of their inspiring triumphs or their admirable philanthropy, and so we are not in awe of them. We aren't seeing their tension after a disappointing job interview or their sadness after their lover leaves. We practice wishing them well anyway, not knowing any of this, but simply because they exist and because we do know the beauty, the sorrow, the poignancy, and the sheer, unalterable insecurity of existence that we all share.

On trains and on the streets, in our homes and in our communities, we practice paying attention—through developing mindfulness, through developing loving-kindness, through letting go of projections—because a more complete attention proffers many special gifts. These gifts can penetrate through the exigencies of social roles and even through terrible hurt. They can remove the seeming hollowness of chance encounters.

Paying attention in this way provides the gift of noticing, the gift of connecting. We find the gift of seeing a little bit of ourselves in others, of realizing that we're not so awfully alone. We can let go of the burden of so much of what we habitually carry with us and receive the gift of the present moment.

Through paying attention we learn that even when we don't especially know or like someone, we are nonetheless in relationship with them. We come to realize that this relatedness is in itself like a vibrant, changing, living entity. We discover the gift of caring, of tending to this force of life that exists between us, and we are immeasurably enriched by that.

Where the Buddha Lives

Lin Jensen

*"Chop wood, carry water." "Ordinary mind is the Way." "Wash your
bowl." These are among the best-known Zen koans, reflecting the
practical, earthy personalities of the ancient Chinese Buddhist masters.
Yet their simplicity is deceptive, for they can easily lead us into the traps
of interpretation or literalness. Lin Jensen warns us that we shouldn't read
too much philosophical "meaning" into these koans, yet they're teaching
something much deeper than mere awareness of the moment.*

The Buddha's household encompasses the whole universe yet
manifests in its entirety in single neighborhoods and individual
houses. The Buddha's household is none other than our own, and
the Buddha has taken up residence there—and in our collective
body and mind as well. We are one family under one roof sharing
one mind.

Consider this fragment of ancient koan, one of the many teaching stories that characterize the long family history of Zen:

> Chao-chou asked, "What is the Tao?"
> Nan-ch'uan said, "Ordinary mind is the Tao."

The human mind is the universe's consciousness, the instrument through which the universe discerns its own presence and knows itself. And through Chao-chou's question, the universe is questioning itself, inquiring into the circumstances of its own nature. It's as if with the advent of the human mind, the universe had at long last shrugged off its primeval sleep and awakened, asking at long last, "What am I?" Nan-ch'uan answers, for the whole universe, saying essentially, "*Just this* is what I am." Both question and answer are a consequence of the human capacity to reflect. We awakened here on this spinning planet in this inconceivable circumstance, only to discover that we *are* this very planet and circumstance. And from that awakening arose the deep and abiding human longing to know where we come from and where we belong. And it is this that spurred Chao-chou to ask of his teacher, Nan-ch'uan, "What is the Tao?"—what is the way home? In our isolating self-awareness, we are like uprooted trees bearing with us a teasing recollection of native soil.

This longing for home is the basis of religious inquiry. Yet, ironically, it is a longing that often mistakenly takes us not nearer but farther from home, setting us out on mental pilgrimages of fanciful metaphor and grand aspirations. We abandon our place at the kitchen counter in favor of kneeling at temple altars. We leave off cooking and lawn mowing for the sake of ceremonial ritual. We light incense and don robes of black, of brown, of purple with gold brocade. We aspire to heaven in preference to earth. In short, we shun the ordinary.

While priests and teachers of many religious traditions offer the spiritual aspirant access to various exotic heavens, Zen offers a one-way ticket to the heaven of the ordinary. And while most religions aspire to a specialized state of mind, a state more holy than that accorded to ordinary mind, Zen insists that the ordinary mind is as holy as it gets. When the Emperor Wu of China asked Bodhidharma, "What is the holiest principle of Buddhism?" Bodhidharma replied, "Nothing holy in it," refusing to isolate holiness in principle of any sort and leaving the emperor with nothing but the ground under his feet.

Zen has been insistent on this matter. When students have asked various Zen masters, "What is Buddha?"—a question tantamount to asking, "What is God?" or "What is the Tao?"—the answers have invariably pointed to the most mundane possible circumstances:

Yunmen said, "A dried shitstick."
Ma-tsu said, "This very mind."
And a mature Chao-chou lived to say, "The oak tree in the courtyard."

An old story tells of a Zen master who was harvesting flax, when a monk asked him this question. The master held up a handful of flax, showing the questioner that a handful of flax, the dirt under one's feet, or even one's soiled gloves are the living body of the Buddha. My teachers taught me to give to all my surroundings the same care and respect I might give to the temple altar. Every object you or I touch is Buddha, and every house—including a homeless shelter or a prison complex or the downtown mall with its sprawling parking lot—is the exact place where the Buddha takes up residence. And we are all keepers of the Buddha's house. The proper labors of a Buddhist begin and end right here on our own familiar, native ground.

D. T. Suzuki, in *An Introduction to Zen Buddhism*, tells of a monk named Yecho who asked, "What is Buddha?" and was told, "You are Yecho." Suzuki also reports another curious response of a master who simply answered, "No nonsense here." I particularly like this last response because it exemplifies Zen's overriding attitude of no-sense at all, not even nonsense, an attitude that resists ascribing unwarranted meaning or sense to reality itself. If Zen could be said to have a motto—and it can't!—the motto would be "Add nothing extra."

Zen is pared down to a simple household thing—and its practice applies to the place where we actually live out our lives. Buddhism in general is a religion that asks us to stay at home where we can attend to our lives firsthand and are truly present in our own skins, honoring the mind and body we were born with. While the old monks followed a tradition of leaving home (and so split up a lot of families), they ironically managed nonetheless to preserve the attributes of household in their several temples, monasteries, and encampments.

Followers of Buddhism have always been studious to engage the ordinary lives and labors of human life. Huineng, for example, who would eventually become the sixth Zen ancestor, was first put to work in the harvesting shed to husk rice before receiving the attention of his teacher. A monk newly arrived to Nan-ch'uan's monastery came upon the master working in the garden one day, and not knowing he was addressing the master himself, asked, "What is the way to Nan-ch'uan?" Nan-ch'uan held up his sickle and said, "This sickle costs thirty cents." The monk said, "I didn't ask about a sickle. I asked about the way to Nan-ch'uan." Nan-ch'uan added, "It cuts very well." Seeking instruction in the Buddha Way, the monk received exactly that. This very sickle, this grass, this simple labor is the truth you're looking for.

In our human capacity for self-reflection and personal assessment, we have felt the hunger of the spirit for its home and have tended to look toward the heights—toward Olympus, Sinai, Sumeru; toward celestial cities of gold; toward the promise of imagined utopias of rest and spiritual fulfillment. But we have done so at the neglect of the spirit's true home. We have disparaged the heaven of the ordinary in favor of wholly fanciful and insubstantial abstractions. But the living spirit is not so airy a thing. In order to live, spirit requires a body and a place of the concrete sort that makes up the everyday pattern and substance of our actual lives.

Among the forty-eight koans recorded in the *Gateless Barrier* is an exchange so simple that one might easily pass by it, were it not that its very simplicity draws to it a certain curiosity and wonderment:

> A monk said to Chao-chou, "I have just entered this monastery. Please teach me."
>
> Chao-chou said, "Have you eaten your rice gruel?"

The monk said, "Yes, I have."
Chao-chou said, "Wash your bowl."
The monk understood.

Several of Chao-chou's dialogues with students have been re-corded in various koan collections and subsequently annotated and interpreted by later teachers right down to the present time. This particular conversation between Chao-chou and a monk is purport-edly given just as it took place, with the exception of the comment that the monk understood, which is editorial. I don't know what the monk understood or how anyone other than the monk could claim to know that there was any understanding at all.

After all, washing a bowl is not something you understand but rather something you do. The problem for me with the claim that the monk "understood" is that it leads to speculation about what the monk understood, and this in turn encourages interpretations that attribute meaning to the dialogue in such a way that a simple line like "Have you eaten your rice gruel?" is rendered as a metaphorical equivalent to "What is the state of your enlightenment?" And from this it follows that the monk's "Yes, I have" means something like "Yes, I'm enlightened," instead of simply "Yes, I've had breakfast." And the worst of all, and the place where I depart from all such in-terpretation, is when Chao-chou's "Wash your bowl" is read as an instruction in purification, urging the monk to rid himself of the pride of enlightenment.

I was fortunate to train for a few years with one of the best koan masters I'm ever likely to meet. He would set me to working on a particular koan, and when I came to offer him my response, he never allowed me to explain how I'd arrived at such a response, cutting off explanations of any sort. While I was often anxious to convey to him what "meaning" I'd derived from the koan, he saw no meaning there at all and judged the whole notion of such meaning as extraneous to the purpose at hand. Nothing in his world stood for something else. A thing or event didn't "mean" something; it was just what it was in and of itself. In his work with me, this koan master beat down every attempt of mine to make meaning out of Chao-chou's telling the monk to wash his bowl. "What did Chao-chou mean by 'Wash your bowl'?" he demanded, challenging me to name whatever meaning I'd claimed to find there. In the end, there was no meaning, and "Wash your bowl" was all I could ever make of it. My journey with this teacher was loosening my hold on the necessity to attribute meaning and explanation to the facts of my life.

To attribute meaning to an event or to a lifetime of events is an expression of dissatisfaction with things as they are. This is true of even the subtlest attribution. If I wash dishes as a practice in Zen mindfulness, I indulge my resistance to simply washing them in order to get them clean. I want the washing to be more significant than I think it to be, and so make a spiritual project of it. We want our lives to have meaning, and we complain inwardly and sometimes outwardly as well if what we do and what we are appear meaningless. Well, our lives *are* meaningless in any sense of their constituting a meaningful narrative plot of some sort, and when we strain to make them otherwise, we're merely indulging a story we like to tell ourselves. You and I don't manifest in the universe as meaning, we manifest as living human beings. We're not here to represent something else. We're here in our own right. A human being, or a sink full of soapy dishes for that matter, is complete in itself without the aid of fictional enhancement.

Still, the monk asked to be taught, and unless we are to assume that Chao-chou ignored the request, then Chao-chou's "Wash your bowl" was a teaching. If so, it was a teaching in reduction, and Chao-chou, in turning the monk back toward his own natural life, was showing him that everything he might ever want to know or be was already present in his person, nothing hidden from view. I've had lots of occasions when the person I wanted to be or thought I ought to be was missing somehow—which is just another way to say that I was dissatisfied with who I was and what I was doing. These were times when life didn't add up to my expectations.

I was hit with a spell of such misgivings when I was asked by my Soto teachers to found a sangha in my hometown and was first set to teaching Zen. I'd taught college literature and writing for thirty years at the time, but there seemed such a mystique surrounding the function of a Zen teacher that I took it on as a sort of role I was required to fulfill. I couldn't seem to simply show up in my own person and do what was asked of me. I imagined instead that I had to be a distinctly different sort of person to succeed at it. And when I began to teach and the sangha quickly swelled to three times its anticipated attendance, my sense of inadequacy grew with the increased numbers. At times I was profoundly beset with the doubt that I had any qualifications at all to teach Zen and felt fraudulent and utterly lacking in spiritual significance. I see now that the fact that I doubted wasn't a problem. The problem was that I thought I shouldn't doubt. I thought that a Zen teacher should know what he was doing without any of the uncertainties I was experiencing. I ought to be different than I was. I ought to be better.

Arguing with myself in this way came, in time, to feel somehow unkind and ungenerous. And trying to improve myself turned out to be just about as effective as trying to improve the shape of my ears. And the reason for that seemed to be that I was starting from the wrong end of things. Satisfaction has its genesis in acceptance rather than resistance; it's more a matter of noticing what's right than one of noticing what's wrong. Regardless of what I might prefer, this is who I am, and this is my world. It is only from this exact person in this exact place that I can step forward into the next moment. It's cranky of me to complain about talents and circumstances. So I've quit trying to size myself up in quite that intentional way. And I find that if I don't insist otherwise, I naturally move along with events in their native progression.

Like Chao-chou's monk, there's nothing I need to be taught in order to be who I am. I couldn't even think, let alone say, such a thing before, nor trust the truth of it. To do so would have felt like an expression of the worst kind of self-satisfied hubris, a smug sense of undeserved accomplishment. I hadn't yet learned the humility required to accept myself as I am. I hadn't touched the deeper wonder of receiving the gift of life and the debt of gratitude I owe for it.

When I remember these things, I quit fussing over myself and my situation. I just wash my bowl whenever it needs it and leave it at that.

Wisdom of the Rebels

An interview with Tom Robbins

The novelist Tom Robbins's spiritual heroes are the Zen rebels, Sufi saints, and wild yogis of the "crazy wisdom" tradition, as he interprets it. Like them, Robbins cuts through self-serious, conventional mind with humor, insight, and a little bit of weirdness. The following interview between the Shambhala Sun's Andrea Miller and Robbins was conducted via fax.

How would you define crazy wisdom?

Tom Robbins: The quick and easy answer is that crazy wisdom is the deliberate opposite of conventional wisdom. Like most quick and easy answers, however, that one isn't really satisfying.

For want of a precise definition, we might consider that crazy wisdom is a philosophical worldview that recommends swimming against the tide, cheerfully seizing the short end of the stick, embracing insecurity, honoring paradox, courting the unexpected, celebrating the unfamiliar, shunning each and every orthodoxy, volunteering for those tasks nobody else wants or dares to do, and perhaps above all else, breaking taboos in order to destroy their power. It's the wisdom of those who turn the tables on despair by lampooning it and who neither seek authority nor submit to it.

What's the point of all this? To enlarge the soul, light up the brain, and liberate the spirit. Crazy wisdom is both transformative and transcendent.

You seem to be particularly partial to Zen Buddhism. Is it Zen's version of crazy wisdom that appeals to you, or are there other elements that draw you to it?

The branch of Zen Buddhism that has long interested me is Rinzai, the sect that eschews the mind-quieting practice of meditation in favor of the mind-blowing activity of wrestling with koans. Koans, of course, are those carefully crafted riddles that can never be solved by means of anything remotely resembling deductive logic.

On a purely intellectual level, attempting to solve koans is a perfect manifestation of crazy wisdom at work. It's important to emphasize, however, that, unlike Zen, crazy wisdom is not a practice; it's an attitude (an attitude I seem to have had since birth).

In general, I'm attracted to Zen's focus on absolute freedom and all-embracing oneness, its reverence for nature, and its respect for humor. When Zen or tantric masters visit North America, they're often astonished by how earnest, how overly serious, Westerners are about their spiritual practice. They'll go to a *zendo* in Minnesota, for example, and wonder aloud why nobody there is laughing. This led Chögyam Trungpa, in a lovely expression of crazy wisdom, to squirt righteously zealous meditators with a water pistol.

To be uptight about one's Zen practice, to become attached to it, is to miss the whole point of it; one might as well hook up with one of the fear-based, authoritarian, guilt-and-redemption religions.

Can you give me some examples of crazy wisdom that interest you? I realize that you talked a lot about crazy wisdom in your Harper's *essay "In Defiance of Gravity," but it would be nice to have more of a taste of what you mean.*

I'm a wordslinger not a scholar, I have a monkey mind, not a monk mind, but I think you can trust me when I report that just as Zen evolved in China from a comingling of Buddhism and Taoism,

there occurred in Tibet a dynamic meeting between Buddhism and
Bön, the ancient Tibetan shamanic religion. The Buddhist masters
who had infiltrated Tibet (around the eighth century) were eccentric
mahasiddhas out of the tantric lineage in India, and the Bön sha-
mans, having a natural affinity, took to their crazy-wisdom ways like
Homer Simpson to donuts, maybe even improving (if *improving* is
the right word) on their radical approach to ultimate awareness.

The Tibetan siddhas soon acquired a reputation as the wildest
of spiritual outlaws. Siddhas slept naked in the snow, hung out in
graveyards, nibbled on dung, drank wine from skulls, publicly engaged in kinky sex, and missed no opportunity to ridicule dogma.
Believing in the possibility of instant karma, they employed shock
tactics to jolt people into spontaneous enlightenment.

When a latter-day Japanese roshi would define buddhahood as
"dried shit on a stick," or answer the question, "What do you do
when you meet your master coming through the woods?" by advis-
ing, "Hit him over the head with a stick," you'd know they'd been
infected with the virus of crazy wisdom.

Whether it sprang up independently in Persia and Turkey or
was carried there by travelers along the Silk Road, I haven't a clue,
but crazy wisdom permeates Sufism. One of my favorite Sufi stories
concerns a man who, feeling in need of spiritual guidance, petitions
for an audience with a renowned master. After a long wait, the request is granted, but the man is allowed to ask only one question. He
asks, "What is God really like?"

The master answers, "God? God is a carrot. Ha ha ha ha ha!"

Feeling mocked and insulted, the man goes away in a snit. Later,
suspecting that he must have misunderstood something, he requests
a second interview, and after several years it, too, is granted. "What
did you mean," the fellow asks, "when you said God is a carrot?"

The master looks at him in amazement. "A carrot?" he bellows.
"God is not a carrot! God is a radish!" And again he laughs uproariously.

Turned away, the fellow broods over this outlandishness for
many months. Then, one day, it dawns on him that the master was

saying that God is beyond definition and can never be described, that anything we might say is God is automatically not God. At that moment, the man was powerfully awakened.

Examples of crazy wisdom also abound in the modern West, ranging from Joris Karl Huysmans sewing his eyelids shut because he believed that at age thirty, he'd already seen so much it would take him the rest of his life to process it all, to Muhammad Ali dancing in his undershorts at the Houston Induction Center after committing a felony by refusing to be conscripted into the army.

Unfortunately, however, crazy wisdom in the West is almost always devoid of a spiritual dimension.

What influences or happenings in your life first prompted you to have a spiritual attitude?

When I left home at age seventeen, I quit attending church because church had been providing me with nothing beyond an anesthetic numbing of the backside and the brain. By my midtwenties, I'd completely rejected my Southern Baptist faith on the grounds that it was a bastion of fascist-tinged hypocrisy based on misinterpretation of Levantine myth and watered-down compromises of the teachings of Jesus. Around that time, I began peeking into Asian systems of liberation, but it wasn't until my early thirties that I was literally propelled into the spiritual zone by the oceanic blast of psychedelic drugs.

Traditionalists won't like hearing this, but the fact is, tens of thousands of Westerners became receptive to and enamored of Buddhist and Hindu teachings as a direct result of LSD.

Over time you have changed your mind about whether or not Americans can thoroughly and successfully adopt Asian philosophies such as Buddhism or Taoism. What is your opinion now?

There are numerous paths to enlightenment. In Asia, the paths have been worn smooth by millions of experienced feet. The Western seeker, while he or she may have ready access to guides, maps, and road signs imported from Asia, must nevertheless stumble along overgrown, unfamiliar trails pitted with potholes and patrolled by our indigenous cultural wolves.

Americans may hold Buddhist ideals in our hearts and minds, but they're not yet in our genes. That takes time. Meanwhile, Asians are becoming increasingly Americanized. Who knows where this exchange will lead?

In your first novel, Another Roadside Attraction, *your character Marx Marvelous contemplates what religion would take Christianity's place if Christianity were suddenly to disappear. Can you describe the faith that you think might develop in such a situation?*

Suppose that from the environmentalist movement there should spring a revival of mystical nature worship, and suppose that this new nature religion should receive an infusion of crazy wisdom sufficient to keep it honest and amusing, free from any trace of dogma. Wouldn't that be the wildcat's meow?

Your book Still Life with Woodpecker *explores how to make love stay. How would you define love?*

Love is a carrot. No, no, it's a radish. Listen, better brains than mine have skidded off the road in pursuit of that elusive subject. I can say this much with confidence: genuine love, while it lasts, is a transformative emotional state that makes of the loved one an irreplaceable being. There's something magical, magnificent, and very sweet about that.

Still Life with Woodpecker *was published almost thirty years ago. Since writing it, have you learned anything new about how to make love stay?*

Well, I've learned that in asking how we can make love stay, I posed the wrong question. Romantic love moves around. That's what it does. Indifferent to misguided human cravings for permanence and certainty, it stages its glorious show, then folds its tent and leaves town. Or, at least, it stops buttering the popcorn. Perhaps it's both insulting and injurious to romance to try to hold on to it.

Ah, but there's another kind of love that does stay—and most Buddhists are familiar with it. When you "fall" into universal love, you're "in" love all the time, external events notwithstanding; you live and breathe in love. Even then, should your romantic partner decamp, you might feel sad or even angry for a while, but you won't sit up night after night swilling tequila and listening to heartbreak music.

It should be noted that there are relationships between mature, grounded, personally evolved individuals (people whole enough not to cling or be needy) that do last and sometimes manage to embody both the romantic and the spiritual.

In Wild Ducks Flying Backward, *you say that the word* spiritual *has become highly suspect. Why do you say that? How and why did the word degenerate?*

When a blue-collar, average Joe hears the word *spiritual,* he'll frequently hee-haw and spit. It sounds sissy, elitist, and heretical to him, a threat to his masculinity and a contamination of the patriotic and religious detergents with which his brain has been thoroughly washed. When cool urban cynics hear the word, they sneer. It's an affront to their existential hipness.

For many others, it's a reminder of the legions of charlatans, frauds, and self-deluded dilettantes who are making money by hawking various brands of "spiritual" guidance. Then, too, there are the innocent airheads who go about broadcasting embarrassing streams of woo woo in their everyday lives (and who are frequently the victims of the con-artist gurus).

These folks—some greedy, some ignorant, some just sweetly naive—have all contributed to the aura of suspicion that surrounds the word *spiritual* in contemporary American society. That's indeed unfortunate, because spirituality, when pure, connects us to the god-head with infinitely more efficacy and grace than does religiosity.

What is the most spiritual place you have ever visited?

An uninhabited savannah deep in Africa, a hundred miles from any artificial light, where, while lions coughed and night birds sang, I gazed at a dozen wheeling constellations and millions of ancient sparkling stars.

If it were true, after all, that humans were made in the image of God, what exactly do you think God would look like?

God is a carrot. Wait a second, that's not right. God is a radish!

Where Is God When Stick Hit Floor?

Rabbi Rami Shapiro

Now here's some meshuga-wisdom action. Rabbi Rami Shapiro confronts Joshu Sasaki Roshi, the grand old man of American Zen, and ends up on his tuchus.

"Where is God when stick hit floor?" Joshu Sasaki Roshi, my Zen master, asked over and over. Unfortunately, I wasn't listening.

This was the second day of a *sesshin*, a Zen meditation retreat, and my first opportunity to experience *sanzen*, a one-on-one meeting with the roshi. The purpose of sanzen is to work on a koan, a Zen puzzle designed to open you to the profound simplicity of reality. I knew this as I prepared to meet with Roshi. What I didn't know was that Roshi spoke English.

All my previous encounters with Sasaki Roshi had been through a translator. Roshi lectured in Japanese, and the translator relayed his words in English. I assumed that was because Roshi spoke no English. So as I sat across from him in sanzen, I had no expectation of actually speaking with the man.

Roshi sat in front of me, his right hand tapping a gnarled piece of mahogany on the hardwood floor between us. His lips moved, sounds emerged, but I heard no question.

"Where is God when stick hit floor?"

My mind wandered. I'd signed up for this retreat because I was a Zenophile. I'd read every book by D. T. Suzuki and Alan Watts I could find. I'd purchased a set of meditation cushions, and I sat *zazen* every day. All I cared about was enlightenment, and this sesshin was going to be great. A real Zen master, authentic Japanese chanting, simple vegan meals—man, this was the fast track to enlightenment. The Buddha pulled it off in eight days sitting under a tree; no way I couldn't do it in a Zen center with hot and cold running water.

"Where is God when stick hit floor?"

What was this guy mumbling about? He must know I don't speak Japanese. My knees were getting stiff supporting my weight on the floor. Nice floor. Well polished. This was cool. Sitting across from a Zen roshi. Right out of one of my Zen books. What is the sound of one hand clapping? What was your original face before you were born? Does a dog have buddhanature?

"Where is God when stick hits floor?"

Oh, my God! Roshi spoke English! In fact, he had been speaking English this whole time. His Japanese accent was so thick, I hadn't recognized his speech as English. How many times had he asked me this question? The Zen master was giving me a koan, for God's sake, and I was ignoring him!

"Where is God when stick hit floor?"

"Uh, God is here?"

For a second I thought Roshi was going to nod, say the Japanese equivalent of "Good boy," and give me a gold Zen sticker. Instead, he slapped my forehead lightly with his palm as if to say, "*Meshuggener!* Have you learned nothing from all I've taught you? From you I get no *nachas*." Or that's what he would have said if he'd been my rabbi, who found me equally dense and inattentive. Roshi scowled, picked up a brass bell, and rang me out of his room. "More zazen!"

During a Zen retreat, sanzen always comes during *kinhin,* walking meditation. That way you can gracefully exit the sitting room and make your way to the roshi's sanzen room. In this particular retreat, a line of chairs were assembled outside the sanzen room. Moving up the row, chair by chair, was a highly ritualized process. As the person sitting in the forwardmost chair left to enter Roshi's room, the rest of us would stand, bow, and advance one chair.

Upon entering the sanzen room, there was more elaborate bowing. You bowed from the waist, then got down on your knees, and then fell on your face, lifting your hands, palms up, off the floor three times. Then you stood, moved forward a bit, and repeated the process. It took three complete bowing cycles to reach Roshi. When done right, you ended up sitting on your knees directly in front of him, your knees only inches from his.

This wasn't the Zen I'd read about in Alan Watts's books. His Zen was far looser and iconoclastic. So I expected to go to sanzen, give Roshi a hug, and share with him some of my deeper thoughts on the meaning of life. But tradition was tradition, and I didn't mind. In fact, it seemed to make the whole procedure more powerful. Most likely this was because I didn't grow up with it.

As a Jew, I knew other traditions. Once, when my sister's boyfriend joined the family for dinner, my mother made brisket. The boyfriend, thinking we'd forgotten to supply the obvious beverage, brought a carton of milk out from the refrigerator. Sensing immediately that he was about to violate the law about strict separation of meat and milk, we all started shouting at him.

But that was Jewish tradition. *Narishkeit*—silliness. What does it matter if you have milk with a piece of brisket? What did Moses know about brisket? Jewish law is tedious. That's why we have Reform Judaism to knock some sense into the tradition.

For me, though, Zen was another matter. Screw up the bowing and get tossed out on your ear? No problem. It was tradition. There is no such thing as Reform Zen. So I didn't mind the rules of Zen. The only thing I minded was seeing Roshi one-on-one.

Time after time, I went to sanzen hoping to impress Roshi with my Zen knowledge. I mean, I had a 4.0 GPA. How hard could this koan business be?

"Where is God when stick hit floor?"

It's really quite simple: God is here. God is everywhere. Didn't Roshi get that?

Now, Zen folks don't talk a lot about God. Roshi was doing this for my sake. He knew I was Jewish, and he knew I was considering going into the rabbinate. So, being a master of *upaya*, skillfully teaching truth from the illusions at hand, Roshi spoke to me of God. Or, more precisely, he spoke to me about where the hell He was when the *farschtunkenah* stick hit the goddamned floor.

I tried haiku. That ought to impress him:

stick in hand
stick on floor
sunlight slips through slatted blinds

"More zazen," was his response.

I tried Nargarjuna's fourfold negation of reality: "There is a stick. There is no stick. There is neither stick nor no stick. There is . . ." I couldn't remember what came next.

"More zazen."

I must have visited the guy a dozen times, and I still couldn't figure out what the hell he was looking for. At last, I gave up.

While sanzen is mandatory in many sesshin, Roshi made it voluntary. I didn't have to see him if I didn't want to. And I certainly didn't want to. But then it hit me: I was telling him where God was. I had to show him. OK. One more time.

I took a seat in line to see Roshi, and I rehearsed in my mind what I would do. Do—not say. There was nothing to say. Zen is the transmission from mind to mind beyond words. I'd read that someplace. It was my Jewish head trapped in words that was causing me all these problems. This time, though, I'd nail it—no words.

Thus far I'd focused my answers on the universality of God when the stick hit the floor. But what I had to do was show Roshi that the stick was irrelevant. God was, is, and always will be, whether the stick hits the floor or not. How could I demonstrate this deep insight? By grabbing that little stick and ripping the sucker out of the old man's hand, that's how. My stick. My God. My answer. My God, I'm brilliant!

Roshi rang in the next person, and in my mind, I calculated the precise distance between Roshi and the door. I figured out how much I'd have to space my bowing so that I'd end up in comfortable reach of the stick with enough leverage to wrench it out of his hands. Roshi was small, plump, and old. I had height and youth on my side. Plus, I had the element of surprise. I mean, no one would ever have tried this before. Roshi rings me in.

"Where is God when stick hit floor?

Hits. Hits the floor. I am a stickler for grammar, but it didn't matter—here was the stick, coming down. I lunged for the wood, wrapped my fingers around it, and yanked, breaking Roshi's grip. Then, triumphant, I sat back with the stick in my hand, proclaiming to the amazed and humbled Zen man: "No stick, no sound, just God!"

At least, that's what was supposed to happen.

Short, round Zen masters are often stronger than they look. I did manage to grab the stick, but Roshi didn't let go. Instead, he grasped my wrist and flipped me over his shoulder. I let him keep the stick; I was busy tumbling onto the floor behind him.

"More zazen," he said, as I bowed and left.

How embarrassing. The old guy tossed me around like I was a sack of flour. My butt hurt, my ego was bruised, and I was through with Zen forever. Except I couldn't leave. No one left sesshin. But so what? All I had to do was put in my time on the cushion and wait the whole thing out. Who cares that I can't get enlightened? It isn't as if it will go on my permanent record.

After a while I stopped fuming. I was bored. I just sat there. Hours passed. Then during the next round of walking meditation, Roshi rang the bell signaling sanzen. Just in case I forgot, my mind started yelling at me, "We aren't going in there! No way in hell are we going to submit ourselves to the embarrassment of trying to answer that stupid koan. Where is God when the stick hits—*hits*—the floor? Who cares?"

"Where is God when stick hit floor?"

Roshi was right in front of me, sitting on his cushions, tapping his stick on the floor. I had no idea how I'd gotten there. Without realizing it, I must have walked out of the meditation hall, taken my place in the sanzen line, moved up chair by chair, and performed the intricate bowing. One mistake in the ritual and I'd have been sent back to the meditation hall. No mistakes, save one: what was I doing back in sanzen?

"Where is God when stick hit floor?"

I don't know exactly what happened next. I can only reconstruct my actions based on where I found myself afterward. It seems that the instant Roshi's stick touched the floor, I flung myself at his feet, screaming at the top of my lungs, "God is here!" I suspect this is what happened, because when I regained awareness I was lying next to Roshi, my throat raw and my ears still ringing with the scream.

I scrambled to my knees, retook my place across from Roshi, and waited to be forever banished. But the old man was laughing hysterically. I'd like to believe he was laughing with me, except I wasn't laughing. I was on the verge of tears. Roshi thought that was funny as well.

"Goodah ahnsa," Roshi laughed. "Goodah ahnsa! Seventy-five percent. Now, more zazen."

Seventy-five percent? C? I hadn't gotten a C since freshman German. What would it take to get a B out of this guy? I never found out. Despite additional sesshin since then with Roshi and others, when it comes to enlightenment, I'm average. It's the best I've ever done.

As fierce and formal as he could be during sesshin, Sasaki Roshi could be just as relaxed and jovial after it was over. I watched as my fellow Zen students hugged Roshi and thanked him for the sesshin. Though I hadn't gotten enlightened, I hadn't flunked either. So I wanted to say good-bye too. But I should have known better. Once

I got within reach, Sasaki Roshi pinched my butt and said, "Roshi or rabbi—choose now!"

I hated that. Not the pinching, though that hurt, but the choosing. I had thought that I could integrate the two traditions. Yet here was Roshi, my ass in his hand, telling me to choose.

Roshi had commented on the size of my bottom earlier in the sesshin while he was using my rear end as a model of how to sit—or rather, how not to sit. He'd lovingly (I guess) commented on the fact that my bottom covered so much of the cushion that it was hard to use me as a visual aid. Now he was telling me that, as wide as my tuchus was, it was not wide enough to sit in both the *zendo* and the shul.

I looked at Roshi and smiled. "I am going to be a rabbi," I said with conviction. "Thank you, Roshi, for showing me that."

Roshi smiled and pinched my tuchus even harder. "Good," he hissed. "Be Zen rabbi!"

Old Friend from Far Away ⌇

Natalie Goldberg

Natalie Goldberg's best seller Writing Down the Bones *inspired thousands to take up writing as a spiritual practice. Here she offers some lessons on exploring and understanding ourselves through the art of writing personal memoir.*

There is nothing stiff about memoir. It's not a chronological pronouncement of the facts of your life: born in Hoboken, New Jersey; schooled at Elm Creek Elementary; moved to Big Flat, New York, where you attended Holy Mother High School. Memoir doesn't cling to an orderly procession of time and dates, marching down the narrow aisle of your years on this earth. Rather, it encompasses the moment you stopped, turned your car around, and went swimming in a deep pool by the side of the road. You threw off your gray suit. A swimming trunk in the backseat, a bridge you dived off. You knew you had an appointment in the next town, but the water was so clear. When would you be passing by this river again? The sky, the clouds, the reeds by the roadside mattered. You remembered bologna sandwiches made on white bread; you started to whistle old tunes. How did life get so confusing? Last week your seventeen-year-old told you he was gay, and you suspect your wife is having an affair. You never liked selling industrial-sized belts to tractor companies anyway. Didn't you once dream of being a librarian or a pastry chef? Maybe it was a landscaper, a firefighter.

Memoir gives you the ability to plop down like the puddle that forms and spreads from the shattering of a glass of milk on the kitchen floor. You watch how the broken glass gleams from the electric light overhead. The form of memoir has leisure enough to examine all this.

Memoir is not a declaration of the American success story, one undeviating road, the conquering of one mountaintop after another. The puddle began in downfall. The milk didn't get to the mouth. Whatever your life, it is urging you to record it—to embrace the crumbs with the cake. It's why so many of us want to write memoir. We know the particulars, but what really went on? We want the emotional truths under the surface that drove our life.

In the past, memoir was the country of old people, a looking back, a reminiscence. But now people are disclosing their lives in their twenties, writing their first memoir in their thirties and their second in their forties. This revolution in personal narrative that has unrolled across the American landscape in the last two and a half decades is the expression of a uniquely American energy: a desire to understand in the heat of living, while life is fresh, and not wait till old age—it may be too late. We are hungry—and impatient—now.

But what if you are already sixty, seventy years old? Eighty, ninety? Let the thunder roll. You've got something to say. You are alive, and you don't know for how long. (None of us really knows for how long.) No matter your age, there is a sense of urgency to make life immediate and relevant.

Think of the word *memoir*. It comes from the French *memoire*. It is the study of memory, structured on the meandering way we remember. Essentially it is an examination of the zigzag nature of how our mind works. The thought of Cheerios ricochets back to a broken fence in our backyard one Nebraska spring, then hops over to the first time we stood before a mountain and understood kindness. A smell, a taste—and a whole world flares up.

How close can we get? All those questions, sometimes murky and uncomfortable: Who was that person who was your mother? Why did you play basketball when you longed to play football? Your head wanted to explode until you first snorted cocaine behind the chainlink fence near the gas station. Then things got quiet and peaceful, but what was that black dog still at your throat?

We are a dynamic country, fast paced, ever onward. Can we make sense of love and ambition, pain and longing? In the center of our speed, in the core of our forward movement, we are often confused and lonely. That's why we have turned so full-heartedly to the memoir form. We have an intuition that it can save us. Writing is the act of reaching across the abyss of isolation to share and reflect. It's not a diet to become skinny, but a relaxation into the fat of our lives. Often without realizing it, we are on a quest, a search for meaning. What does our time on this earth add up to?

We hope for a linear method of writing. Do A, B, C, and voilà— your memoir is before you, sprung like a cake from a pan. But look at your life: A often doesn't lead to B or C. And that's what makes it compelling—how things worked out in the wrong places or were a disaster where they were supposed to bring happiness. Even if you managed to narrow your life to one thin line—born, went to school, worked a job from nine to five, saved your money, ate a single lamb chop and baked potato on Saturday night—there were still dreams and nightmares, the gaping hole of death at the end, the sudden unmistakable crush on the woman with pale eyes who worked the register at the employee cafeteria.

And because life is not linear, you want to approach writing memoir sideways, using the deepest kind of thinking to sort through the layers; you want reflection to discover what the real connections are. A bit of brooding, pondering, contemplating, but not in a lost manner. I am asking you to make all this dynamic. Pen to paper gives muscle to your deliberations.

The title *Old Friend from Far Away* comes from the Analects by Confucius. We reach back in time to another country. Isn't that what memory is?

To have an old friend visit
from far away—
what a delight!

THE FOUR-LETTER WORD

Let's dare talk about love for a moment, shall we?

Being in love is a loss of control. Suddenly your life is dependent on the eyebrow twitch of Joe Schmo. It's terrible—it's thrilling. Everyone wants it.

No one says it, but writing induces that state of love. The oven shimmers, the faucet radiates, you die into the mouth that only you see. Right there, sitting with your notebook on your lap, even the factory town you drove through heading north to Denver, the town you hated and prayed no flat tire, no traffic jam would hold you there, even that place while writing about that trip, that day, that year, you caress now. Your life is real. It has texture, detail. Suddenly it springs alive.

Hardly moving, only the pen, hand, wrist, lower arm in a quiet stir, yet love is exuding from your every cell. You are like a great mountain, a buddha. You are yourself.

Tell me about a breakfast you were once privileged to have. Eggs over easy? Grapefruit? One thin slice of toast? Not even that. You ate a pickle—and it never tasted so good. You vowed to eat pickles for breakfast for the rest of your life. Then what happened? Tell me. Be specific. Go.

WILD AT HEART

In the essay "Wild at Heart," in a book called *The Poem That Changed America: "Howl" Fifty Years Later,* Vivian Gornick writes,

Allen Ginsberg was born in Newark, New Jersey, in 1926 to Louis and Naomi Ginsberg; the father was a published poet, a high school teacher, and a socialist; the mother, an enchanting free spirit, a passionate communist, and a woman who lost her mental stability in her thirties (ultimately she was placed in an institution and lobotomized). Allen and his brother grew up inside a chaotic mixture of striving respectability, left-wing bohemianism, and certifiable madness in the living room. It all felt large to the complicated, oversensitive boy who, discovering that he lusted after boys, began to feel mad himself and, like his paranoid parents, threatened by, yet defiant of, the America beyond the front door.

None of this accounts for Allen Ginsberg; it only describes the raw material that, when the time was right, would convert into a poetic vision of mythic proportion that merged brilliantly with its moment: the complicated aftermath of the Second World War. . . .

Let's look at this. The first paragraph is a detailed list of the specifics of Allen Ginsberg's early life. Yes, he was born in Newark; yes, yes, his father was what Gornick says he was and his mother is described aptly. It is true he was inclined to love boys when he was young. But then the stunning line: "None of this accounts for Allen Ginsberg." Huh? I thought in writing we build up the details and create a picture of who we are. This is exactly the problematic trick.

You can be told what materials make a hand—the skin, the fine bones, the nails, the persnickety thumb—but then all the ingredients fuse and explode. Whose hand is this? A leap happens. Allen Ginsberg became a huge figure who changed the face of poetry. Notice, too, it is not only Allen Ginsberg, the man, who created himself, but also his work that met the moment—he ignited with his time. Something dynamic happened.

We don't live in a vacuum. That extra ingredient—the flint snapping across the rough edge of our era, the day the news broke, the flavor of our decade, our generation—makes the spark spring up. You never talk just for yourself. A whole flame shoots through you. Even if you're not aware of it, even though your sorrow, your pain, is individual, it is also connected to the large river of suffering. When you join the two, something materializes.

When Bob Dylan sat in the third-row first seat in B. J. Rolfzen's English class in Hibbing High School, his public school teacher had no idea that this quiet boy would, two years after he left his family at eighteen, write some of the best songs of the twentieth century.

Allen Ginsberg and Bob Dylan were brought up thousands of miles apart. Bob Dylan had stable, middle class parents. His father sold electrical equipment, stoves, refrigerators to iron ore miners in northern Minnesota. His mother belonged to B'nai B'rith. But "none of this accounts for" Bob Dylan. Dylan took a leap into another life. As an adult fourteen years older than Bob Dylan, Allen Ginsberg heard Dylan's songs and knew the torch of inspiration, of freedom, had been passed on to the next generation.

We each are endowed with original mind, which is like a river under the visible river, unconditioned, the immediate point where our clear consciousness meets the vast unknown; yet we've blown smoke screens to cloud it. Fake images, false illusions. When Allen Ginsberg sat down one night in his twenties to write what was really on his mind, he replaced the rhymed poesy he'd learned from his father and from school. That decision was the beginning of one of the most famous poems in our language. Imagine! The power of writing what's truly on your mind. What you really see, think, and feel. Rather than what you are told you should think, see, and feel. It causes a revolution—or at the very least, a damn fine poem.

Raw material is poured into a burning vat and something different comes out. Maybe in past generations when people didn't leave home and raised their children near their parents in the same town where they grew up, and if your father was a steelworker, you became a steelworker, or if your mother was a secretary, you became an office manager, you might not have had the luxury of wondering about yourself. You might not ponder how A became B and produced C. It might all have been obvious. But I bet that even a third-generation physician on his way to work in his hometown who suddenly notices the glint off a parking meter, stops still and questions, "Who am I?" and is left in this swirl that doesn't make sense. One lives and then one dies? Who thought this scheme up anyway?

We go back to our past to piece things together. "I always loved coffee ice cream, roast beef, and hopscotch." It still makes us happy to remember these things, but how did they lead to moving from the sprawl of a city on the East Coast to listening to mourning doves on a dead branch outside our kitchen door in the vast West? Can we turn around fast enough to catch a glimpse of our own face?

In some ways writing is our attempt to grasp what went on. We want an answer. We want things to be black and white, to be obvious and ordered. Oh, the relief. But have you noticed, it doesn't work that way? We live more in the mix of black and white, in the gray, or in the brilliant colors of the undefined moment.

Can we bear to hang out in incongruity, in that big word *paradox*? How did I end up with the partner I have, the children that sprang from me? How can I love my father, who betrayed me? This isn't a call to ditch it all, even though nothing makes sense. Instead, don't reject anything—the person who did something unforgivable, the white rose at the edge of your driveway, the split pea soup you never liked.

There are no great answers for who we are. Don't wait for them. Pick up the pen and right now, in ten furious minutes, tell the story of your life. I'm not kidding. Ten minutes of continuous writing is much more expedient than ten years of musing and getting nowhere.

Include the false starts, the wrong turns, the one surprising right thing that happened. A lot of it is ungrabbable—but you might sense an aroma, a whiff of something. Always in writing, at the back of words are no words, behind you is nothing. That nothing holds us up. Embrace it.

In 1997, at the age of seventy, Allen Ginsberg heard from his doctor that he only had a short time to live, and he cried. Then, sitting in his hospital bed, he picked up a pen and worked on a poem he was writing. That man had an abundant heart. His death was important, but so was a poem. Soon before the end, he stayed up into the morning hours, making long-distance calls to friends to say good-bye, to ask if they needed anything, were they taken care of, should he leave them funds in his will.

I tell you all this because there is a sea of possibility out there. Again, I say, pick up the pen and find it for yourself. Don't begin with an idea: begin to understand your life—and death—with the point of the pen touching paper.

JUST SITTING—OR DO THE NEOLA

Let's try something else, too. Drop it all—forget about the technique. Throw the anchor out the window or into the center of the Indian Ocean. Just sit for twenty minutes. Don't worry if fifteen of the twenty are spent obsessing about your wedding dress and it turns out you're sixty and in all likelihood you won't marry again. Or you drifted off to a deep desire to suddenly cut your toenails, and you thought about it over and over—where you would get the clippers, how you'd bend over the tub rim. Oh, such fine detail.

For the first few years, every retreat I sat, I imagined making a pot roast. I'd carefully peel the onions, get out the cutting board. Add carrots, brown the meat. It made no sense. I never cooked one when the retreat was over—or thought about it in my daily life.

This is the mind. If you were only present to the sitting for a moment in the full twenty minutes, you did not fail. There is no success or failure, no great place you are going. You are "just sitting." To wander, to obsess, to lust—you get a flavor of the mind, a direct meeting. Without acting on any of the thoughts, you get to see how they rise up and—if you're lucky—pass away. Sometimes we get stuck. You get to observe the nature of being stuck.

But eventually with this just sitting, thoughts are only another thing, like snow out the window. They get your attention for a moment, and then they don't. We need to give enough space in just sitting for our thoughts to settle. Let the mind quiet of its own accord. It takes time to become who we are.

It's like shaking up vinegar and oil. Put down the bottle and wait for the vinegar to sink to the bottom, for the oil to become clear. Sit still and watch it happen inside you.

In just sitting, you can drop any exact effort. There is a sound. You hear the sound. You feel hands on thighs. Then you might notice your breath. Finally you are propelled into the deep unknown: open space between sound or feeling or the vagaries of your thoughts. Just here.

I'd been taught just sitting in a very formal way, but it didn't become mine until thirty years later, when it seemed I gave up everything for a few months. Daily I went to a café called Bread and Chocolate and sat at a table near a big window, holding on to a tall cup of steaming water, taking an occasional sip and nibbling at a chocolate chip cookie that had to last an hour. It was then that I dropped all effort, even discursive thinking came and went. I wasn't caught by anything.

Maybe it was all the practice before that brought me to this place. Maybe I was finally exhausted. But you don't need thirty years to discover it.

I have a student named Neola. Isn't that a fine name? When I first met her, I immediately started a little ditty: "Roll over, Mineola . . ."

When nothing else seemed to work for her, I suggested she go to a café and just sit. I created a shorthand for just sitting: "Do the Neola," I told the class.

Neola loved having something named after her. And when a practice is your namesake, you have to get good at it. I told her to write me a postcard from one of the cafés. Then I gave her another instruction to confound her: always follow the person behind you.

Ridiculous? No? Yes? You figure it out. Don't exclude anything, including the dog's bark, a dozen roses and daylilies, the wails in Iraq, the cement, the nothing that was your life. Being right on the point, the point being there is no point. You go out between breaths. Your notebook becomes luminous. You suddenly know what to write.

One of the students said, "'Do the Neola' sounds like a dance."

Yes. A dance. The great dance.

There Is Much We Do Not Know about the Feelings of Butterflies ☵

Liza Dalby

"Death—" said an old Zen master, "he who penetrates here is truly a great man." If religion and philosophy are a response to anything, it is the question of death. It is the great koan. Ethnographer Liza Dalby returns to Japan, where she was one of the few Westerners to apprentice as a geisha, and on a visit to the gravestone of her "geisha mother," wonders whether the answer to the koan of death is a butterfly.

Last fall I returned to Kyoto, a city where I had once lived and researched the subject of Japan's geisha tradition. I still have many friends there, including *geiko* (as the Kyoto geisha call themselves) current and retired. Whenever I visit Kyoto, there are two old friends in particular to whom I always pay my respects. One is my geisha sister, Ichiume, who was put in charge of my training; the other, my geisha mother, Kiyo Hasui, who invited me to join the community of Pontochô as a participant observer. Both of them are dead. Twenty-four-year-old Ichiume died in 1979 in a fire accidentally started in the traditional wood-and-paper teahouse where she lived. Kiyo Hasui passed away twelve years ago at age seventy-three.

In Japan, almost everyone is Buddhist when they pass away. In fact, to say someone "has become a buddha" (*hotoke ni natta*) simply means he or she has died. It has always seemed to me that in Japan, the dead are never very far away. Often, memorial tablets are set up in a votive altar called a *butsudan* kept in the home. Every day, fruit or flowers are offered and incense burned. Many of my Japanese friends sit in front of the butsudan when they are worried and tell their troubles to deceased family members. On special death anniversaries, people go to the cemeteries as well. If, like me, you are in town once every couple of years, you visit friends' graves when you can.

There is an etiquette for these visits to the cemetery. First, you announce yourself at the priest's house. Someone answers—usually his wife—and you tell her who you've come to visit. You may request her to write out your friend's Buddhist after-death name on a thin strip of wood, along with a Siddham-script mantra and your name. You will place this in a rack behind the stone—it's like leaving your calling card. You will fill a short bucket with water, pick up one of the ladles hanging next to the faucet, and carrying the flowers and incense you've brought, step your way through the narrow paths between the family plots. When you've reached your friend's stone, you can remove faded flowers from the granite vases, tidy up, change the water, add your new bouquets. You insert your wooden slat into the rack, looking at the names written on the old ones. Who else has visited? When did they come? You light several sticks of incense, then ladle the rest of the water over the headstone.

"It soothes the hotoke" is how this custom was once explained to me. Unless, of course, it is the middle of winter. When Hasui-san and I visited Ichiume's grave in December one year, she held my arm back.

"Not too much," she said. "The hotoke will catch a chill."

The way Buddhism is popularly practiced in Japan, the hotoke is clearly spoken of, thought of, and treated as a person's soul. The mental connections of the living to the dead are so strong they create the hotoke's reality. Incorporeal though it may be, it can be affected by the physical world—for example, a splash of cold water. One could say this belief contradicts the philosophy of classic Buddhism in which the existence of a permanent self, living or dead, is considered to be an illusion. Nevertheless, despite sectarian differences among the different branches of Mahayana Buddhism in Japan, most Japanese think of the hotoke as but a transformed version of a person's essential self.

So, in Kyoto for a few days in early October, I bought some incense and picked up a bouquet of chrysanthemums, carnations, roses, and evergreen sakaki leaves at a florist near Shin'enji, a small, not-at-all-famous Pure Land temple in north-central Kyoto. The priest's wife recognizes me by now.

"It's so sad," she says as we fill the bucket at the hose bib and walk back toward my geisha mother's stone.

"No one comes to visit her, except her old friend Yoshiko. But she only comes once a year at Obon."

"What about her son?" I ask.

"Nobody's seen him in ages," she replies. "He's just disappeared."

Sure enough, at the stone there is only one other wooden strip, left there last August by Hasui-san's old colleague and fellow geisha, Yoshiko.

"Look, a butterfly has joined us," I murmur to the priest's wife as she excuses herself to go back to the house. From my childhood as a butterfly collector, I recognize a fritillary, somewhat tattered now in autumn.

I stand in front of the stone, thinking about how vivacious Hasui-san was when I knew her—how well connected, how many friends she had, how she loved a party. Compared to the other monuments bristling with visitors' wooden strips, her stone seems sad and neglected. Then I notice the butterfly again. It has landed directly on top of the smooth granite stone in front of me, almost at eye level. I look around. I am the only person in the graveyard. There are no other butterflies. Perched on the stone, slowly pumping its wings, it shows no inclination to fly away. I take out my video camera, and now the butterfly turns to face me. A breeze arises, and I see it brace its tiny hooked feet in an effort not to be blown off the slippery granite.

And I swear it looks straight at me with its speckled jewel eyes. We regard one another, this butterfly and I, and I have the uncanny feeling that it is trying to communicate. Finally, a puff of wind blows it off the stone.

"That was exceedingly odd," I think to myself. I put down my camera and proceed to change the flowers, light incense, and ladle water. And then the butterfly is back. Now it lands on the flowers, again opening and closing its wings. This time I extend my hand, and the butterfly climbs on my finger. Once again we look at one another for about ten seconds before it flies off.

When I told Japanese friends about this strange encounter, they were all quite certain that the butterfly was the soul of my geisha mother, grateful to have been visited. I discovered through these conversations that their interpretation was grounded in a long-standing belief about a connection between souls and butterflies. It turns out the idea of the soul as butterfly is widespread throughout the world. The ancient Greek word *psyche* referred to both the butterfly and the soul. In China, the sage Zhuangzi dreamt he was a butterfly, but upon waking puzzled whether he might now be a butterfly dreaming he was Zhuangzi. In our own time and scientific tradition, psychiatrist Elisabeth Kubler-Ross noted that children who have had near-death experiences often report dreaming of becoming a butterfly.

Butterflies do not seem to be part of classic Buddhism, but in Japanese Buddhist tradition, the priest Rennyo, the fifteenth-century revitalizer of the Pure Land sect, recorded a dream after the death of his daughter in which he saw three blue lotus flowers rise from the white bones of the cremation pyre. Suddenly, an inch-high golden image of the Buddha appeared and changed into a butterfly that flew up toward the western sky.

Since I happened to have pictures of my geisha mother on my laptop, I added them to the video I'd taken in the cemetery and uploaded it to YouTube as "Butterfly from Beyond." I also wrote to two Japanese entomologists, asking their opinion of the behavior of this butterfly, in fact a type of fritillary called *tsumagurohyômon* (black-hemmed leopard spot) in Japanese. "This species does well in degraded urban habitats," one wrote back. "They are often seen in small green spaces in the middle of a city."

"It was sunning itself," wrote the other. "Its landing on that particular stone is coincidence." I thought someone might write that experiences like mine were common—perhaps because Japanese fritillaries are attracted to people (unlike those I pursued with my net as a child). But no. Neither one mentioned that.

The fact that the butterfly was in this urban graveyard may not have been remarkable, yet it seems to me that—of all the headstones, of all the flowers there—its choosing me specifically is. "There is still much we don't understand about the habits of butterflies" is how entomologist S. Ueyama ended his e-mail. "But if some people wish to see the butterfly fluttering down to the stone as a person's soul, there's nothing wrong with that."

I believe one must welcome such experiences. Not look for them, necessarily, but when they happen, pay attention, appreciate, and cherish them, even without fully understanding. There is much we do not know about the feelings of butterflies.

Of Course I'm Angry!

Gabriel Cohen

*As his marriage falls apart, Gabriel Cohen obsesses over all the things his
wife has done to make him angry. But a chance encounter with Buddhism
shows him that the anger is his alone, and that it never serves any good
purpose after all.*

Three years ago I was standing in a real estate office, filling out a
rental application, when out of the corner of my eye, I saw a big man
enter and approach the realtor. The stranger muttered something,
then shoved the young man. I thought he was just kidding—a friend
roughhousing?—until he pinned the realtor against a wall and
started punching holes in the Sheetrock, four of them, circling the
frightened man's head.

Breathless, I ran out to the store next door and urged the woman
behind the counter to call the police. "The guy next door is about to
be killed!"

I tiptoed back to check on the realtor. Thankfully, his assailant
had disappeared, leaving him alive and unhurt, but the man was still
trembling.

"Who was that?" I asked. "Some crazy person off the street?"

"No," the realtor replied. "His ex-wife used to work here. He
was drunk, and he was looking for her."

I walked out of the office into a New York heat wave, a day so hot that the asphalt was threatening to melt. I was in the middle of the worst period of my life: a month before, my own wife had suddenly—without warning or apology—walked out of our marriage.

I thought about that stranger's anger, and I thought about my own.

I considered myself a generally cheerful person, prone to corny jokes and bad impressions of TV characters, but that jovial self-image had been severely tested during the last few months of my marriage. Our landlord had decided to sell the house my wife and I were renting an apartment in. Though she and I had gotten along well for four years, our search for a new home led to all sorts of disagreements, and then to outright verbal fights (which pointed to other hidden problems in our relationship).

After our marriage fell apart, I trudged through the city streets, praying that I could find an affordable place on my own. I spent endless hours playing a mental loop in which I railed against my ex-wife, her friends, and even her therapist. At around that time, fortunately, I stumbled across a poster for a Buddhist talk. I knew little about Buddhism; I saw it as a foreign, esoteric religion full of rituals and chanting, or a New Age fad for rock stars and Hollywood actors. But the title of the talk grabbed my attention: How to Deal with Anger (not, as my preconceptions might have led me to expect, How to Bliss Out and Pretend You're Not Really Angry). Under ordinary circumstances, I would have passed on by, but I was suffering and desperate. What did I have to lose?

That very first talk turned my whole world upside down—or right-side up. I was greatly surprised to hear that if I was angry at my wife, my wife was not the problem. My problem was *my anger*.

I used to think of the spiritual path as a detached, solo journey, like Moses trekking up the mountain or the Buddha wandering off to sit under his Bodhi tree. I imagined how challenging it would be to renounce life's pleasures and meditate in a cave. Now I realize that life offers a much more common but just as powerful spiritual trial: just try getting along with one other person for the rest of your life. Tie the knot. In good times, the rewards are great: the intimacy, the support, the joy of being loved and of loving someone else. Sometimes, though, the positive energy of a marriage seems to derail, to twist, to spiral into a negative whirlwind. It almost appears as if the more good energy you put into a relationship, the more bad feeling can come howling out the other side.

In my case, I was sorely tempted to blame my wife for our problems. After all, I had gone into marriage with the understanding that it would inevitably entail struggling through some hard times; she was the one who had refused to put in the hard work that any relationship requires. I thought she was *making me* feel angry—and heartbroken and betrayed and all that other fun stuff. I mean, I knew my anger was an internal feeling, but it felt as if it was coming to me from her, as if it could leap from one person to the other. I didn't see my anger as a sign of my own irrationality; I thought it made perfect sense. My wife had behaved unreasonably. *Of course* I was getting upset.

As I mentioned, though, that Buddhist talk rocked my view.

It took place in a yoga studio. The teacher held up a book. "How many of you think this exists independently of your mind?"

Everyone in the audience raised their hand.

As the teacher led us to see, though, our only way of knowing the book was there was by filtering our perception of it through our own minds. And that's true of every single thing in our lives: the objects around us, the people, our concepts, *everything*. Our entire experience of life is shaped by how we perceive and how we think.

Normally, we believe that we need to reshape our external circumstances to improve how we feel (more money, a better job, a more accommodating spouse), but that's a huge, never-ending, continually frustrating quest. Buddhism recommends a much more feasible, achievable goal: we can transform our lives by changing how we think about them. As the eighth-century sage Shantideva put it, if we want to avoid stepping on thorns, we can't possibly cover the whole world with leather—but we *can* cover our own feet.

Somehow, I realized early on that being pissed off at my ex was not making me feel better. I needed to find a more positive way out of my suffering. The fact that my emotions only existed inside my own head was great news; it meant that they were not dependent on my ex-wife, on how the legal proceedings developed, or on any other external factors. I could improve my experience of divorce by taking responsibility for my feelings and by learning how to train my mind. And so—like millions of Buddhist practitioners before me—I set out on a journey of internal exploration, observing my thoughts like a scientist peering at electrons buzzing around inside a cloud chamber. I made some fundamental discoveries.

I found that I was not "an angry person"; I was simply a person experiencing angry *thoughts*. Like all thoughts, they were just temporary, just passing through my head like storms through a clear blue sky. They didn't have the power to damage the inherent clarity of my mind. And they couldn't force me to act in an angry way. I learned that it was possible to put a little pause, a breathing space, between an external event and my reaction to it in order to discover a broader range of options.

As I probed deeper, I realized that—in almost every case—my anger arose out of a deep, internal sense of *hurt*. That feeling was uncomfortable, often intolerable, and I would try to get rid of it by projecting it outward. That seemed to offer some sense of relief, but it had pained my wife and damaged our relationship.

Often, my hurt arose out of a perceived sense of injustice. Like legions of foolish men before me, I believed that being right was the essential thing. When conflicts arose, I argued like an expensive trial lawyer. I won some battles, but I lost the war.

I don't want to overstate how angry I was. My wife and I actually got along very peacefully and lovingly for the great majority of our time together. I'm generally pretty upbeat and laid-back, and I have friends who say that they can hardly even *imagine* me angry.

On the other hand, that Buddhist talk made me realize that I was probably underestimating how angry I, and most people, really are much of the time. We tend to believe that anger is an aberration, an emotion that only arises in exceptional circumstances. But pick up any newspaper and you'll see how prevalent it is in the world at large: abuse, assault, murder, war. And it's pervasive in our daily lives. We're peeved that it starts raining just as we decide to go out for a walk. We're disappointed that we didn't win the lottery (even if we didn't buy a ticket!). We're irate because our parents didn't love us enough or loved us too much. We're aggrieved that our life is not turning out as we wish or believe it should. Some of us can't acknowledge our anger; we suppress it and become depressed, or try to salve it with alcohol or food or shopping—or we run away. (If you doubt that there's an unacknowledged current of anger underlying your daily existence, just notice how it flares up the instant someone cuts you off in traffic or steals your parking space. Did it arise out of nowhere, or was it already there?)

Among all our spurs to anger, why is a failed marriage so especially powerful? Partly, it's because our expectations are so high and unrealistic. We buy into a fairy tale that our spouse will relieve us of all our existential suffering and loneliness; we believe that they should make us happy all the time. As Buddhism points out, that's not love; it's an ego-based delusion called *desirous attachment.* When that false ideal falls apart, it's quickly replaced by disappointment and hostility. It's much easier to blame our spouse than to acknowledge the fundamental wrongness of our own view.

It's not a thin line between love and hate; Buddhism says that true love is *never* the cause of suffering. It's a thin line between unreasonable expectations and the stinging disenchantment that arises when they can't be met. A big part of the solution is learning to let go of our expectations of what *should* happen and to be more accepting of what life actually brings. As the thirteenth-century Zen teacher and philosopher Dogen beautifully put it, "A flower falls, even though we love it; and a weed grows, even though we do not love it."

As I developed a practice, I came to understand that my feelings of disappointment and hurt and injustice were all rooted in the same toxic soil: an inflated sense of the primacy of my own needs and desires—what Buddhists call *self-cherishing*. My anger was a childish wail of complaint: "What about *me?*"

A remarkable meditation called *taking and giving* helped me start letting go of my self-centeredness and resentment. As I went to more Buddhist talks, I became familiar with the technique of imagining that I was exhaling my tensions and frustrations as dark smoke and that I was inhaling a clear, blissful light. One day, though, after a talk on anger, the teacher offered an astonishing, counterintuitive exercise. She said that if we were angry with someone, we should imagine breathing in *their* suffering as dark smoke and that we should imagine breathing that blissful light toward *them*. In the early days of my divorce, the last thing I wanted was to imagine that I was taking on my wife's troubles, but when I tried the meditation, it had a profound effect: it helped me to see her as a suffering person in her own right. I had already found that when my heart was full of anger, it held no room for compassion. While doing this meditation, I discovered that the reverse was also true.

In regard to my big desire to be in the right, Buddhism offered another counterintuitive, helpful method: accepting defeat and offering the victory. Instead of always trying to win, I could surrender my own agenda in the service of a greater peace: I could lose battles, and the war might disappear.

Buddhists say that the antidote to anger is patience. One thing that has helped me move toward that goal has been learning to see that things do not inherently exist in the way that I perceive them to (the Buddhist concept of emptiness). That may sound abstract and intellectual, but it's easy to apply to relationships. When Zen master Shunryu Suzuki was asked to sum up the essence of his philosophy, he replied with just three words: "Not necessarily so." If I get riled up now, I repeat those words to myself, a reminder that my perception of what's going on is undoubtedly incomplete and likely faulty. The anger I perceive in someone else may be arising out of hurt; their seeming stubbornness may cover insecurity and fear.

. . .

Did all this new knowledge miraculously enable me to eradicate my anger? Of course not. But at least I started getting better at recognizing it when it first arose and calming myself before I might act on it.

Eventually, I came to see that anger was a false friend. Though it might seem to bolster me, to save me from depression, to keep me moving forward, it worked against me. Each impetuous e-mail, each vengeful riposte, each passive-aggressive refusal to respond—they all came back to bite me in the end. In fact, Buddhism says that acting out of anger is *never* the skillful thing to do.

You might think of certain exceptions. What about anger directed against social injustice? And isn't it necessary and therapeutic to express some anger?

I can think of at least three answers to these objections.

First, anger causes us to perceive its object in a distorted way. We turn the person we're mad at into an ogre. We become unable to see their good qualities, and we get pumped full of a blinding adrenaline that often causes our interactions to spiral out of control. Anger leads us to see things in a polarized, sharply dualistic way. We believe we're good; we believe our enemies are evil.

If you think that's a helpful way to look at conflict, just look at what it has done for the Israelis and Palestinians, Hutus and Tutsis, Armenians and Turks, etc., etc., etc. Of course, it's important to work against injustice, but we need to do so wisely, with clear eyes and a compassionate, understanding view of all sides. As Ghandi, Martin Luther King, Jr., and the Dalai Lama have so ably demonstrated, a calm mind gets better results. These wise leaders were able to see that, just as our anger is a delusion arising out of our suffering, the anger of our "enemies" is also a delusion, like a sickness in their minds. We should fight the delusion, not the people who suffer from it.

Second, though some therapists tout the benefits of expressing anger in a controlled way, such as punching a pillow, recent research in neuroscience contradicts that notion: if you punch a pillow, you're actually exercising your brain's neural pathways for aggression.

Finally, our anger damages us as well as the object of our wrath. It increases our heart rate, elevates our blood pressure, and has other serious health effects. As the saying goes, anger is an acid that corrodes the vessel that holds it. This seems stupidly obvious to me now, but when I was tromping around the streets of Brooklyn, running my resentful little mental loops, I failed to realize that they had absolutely no effect on my wife. I was just working myself into an increasingly agitated state—punching holes, in effect, in a wall that only I could see. I was carrying around an entirely unhelpful burden, and I had to resolve to set it down.

In case I needed a more forceful demonstration of the dangers of anger, life soon provided one. A few minutes after I left that real estate office, I came across another realtor. Miraculously, she drove me straight to a fantastic apartment, in a big old Victorian house with a front porch and a back patio, a stained-glass window, and even a chandelier. By New York standards, the rent was cheap. It wasn't until a few weeks later, just before I moved in, that I found out why. It turned out that my landlord had been having troubles with his own marriage.

One night, in a fit of rage, he had killed his wife.

In my new apartment.

The message could not have been clearer: *this is what can happen if you let anger win.*

Three years of working with Buddhist insights and practice have certainly not turned me into a saint, but occasionally I see evidence of progress.

My writing desk faces a window that looks out on the street. My neighborhood is generally quiet, but several days ago a stranger parked a luxury car directly outside. After a few minutes, its car alarm started going off—the worst kind, the one where the horn continually bleats. I sat there trying to work, getting increasingly frustrated and annoyed. Finally, I wrote a note, and then I marched out and stuck it under the windshield. (What kind of note? Let's put it this way: the salutation read, "Dear Asshole.")

When I came back inside, I sat there listening to the alarm. And I stared at my note. It took a while, but eventually my new training kicked in. At first I thought my blast of anger would cause the owner of the car to feel regretful and ashamed; I finally realized that it would only make him angry in return.

I replaced it with a new note. I did my best to keep my emotions out of it. Calmly, I explained that the car alarm was broken. What else did I have to say? I didn't need to inflate the problem by adding all sorts of self-righteousness and drama; I just called it to his attention, and then I let it go.

At the end of a long path, after extensive mental training, we might hope to become completely free of anger. In the meantime, it can act as a fire that consumes us or a bell that warns us when something is wrong—not with our circumstances, but with the way that we're thinking about them.

The choice is ours.

Long Journey
to a Bow ⊘⟫

Christina Feldman

*Reflecting their egalitarian principles, and sometimes reaction against
their own institutionalized churches, many Westerners have a hard time
accepting what looks to them like Buddhism's conventional religious
hierarchy. But while no one can claim that Buddhism is completely
free of the usual power structures, Buddhist rituals of respect and
devotion express something much deeper. Christina Feldman's long
encounter with the practice of bowing led her to reflect on the deceptive
nature of conceit.*

When news of the impending death of a beloved and esteemed
teacher swept through the village, well-wishers gathered to pay their
last respects and honor him. Standing around the master's bedside,
one by one they sang his praises and extolled his virtues as he listened and smiled weakly. "Such kindness you have shown us," said
one devotee. Another extolled his depth of knowledge, another la-
mented that never again would they find a teacher with such elo-
quence. The tributes to his wisdom, compassion, and nobility
continued until the master's wife noticed signs of restlessness and
kindly asked his devotees to leave. Turning to her husband, she

asked why he was disturbed, remarking upon all the wonderful tributes that had showered him. "Yes, it was all wonderful," he whispered. "But did you notice that no one mentioned my humility?"

The conceit of self (*mana* in Pali) is said to be the last of the great obstacles to full awakening. Conceit is an ingenious creature, at times masquerading as humility, empathy, or virtue. Conceit manifests in the feelings of being better than, worse than, and equal to another. Within these three dimensions of conceit are held the whole tormented world of comparing, evaluating, and judging that afflicts our hearts. Jealousy, resentment, fear, and low self-esteem spring from this deeply embedded pattern. Conceit perpetuates the dualities of "self" and "other"—the schisms that are the root of the enormous alienation and suffering in our world. Our commitment to awakening asks us to honestly explore the ways in which conceit manifests in our lives and to find the way to its end. The cessation of conceit allows the fruition of empathy, kindness, compassion, and awakening. The Buddha taught that "one who has truly penetrated this threefold conceit of superiority, inferiority, and equality is said to have put an end to suffering."

Although I didn't recognize it at the time, my first significant encounter with conceit happened in the very beginning of my practice in the Tibetan tradition, a serious bowing culture. I'm not talking about a tradition that just inclines the head slightly, but a culture in which Tibetans undertake pilgrimages of hundreds of miles doing full prostrations the entire way. In Tibetan communities the serious bowers can be spotted by the callus in the center of their forehead. Walking into my teacher's room in the Himalayan foothills for the first time, I found myself shocked to see people prostrating themselves at his feet. My reaction was visceral; I saw their bowing as an act of self-abasement, and I determined never to do the same. My conceit appeared in the thoughts that questioned what this plump, unsmiling man swaddled in robes had done to merit this attention. The recurrent words *I, me, better, worse, higher, lower, worthy,* and *unworthy* provided fuel for plenty of storytelling and resistance.

Over the years, as my respect and appreciation for this teacher's generosity, kindness, and wisdom grew, I found myself inching toward a bow, often a token bow with just a slight bob of my head. Occasionally I would engage in a more heartfelt bow born of deeper gratitude, but still an element of tension and withholding remained. I continued to practice in other bowing cultures. In Asia, I witnessed the tradition of elderly nuns with many years of practice and wisdom kneeling before teenage monks who had yet to find the way to sit still for five minutes. In Korea, I saw a practice environment where everyone bowed to everyone and everything with respect and a smile. It dawned on me that bowing was not, for me, just a physical gesture, but rather an object for investigation and a pathway to understanding conceit. The bow, I came to understand, was a metaphor for understanding many aspects of the teaching—pride, conceit, discriminating wisdom, and self-image.

My first challenge on this journey was to distinguish the difference between a bow as an act of letting go of conceit and a bow that reflected belief in unworthiness. As Kate Wheeler once wrote, "A true bow is not a scrape." Many on this path—both men and women—carry a legacy of too many years of scraping, cowering, and self-belittlement, rooted in belief in their own unworthiness. The path to renouncing scraping can be long and liberating, a reclaiming of dignity, and a letting go of patterns of fear. Discriminating wisdom, which we are never encouraged to renounce, clearly understands the difference between a bow and a scrape. A true bow can be a radical act of love and freedom. As Suzuki Roshi put it, "When you bow there is no Buddha and there is no you. One complete bow takes place. That is all. This is nirvana."

Conceit manifests in the ways we contract around a sense of self and other; it lies at the core of the identities and beliefs we construct, and it enables those beliefs to be the source of our acts, words, thoughts, and relationships. Superiority conceit is the belief in being better or worthier than another. It is a kind of conceit that builds itself upon our appearance, body, mind, intelligence, attainments, stature, and achievements. It can even gather around our meditative superiority.

We see someone shuffling and restless on their meditation cushion and then congratulate ourselves for sitting so solidly. We might go through life hypercritical, quick to spot the flaws and imperfections in others, sure we would never behave in such unacceptable ways.

Superiority conceit is easily spotted when it manifests in arrogance, bragging, or proclaiming our excellence to the world. On retreat we may find ourselves rehearsing the conversations we will have with our partner, recounting our trials and triumphs, but especially our heroism in completing the retreat where others failed. We can feel remarkably deflated when his only interest is when we're going to take out the garbage. It can be subtle in our inner beliefs in our specialness, rightness, or invulnerability. Superiority conceit looks like a safer refuge than inferiority conceit (thoughts of being worse than another), but in truth, both cause the same suffering. Feelings of superiority have the power to distort compassion into its near enemy, pity, and to stifle the capacity to listen deeply. Superiority conceit disables our receptivity to criticism because we become so convinced in the truth of our views and opinions.

A traditional Buddhist story tells of the time after the Buddha's death when he descended into the hell realms to liberate all the tormented beings imprisoned there. Mara (the personification of delusion) wept and mourned, for he thought he would get no more sinners for hell. The Buddha said to him, "Do not weep, for I shall send you all those who are self-righteous in their condemnation of sinners, and hell shall fill up again quickly."

Inferiority conceit is more familiar territory for many of us, probably because a chronic sense of unworthiness is so endemic in our culture. The torment of feeling worse than others and not good enough is the daily diet of inferiority conceit. A student on retreat came in distress to report that none of her more familiar dramas and agitation were appearing, and she was convinced she was doing something wrong. The teacher suggested that this odd experience could actually be one of calmness and was surprised when the suggestion was met with even more distress and denial, with the student exclaiming, "Calm is not something I can do." Another student experiencing rapture in her practice continued to assert that it was menopausal flashes, unable to accept that she could experience deep meditative states. Inferiority conceit gathers in the same places as superiority conceit—the body, mind, and appearance, as well as in the long list of mistakes we have made throughout our lives.

Inferiority conceit is fertile in its production of envy, resentment, judgment, and blame, which go round and round in a vicious circle of storytelling, serving only to solidify our belief in an imperfect self. This belief is often the forerunner of scraping, as we create heroes and heroines occupying a landscape of success and perfection we believe to be impossible for us. Governed by inferiority conceit, we may be adept at bowing to others, yet find it impossible to bow to ourselves, to acknowledge the wholesomeness and sincerity that keep us persevering on this path. Learning to make that first bow to ourselves is perhaps a step to realizing that a bow is just a bow, a simple gesture where all ideas of self and other, worthy and unworthy, fall away. It is a step of confidently committing ourselves to realizing the same freedom and compassion that all buddhas throughout time have discovered; it is acknowledging that we practice to be liberated. We practice because it seems impossible; we practice to reclaim that sense of possibility. We learn to bow to each moment, knowing it is an invitation to understand what it means to liberate just one moment from the burden of self-judgment, blame, envy, and fear. Letting go of inferiority conceit awakens our capacity for appreciative joy and reclaims the confidence so necessary to travel this path of awakening.

Seeing the suffering of superiority and inferiority conceit, we might be tempted to think that equality conceit is the middle path; however, a closer look shows us that it is more a conceit of mediocrity and minimal expectations. Equality conceit is when we tell ourselves that we all share in the same delusion, self-centeredness, and greed, that we all swim in the same cesspool of suffering. We see someone falling asleep on their cushion and feel reassured. We observe a teacher dropping their salad in the lunch line, and it confirms our view that people are essentially and hopelessly mindless. Sameness can seem both comforting and reassuring. Thinking that others are also struggling on the path can make us feel relieved of the responsibility to hold aspirations that ask for effort and commitment.

Equality conceit can express disillusionment with human possibility. When we look at those who appear happier or more enlightened than ourselves and primarily see their flaws, we are caught in equality conceit. We see those who seem more confused or deluded than ourselves, and we know we have been there. We see our own delusions and struggles reflected in the lives of others and think that we are relieved of the task of bowing. The offspring of equality conceit can be a terminal sense of disappointment, resignation, and cynicism. After Al Gore's documentary, *An Inconvenient Truth,* was released, several newspapers responded by publishing the electric bill of his home. What wasn't mentioned was how the home's electricity was generated by solar power. It seemed there was a driving need to reduce his message and show that we're all hopeless carbon emitters.

All forms of conceit give rise to the endless thoughts and storytelling that solidify the beliefs we hold about ourselves and others. Liberating ourselves from conceit and the agitation it brings begins with our willingness to sensitize ourselves to the subtle and obvious manifestations of conceit as they appear. The clues lie in our judgments and comparisons, the views we construct about ourselves and others. Suffering, evaluating, envy, and fear are all signals asking us to pause and listen more deeply. We learn to bow to those moments, knowing they are moments when we can either solidify conceit or liberate it. Instead of feeding the story, we can nurture our capacities for mindfulness, restraint, and letting go. Instead of volunteering for suffering, we may be able to volunteer for freedom. It is not an easy undertaking, yet each moment that we are present and compassionate in the process of conceit building is a moment of learning to bow and take a step on the path of freedom.

Life is a powerful ally because it offers us the opportunities to let go of the conceit of self. There are times when our world crumbles. Unpredictable illness and other hardships come into our lives, and we face the reality once more that we are not in control. Sometimes there is simply no more that "I" can do. In those moments, we can become agitated, or we can acknowledge that we are meeting the First Noble Truth: at times there is unsatisfactoriness and suffering in life. When we face the limitations of our power and control, all we can skillfully do is bow to that moment. The conceit of self is challenged and eroded not only by the circumstances of our lives but also by our willingness to meet those circumstances with grace rather than with fear.

A teacher was asked, "What is the secret to your happiness and equanimity?" She answered, "A wholehearted, unrestricted cooperation with the unavoidable." This is the secret and the essence of a bow. It is the heart of mindfulness and compassion. To bow is to no longer hold ourselves apart from the unpredictable nature of all of our lives; it is to cultivate a heart that can unconditionally welcome all things. We bow to what is, to all of life. By liberating our minds from ideas of better than, worse than, or the same as, we liberate ourselves from all views of self and other. The bow is a way to the end of suffering, to an awakened heart.

Healing Ecology ⤷⤷

David Loy

*The scholar and activist David Loy has found unique and effective ways
to present Buddhism's analysis of the human condition. He points to the
"lack" we feel at the center of our being, which is a source of suffering
when we try to solidify it but the nature of enlightenment when we accept
it as openness and freedom. Loy is especially effective in extending that
analysis into the realms of economics, politics, and society, where he
finds the same forces at play on a larger, collective scale. Here, he asks
how Buddhism can help us address the world's ecological problems.*

> We are here to awaken from the illusion of our separateness.
> —THICH NHAT HANH

> I came to realize clearly that mind is no other than mountains
> and rivers and the great wide earth, the sun and the moon and
> the stars.
> —DOGEN

What can Buddhism contribute to our understanding of the ecological crisis? As a complex religious tradition or group of traditions,
Buddhism naturally has a lot to say about the natural world. Pas-
sages in many Buddhist texts reveal sensitivity to the beauties of

nature and respect for its various beings. A good example is the *Jat-aka* tales ("birth stories") that describe the previous lives of the Buddha before he became the Buddha. In many of them he is born as an animal, and in some of the best-known tales the Buddha sacrifices himself for "lower animals," such as offering his rabbit body to a weak tigress so that she can feed her starving cubs. By implication, such fables challenge the duality usually assumed between humans and "nature"—as if we were not part of nature! They suggest that the welfare of every living being, no matter how insignificant it may seem to us, is spiritually important and deserving of our concern. All beings in the Jatakas are able to feel compassion for others and act selflessly to help ease their suffering. In contrast to a Darwinian "survival of the fittest," which is often used to justify our abuse of other species, its stories offer a vision of life in which we are all interconnected, parts of the same web of life, and therefore also interresponsible, responsible for each other.

This compassion is not limited to the animal realm. If we can believe the traditional biographies, the Buddha was born under trees, meditated under trees, experienced his great awakening under trees, often taught under trees, and passed away under trees. Unsurprisingly, he often expressed his gratitude to trees and other plants. Some later Buddhist texts explicitly deny that plants have sentience, but the Pali Canon is more ambiguous. In one sutra, a tree spirit appears to the Buddha in a dream, complaining that its tree had been chopped down by a monk. The next morning the Buddha prohibits sangha members from cutting down trees. Bhikkhu monks and bhikkhuni nuns are still forbidden from cutting off tree limbs, picking flowers, even plucking green leaves off plants. What would the Buddha have to say about our wanton destruction of whole ecosystems?

Yet great sensitivity to nature is hardly unique to Buddhism. In general, the Indian traditions have identified more with the natural world than have the Abrahamic traditions (Judaism, Christianity, Islam), which have emphasized the uniqueness of human beings and our dominion over the rest of creation. All these traditions teach "do not kill," but the Abrahamic commandment protects other human beings, whereas the Indian traditions stress the sanctity of all life. Nevertheless, the West has also celebrated many important counterexamples: for example, Saint Francis in the Middle Ages; more recently, romantic poets and visionaries; and today, environmental movements such as deep ecology. What special perspective, if any, does Buddhism offer to our understanding of the biosphere, and our relationship to it, at this critical time in history when we are doing our utmost to destroy it?

To answer that, we have to go back to a more basic question: what is really distinctive about Buddhism? The four noble (or "ennobling") truths are all about *dukkha* (suffering), and the Buddha emphasized that his only concern was ending dukkha. To end our dukkha, however, we need to understand and experience *anatta*, our lack of self, which seen from the other side is also our interdependence with all other things.

There are different ways to explain anatta, yet fundamentally it denies our separation from other people and, yes, from the rest of the natural world. The psychosocial construction of a separate self in here is at the same time the construction of an "other" out there, that which is different from "me." What is special about the Buddhist perspective is its emphasis on the dukkha built into this situation. Basically, the self is dukkha.

One way to express the problem is that the sense of self, being a construct, is always insecure, because inherently ungrounded. It can never secure itself because there is no-thing that could be secured. The self is more like a process, or a function. The problem with processes, however, is that they are always temporal, necessarily impermanent—but we don't want to be impermanent, something that is changing all the time. We want to be real! So we keep trying to ground ourselves, often in ways that just make our situation worse. For Buddhism the only true solution lies in realizing our nonduality with others and understanding that our own well-being cannot be distinguished from their well-being.

That brings us to the really interesting question, ecologically. Does this basic insight about the intimate connection between sense

of self and dukkha also apply to the sense of separation between us
and them? The issue here is whether "separate self equals dukkha"
also holds true for our biggest collective sense of self: the duality between us as a species, Homo sapiens, and the rest of the biosphere.

Expressed in that way, the question seems rather abstract, but if
this particular parallel between individual and collective selves
holds, there are two important implications. First, our collective
sense of separation from the natural world must also be a constant
source of collective frustration for us. Second, our responses to that
alienation, by trying to make our collective species–self more real—
in this case, by attempting to secure or "self-ground" ourselves tech-
nologically and economically—are actually making things worse.

These are pretty big claims. What are they really pointing at?
"Our species' alienation from nature is an ongoing source of collective dukkha." What can that mean?

Earlier I referred to the way that the Abrahamic religions assign
humans to a special place and role in creation, superior to all other
creatures. Western civilization developed out of the interaction between Judeo-Christianity and the culture of classical Greece (inher-
ited by Rome). Greece emphasized our uniqueness in a different
way: by distinguishing the conventions of human society (culture,
technology, etc.) from the rhythms of the natural world. What is important about this distinction is the realization that whatever is social convention can be changed: we can reconstruct our own societies
and in that way (attempt to) determine our own collective destiny.

Today we take that insight for granted, yet it's not something
that most premodern, traditionally conservative societies would
have understood. Without our sense of historical development, they
have usually accepted their own social conventions as inevitable because also natural. This often served to justify social arrangements
that we now view as unjust, but there is nevertheless a psychological
benefit in thinking that way: such societies shared a collective sense
of meaning that we have lost today. For them, the meaning of their
lives was built into the cosmos and revealed by their religion, which
they took for granted. For us, in contrast, the meaning of our lives

and our societies has become something that we have to determine for ourselves in a universe whose meaningfulness (if any) is no longer obvious. Even if we choose to be religious, we today must decide between various religious possibilities, which diminishes the spiritual security that religions have traditionally provided. While we have a freedom that premodern societies did not have, we lack their kind of "social security," which is the basic psychological comfort that comes from knowing one's place and role in the world.

In other words, part of the rich cultural legacy that the Greeks bequeathed to the West—for better and worse—is an increasing anxiety about who we are and what it means to be human. There is a basic tension between such freedom (we decide what to value and what to do) and security (being grounded in something greater that is taking care of us), and we want both. As soon as one of them is emphasized, we want more of the other. In general, however, the modern history of the West is a story of increasing freedom at the cost of decreasing security, in the sense that loss of faith in God has left us rudderless. Thanks to ever more powerful technologies, it seems like we can accomplish almost anything we want to do—yet we don't know what our role is, what we should do. That continues to be a source of great anxiety, not only for us individually but collectively. What sort of world do we want to live in? What kind of society should we have? If we can't depend on God to tell us, we are thrown back upon ourselves, and our lack of any grounding greater than ourselves is a profound source of dukkha.

I think that is how we can understand the first implication mentioned earlier: the claim that our collective sense of separation from the natural world is a continual source of frustration. The stronger our alienation from nature, the greater our anxiety. Aren't the narcissism and nihilism that have become so common today expressions of that anxiety? It's the same as our individual problem: the stronger my personal sense of alienation from other people, the more likely that I will become anxious or depressed. Recently psychologists have been realizing that, once a very basic level of food and shelter has been attained, the most important factor determining happiness is our relationships with other people. Might that also be true collectively? What does that imply about our species' estrangement from the rest of the biosphere?

We have yet to consider the second implication mentioned earlier, that our collective response to this collective dukkha is just making things worse. What does that mean?

First, let's remember how things go wrong individually. We usually respond to the delusion of a separate self by trying to make that sense of self more real—which doesn't work and can't work, since there is no such self that can be isolated from its relationships with others. Since we don't realize this, however, we tend to get caught up in vicious circles. I never have enough money or power, I'm never famous enough, attractive enough. . . . Is there a collective parallel to these sorts of compulsions?

Consider our attitude toward economic growth and technological development. What motivates them? Obviously, we enjoy our comfort and wealth—but when do we have enough? When will our GNP be large enough? When will we have all the technology we need? Perhaps we are deceived by the word *progress,* because of course one can never have enough progress if it really is progress. Yet why do we think that more is always better?

When we think about our collective response from this perspective, I think the motivation becomes clear. Lacking the security that comes from knowing one's place and role in the cosmos, we have been trying to create our own security. Technology, in particular, is our collective attempt to control the conditions of our existence on this earth. We have been trying to remold the earth so that it is completely adapted to serve our purposes, until everything becomes subject to our will, a "resource" that we can use. Ironically, though, this hasn't been providing the sense of security and meaning that we seek. We have become more anxious, not less. That's because technology can be a great means, but in itself, it's a poor goal. Ask any dictator: once you crave power, you can never have enough security to feel safe yourself.

Technology and economic growth in themselves can't resolve

the basic human problem about the meaning of our lives. Since we are not sure how else to solve that problem, however, they have become a collective substitute, forms of secular salvation that we seek but never quite attain. Yet again, means have become ends. Because we don't really know where we want to go or what we should value, we have become obsessed with control. That is why we can never have enough technological or economic development.

If the previously mentioned two implications are true, something like the ecological crisis is inevitable. Sooner or later, one way or another, we will bump up against the limits of this compulsive but doomed project of endless growth. That does not mean there is no solution. It does mean that we need to understand the roots of the problem better and find ways to address those roots more directly. Since our increasing reliance on technology as the solution to life's problems is itself a large part of the problem, the ecological crisis does not call for a primarily technological response (although technological changes are certainly necessary). Dependence on sophisticated, ever more powerful technologies tends to aggravate our sense of separation from the natural world, whereas any successful solution (if the parallel still holds) must involve accepting that we are part of the natural world. That, of course, also means embracing our responsibility for the well-being of the biosphere, because its well-being ultimately cannot be distinguished from our own well-being. Understood properly, our taking care of the earth's rain forests is like me taking care of my own leg.

So is the solution somehow "returning to nature"? We cannot return to nature because we have never left it. The environment is not really an environment. The word *environment* literally means "the conditions within which a person or thing dwells." That way of describing the natural world is already dualistic, because it dichotomizes between us and where we are located. The environment is not merely the place where we live and act, for the biosphere is the ground from which and within which we arise. The earth is not only our home, it is our mother. In fact, our relationship is even more intimate, because we can never cut the umbilical cord. The air in my lungs, like the water and food that pass through my mouth, is part of a great system that does not stop with me but continually circulates through me. My life is a dissipative process that depends upon and contributes to that never-ending circulation. Eventually I too will be food for worms.

According to this understanding, our problem is not technology in itself but the obsessive ways that we have been motivated to exploit it. Without those motivations, we would be able to evaluate our technologies better in light of the ecological problems they have contributed to, as well as the ecological solutions they might contribute to. Given all the long-term risks associated with nuclear power, for example, I cannot see it as anything but a short-sighted solution to our energy needs. In place of fossil fuels, the answer will probably be—I'm inclined to say, will have to be—renewable sources of power (solar, wind, etc.) along with a radically reduced need for energy. As long as we assume the necessity for continuous economic and technological expansion, the prospect of a steep reduction in our energy needs is absurd. A new understanding of our basic situation opens up other possibilities.

But wait a moment. How does any of this resolve the basic problem outlined earlier—the anxiety that plagues us today because we have to create our own meaning in a world where God has died? Like it or not, individual and collective self-consciousness has alienated us from premodern worldviews and the "natural" meaning of life that they provided. Nor would we want to return to such worldviews—often imposed and maintained by force—even if we could. But what other alternatives are possible? Or are we just fated to endure this existential kind of dukkha?

This objection helps us to see that any genuine solution to the ecological crisis must involve something more than technological improvements. Again, if the root of the problem is spiritual, the solution must also have a spiritual dimension. And again, this does not mean a return to premodern religious conviction, which is impossible for us today. Buddhism shows another way, which de-emphasizes

the role of dogma and ritual. The Buddhist approach is quite prag-
matic. The goal of the Buddhist path is wisdom in service of personal
and social transformation. This, however, is quite different from the
sort of rational self-reformation that Greek thinkers sought. When
we meditate, for example, we are not transforming ourselves. We are
being transformed. Quiet, focused concentration enables something
else to work in us and through us, something other than our usual
ego-self. This opens us up and liberates a deeper grounding within
ourselves. Our lack of self (anatta) is what enables this process.

This "something else" frees us from the compulsion to secure
ourselves within the world. We do not need to become more real by
becoming wealthy or famous or powerful or beautiful. That is not
because we identify with some other spiritual reality apart from the
world. Rather, we are able to realize our nonduality with the world
because we are freed from such fixations.

How does that affect the meaning of one's life? Although living
beings are numberless, the bodhisattva vows to save them all. He or
she assumes the grandest possible role on a path that can never come
to an end. Although such a commitment is not compulsory, it follows naturally from realizing that none of those beings is separate
from oneself.

So we conclude with one final parallel between the personal and
the collective. We discover the meaning we seek in the ongoing,
long-term task of repairing the rupture between us and mother
earth, our natural ground. That healing will transform us as much as
the biosphere.

Mindfully Green 🌀

Stephanie Kaza

Environmental progress—like all real change—starts within, as each of us decides to change the way we live. Yet the ecophilosopher and Zen practitioner Stephanie Kaza argues that environmentalism must be about more than the personal actions we take or the public policies we support. To be truly transformative, it must change the way we see ourselves, our world, and the relationship between the two. In short, it must be a spiritual path.

At times it can seem like we are making little progress on environmental problems. Over and over I hear these questions: "What can one person do? What should I do?"

My answers have come a long way from the early eco-enthusiasm of the 1960s. We felt sure we could save everything if people only knew how much was at stake. Today we face environmental concerns with more awareness, recognizing the political, economic, and social constraints that limit our actions. The more we understand ecosystem complexities and human inequities, the more we realize how much effort it will take to turn the ship toward a sustainable future.

Truthfully, we can't even begin to realize how much effort it will take. In the last few years there has been a deluge of books on the market and Internet websites offering "easy steps" to being green. People everywhere are wanting to do the right thing; there is a hunger for information and guidance. Most often the focus at this first stage of response is personal: "What can I do to create a green lifestyle? How can I live in a more ecofriendly manner?" The guidebooks point out ways to save energy, make wise food choices, and consider green products. These are important steps in the right direction; they offer a way to begin living with the earth's health in mind. But we will need to take this conversation much further if we are truly to address the state of the world today.

As I have spoken to audiences around the country, I have been struck by what could be called "green zeal," an almost fervent sense of engagement with environmental concerns. People feel passionately about protecting rain forests and whales; they want everyone to know that polar bears and penguins are threatened. Behind the passion is a deeply felt need to do something right, to find a way to correct our past environmental errors. Almost no point on the globe is free of human influence now; we have left our mark in virtually all of the world's ecosystems. People today feel the sorrow of these thoughtless actions in the past—the once-expansive forests so diminished, the native peoples decimated. There is a great well of shame and grief wanting relief from the painful consequences of our own shortsighted actions. This manifests as a need for healing, for making life changes that will take us in a kinder direction, one that can sustain our own lives as well as the rest of life on earth.

Our anxiety over an uncertain future has become particularly acute with the new understanding that climate change will affect us all. We have the sense that global support systems are lurching out of control, that things have gone too far, that we may already be in serious danger. Climate advocates are urging government leaders to invest in a green vision for a more hopeful future. Businesses are making energy and waste audits to cut costs and improve long-term economic viability. Voters are calling for a "green jobs" economy to help us make the shift from fossil fuels to renewable energy. Green zeal is necessary to change our ways quickly, to meet environmental goals that would be impossible without global cooperation.

In the midst of so much greening activity, many people are

making significant changes to their lives, taking up what I've come to call the "green practice path." They are changing their lightbulbs, taking the bus, insulating their homes, serving on community boards, and passing along green values to their children. From what I've observed, these efforts are based in much deeper motivation than home improvement. People are thinking deeply about what matters to them and taking their actions seriously. I believe they are bringing their best ethical and spiritual attention to environmental concerns and trying to match their actions to their moral principles.

People come to green practice from many walks of life and are taking initiative in many different arenas. Green zeal is turning up in every corner of the earth. Thousands of people are living their own inspiring stories as they find a way to share their green ethics on behalf of a more peaceful and genuinely happy world. There is no single green path; the path is determined by individual experience, local needs, and personal motivation. The green path is, by and large, a secular practice, open to all who feel the call. It seems to me to reflect what the Dalai Lama calls an "ethics for the new millennium," an ethics built on compassion, restraint, and acceptance of universal responsibility for the well-being of the earth.

If we engage green living in more depth, it becomes an expression of our deepest moral values. The "work" of green living becomes less a chore and more a locus of ethical development. We conserve water not because we *should* be frugal but because we respect the earth's resources. This shift in thinking and understanding can be quite profound. The conversation moves from personal sacrifice to real consideration of the nature of our connection with the earth. When we come to see ourselves as part of the great web of life, in relationship with all beings, we are naturally drawn to respond with compassion.

A PATH OF PRACTICE

When people start out on the green path, environmental issues can feel like a separate world, something very much apart from their own lives. That sense of separation makes it harder to find a way to become part of the work in an effective and meaningful way. In a world of myriad environmental challenges, it is not always clear where to make a contribution. How do you know where to put your effort? How can you tell if your work is making a difference? As you look for a way to address what is disturbing to you about our planetary situation, it is important to keep asking such questions until the appropriate answers arrive.

You might wonder where exactly to apply the green principles we've discussed. Should you work with a nonprofit organization or a government agency? Should you get a new, greener job? Should you work locally, nationally, or internationally? Hardly ever does anyone survey all the possible options and then make a rational decision about "what is best." There is too much going on; there is too much to know. This may seem overwhelming as you step onto the green path, but actually it is a good thing. We have come a very long way since the word *ecology* made its debut in the 1960s. In the twenty-first century, understanding ecology is central to sustaining life on earth as we know it. There are many conversations, many opportunities, and many good causes at every possible scale of engagement. The key is finding the right "fit" with your knowledge, skills, interest, and values. It also helps if someone extends you a hand.

Being naive can be an advantage to the seeker. You approach any new topic of earth-keeping with a fresh mind, a willing curiosity, and your own humble honesty about how little you know. This means you must turn to others to learn more, coming with open hands as a student. Everything you encounter has some value because you don't yet know what will be useful. Beginner's mind is a beautiful gift for those entering the stream or taking up a new phase of the work. By asking for help or information, you take small steps in building relationships with others doing this work. This is very important; it is too easy to become discouraged if you try to go it alone in facing environmental issues. Forging connections with others makes it seem possible to do the work; those with experience are a testimony of success to surviving the challenges.

For some, the call or invitation comes first from the natural world itself. In my own formative years in environmental work, I lived on the edge of a wild area near the University of California in Santa Cruz. I would often go for walks among the coast live oaks on the grassy terraces or down to the dark canyon of the redwood-lined creek. During the long and emotionally demanding process of completing my graduate studies, I took my unshaped questions to the land, letting my feet guide me as I walked. I learned to respond to the pulls in different directions, not knowing where I would end up, trusting the process for its own wisdom. Sometimes I would find myself climbing an oak on the mesa for the big view of ocean and sky. Sometimes I would crawl close to a small spring nestled in moss, feeding the creek drop by drop. I found answers through listening closely, waiting for insight that made sense in a way I could recognize.

Some find the call arising from conversations with friends or from watching a stirring film. A neighbor tells you about her community garden plot; a colleague explains his house-insulation project. After the widespread showing of Al Gore's 2006 film, *An Inconvenient Truth,* many people suddenly felt called to take up the challenge of climate change. For some, the response is quiet and personal, an inner reflection or reckoning: "It's time. I must do something." For others, the process of taking up the green path is social and full of exciting possibility, like the coming together of thousands of students involved in the Focus the Nation actions on climate. The sheer social momentum of so much inspiring activity can galvanize a crowd to new levels of green commitment.

This seeking or calling process generates a need to know more, to see who's doing what, to get your bearings in an unfamiliar universe. These days it is not hard to develop a basic working knowledge of ecological principles and to learn about key areas of concern where people are engaged as citizens and professionals. Information is quite accessible on the Internet or in introductory books or environmental magazines. Many environmental groups welcome volunteers interested in broadening their knowledge base by working with others who know more. It can be tempting to want to study until you feel you know enough to take action. But if you get bogged down with information overload, it might undermine the forward momentum you are trying to generate. To counter this hazard, you should keep an eye on what I call your "juice meter." Which topics and issues generate energy for you? When do you notice your enthusiasm barometer going up? These moments offer important feedback in the learning process; they tell you what to pursue and what to leave for others to pursue. You don't even need to know why something is exciting; you just need to follow that thread to the next step.

In any given problem-solving arena, the question will arise: "What is effective action?" This is another way of asking, "What can I actually do? How can I be effective, given who and what I know now? How can my work have some impact?" These are important questions that should always be kept nearby in evaluating your potential to contribute, which, of course, is constantly changing. The newcomer to any environmental topic has a thousand ideas of "what people should do" to "save the environment." The good news is that most of these ideas are already in progress somewhere. You don't need to reinvent the wheel; you just need to find people who are already acting on your good ideas and join them. Chances are that they will already have assessed the options for effective action and will have developed initiatives that fit the current situation. People with more knowledge and experience, whether they are with the Sierra Club or the Department of Environmental Conservation or the local recycling center, have already given these matters quite a bit of thought.

The most important aspect in the early stages of the green practice path is to find what is personally satisfying and meaningful. Without this, you won't continue the work. It is also crucial to make some friends in the process. Without friends, you will feel isolated and lonely, and the work won't be as much fun. People don't usually think of environmental practice as "fun," but if you are spending time with good people and sharing a sense of purpose, you are having a good time helping to create a more sustainable world. Whether you take up this work in your family setting or as a volunteer, in school or downtown, it is all useful. It is all part of the process of shifting the social paradigm toward active care for the place where you live, the place you call home. Your early experiences with green practice often set the direction for where the path leads you next, which may be further into the fray.

Deepening the Practice

Being a beginner with any environmental topic, by definition, cannot last. The more you know about the environment, the less you can rest in blissful ignorance. It is too disturbing. The more you know about climate change, threatened species, energy needs, and human impact, the more concern you are likely to feel. The more time you spend in beautiful natural areas, the more you find out about the physical and political threats to their well-being. The more you understand about social inequity and environmental injustice, the harder it is to see your own actions in isolation. Environmental knowledge can be a double-edged sword: learning more about the world's suffering often generates alarm and emotional distress. At the same time, that very knowledge can galvanize you to take action and put that knowledge to work to alleviate suffering.

As a beginner you may have ventured into environmental work in a single arena, such as food and diet or caring about a personally significant place. Your shift to green thinking may have come from a single bout of intense commitment or smaller explorations at a gradual pace. If you stay on the green practice path, your range of interests and concerns will expand. If your interest has been sparked through organic foods, you might want to learn more about eating local. If you are concerned about the health impacts of pesticides, you might want to learn more about hormone disrupters. At some point, you realize you are asking the green question more and more often: "What is the environmental impact of this product? Of this housing development? Of this zoning policy?" You realize you are no longer living in a bubble, as if your actions had no impact anywhere. You know they do. Your environmental innocence is gone.

This is how a person enters the next stage of the path of practice. You may not have planned on it. You may find yourself surprised by your own growing convictions. Or you may be wondering how to become a more effective advocate for the environment. As a professor, I am invited to be part of such wonderings as students come to me considering graduate school or midcareer professionals ask about switching fields. Each person arrives in my office carrying a bundle of questions and possible options. They want to think out loud with someone and find something that matches their yearning. I ask them what has brought them this far on the path, and then I try to gauge what level of commitment they imagine for themselves. I listen while they share what they have been thinking about, no matter how tentative their vision. They have come for encouragement, to hear someone say, "Keep going. Yes, you can do more." It is clear they want a wider engagement with environmental concerns in their personal or professional lives, or maybe even both.

Taking up this phase of deeper commitment involves several significant inner processes that inform each other. When the green critique penetrates further into your life, you may need to rethink personal priorities. Every day and every hour, we are making choices that reflect our current priorities. We choose to invest our time, energy, money, and relationships in certain things over others. Rethinking priorities means examining our current patterns and seeing if they really reflect what matters most to us. If environmental concerns come to occupy more of your everyday thoughts and activities, then it makes sense to move them more into the forefront of your activities. For example, you might learn enough about eating local foods to decide to grow some food of your own. This then means investing in a garden plot and in tools, seeds, soil amendments, compost box, and so on. It also requires an investment of your own precious and limited time. As you share the fruits and vegetables of your labors with others, success generates its own momentum and your investment pays off.

Rethinking priorities leads naturally to the second process of personal assessment. From those early stages of beginner's mind, you now have accumulated new skills and knowledge and likely have developed ethical stances in the areas where you have some under-standing. So you ask yourself, "What do I know? What can I actually do? What more do I need to be helpful on another level?" It can be very helpful to talk this through with someone who can be a witness to your personal growth as a concerned earth citizen. As much as you see what you have gained thus far, it will be obvious that there is much more to learn. It is not possible to do it all, no matter how concerned you are. You are only one person with a finite number of hours to give to earth care. So you must make some strategic choices to guide your next steps. For some people, what is appropriate is more education and professional development to prepare for full-time work in an en-vironmental field. This is a common motivation for seeking a gradu-ate degree. Others may need a change of location, a geographical move to bring them closer to a hub of environmental activity, such as Washington, D.C., or one of the rising centers of sustainability, such as Portland, Oregon. Still others may want a major change in lifestyle or more spiritual training to support deeper environmental work.

Complementing both of these processes is self-reflection on the big picture: "What is really important now, both in my own life and in the world?" When I was preparing to take lay ordination vows in the Soto Zen tradition, I was asked to do just this. My Zen teacher had me sit in a room quietly all day by myself, thinking about what it meant to take these vows. I felt somehow there was much more going on than I completely understood. I read the Buddhist precepts and recited the three refuges, settling my mind on accepting this commit-ment as best I could. In late afternoon I took a long, slow walk in the New Mexico landscape, preparing to cross through this gate. The next day, after a light snow had dusted the mountains, I repeated my vows in the presence of the local Zen community and received affirmation from my teacher. Afterward we held a wonderful party, and one of my teacher's senior students called in to offer congratulations. He explained that before this day I had been practicing primarily for my-self, to improve my own physical and mental well-being. Now, with these vows, my practice would be primarily in the service of others.

When you come to take environmental work seriously, you

realize you are doing it on behalf of all beings, not just for your own well-being. Looking at the big picture means understanding the nature of the current threats, seeing who the political players are, finding the initiatives that make the most sense in the long run. It also means really trying to apply global principles of justice and sustainability. We cannot do effective environmental work without taking up the roles of race, class, gender, power, and privilege in perpetuating environmental damage and inequity.

In the last few years the global conversation has shifted to focus on the impacts of climate change. All other environmental work seems to be subsumed or compared to the call to "do something" about climate change. Many of us find ourselves falling short in knowledge or skill to respond to this call and perplexed at how to shift personal priorities. Reflecting on the big picture of climate change, peak oil, and the exploding demand for resources is very unsettling. It is a time of great foment, with many ideas surfacing, many big conversations at play that will affect all of us. We are all being invited into this second stage of the practice path, with no time to waste.

TAKING UP THE PATH

For some people, certainly not all, there will be a third stage of the green practice path. At this point, the practice becomes a "lifeway." In Native American traditions, people speak of everyday practice and culture fused into a way of life, something practiced by the whole community. The lifeway includes ethics, spirituality, social mores, and a deeply tested way of doing things that makes sense. A lifeway is not a religion; it is not something you can adopt or be baptized into. A lifeway is also not an identity in the sense of ethnic or political identity. A lifeway is a way of being in the world that carries strong intention and shared wisdom. People who follow a shared lifeway help each other develop this wisdom and the strength to persevere under duress.

To introduce my class to this idea of lifeway, I invite my friend Amy Seidel to visit as a colleague and role model. Amy is the director of Teal

Farm, a demonstration site in northern Vermont for living sustainably in the future. Each year she gives us a progress report on developments at the farm. Plantings have been designed with a warming climate in mind; the system of solar and micro-hydro sources is set up to feed energy back into the grid. In the main house, there are facilities for bulk food preservation and storage.

I have walked around the site with Amy, marveling at the care and foresight shown in so many details. Amy describes the vision of living close to the land on what it produces. She grounds this vision solidly in ecological principles, looking clear-eyed at a warming planet. She doesn't exhort the students; she just shares what she knows about sustainable practices and how to plan for a green future. It is obvious that she is extending an invitation to the green lifeway to everyone in the room. Afterward the students come down and mob her with questions, eager to learn more.

If you find you are revising your priorities to reflect your environmental concerns and seeking out friendships that support your environmental priorities, you may see that something significant has shifted in your depth of commitment. Thinking about the earth is no longer something you do now and then; it has become a way of life. Nonharming and systems thinking have become second nature to you. In every situation, you look for the green alternative that makes the most environmental sense. Because this is a way of life, you feel morally obliged to look at every aspect of your food choices, your buying patterns, your energy use, your civic contributions to greening your community.

There is no single lifeway to hold up conveniently as a gold standard. You do not necessarily have to be a vegan or vegetarian, or live off-grid or in a green-built house, or have a job influencing environmental policy. You do not have to drive a hybrid car, grow a garden, or wear organic clothing. What marks the green lifeway is not specific choices but depth of commitment and intention. The person in this stage of the practice path takes it very seriously, questioning the impacts of their actions in all that they do. This process of ethical reflection is fueled by a deep and abiding love for the well-being of life on earth.

From this perspective, any aspect of human activity is open to ethical reflection and incorporation into a green lifeway. In new and inspiring ways, people are carrying this process forward into uncharted territory. Churches and temples are trying to green their sanctuaries as part of their congregational lifeway. Universities are looking for ways to green not only their curricula but also their buildings. A local green parenting store opened up recently on our downtown pedestrian marketplace. Green marriages have come into fashion to support couples committed to caring for the earth in all they do. And there is now a green burial movement in the United States, which considers the environmental ethics of our choices in dealing with the dead.

But let me repeat again, lifeway is not lifestyle. It is not about personal choice as a green consumer or the perfecting of green virtue. A lifeway is informed by the wisdom and experience of others and is nourished by building community with others on the green practice path. These may be friends, colleagues, family members, or role models from afar. *Community* may not necessarily mean "neighborhood"; people following this path find each other across the continent and globe. We encourage each other, we lean on each other, and we build on each other's strengths and experiments. When there are setbacks or frustrations, as in the last eight years of the U.S. presidential administration's leadership, we look to others in Europe, India, Australia, and beyond to keep the momentum going and the practice path strong. Experimental communities in places such as Auroville, India, model visions of the future where practicing a green lifeway is backed by infrastructure as well as intention.

Some time ago, I came to the realization that no matter how committed I was to a green lifeway, this work would not be completed in my lifetime. The forests would not all grow back, the energy grids would not all go solar, the roads would not all have bike lanes before I left this world. At the time, I thought that was discouraging, but mostly it was deeply sobering. It led me to see that it is very important that I pass the green spark on to the next generation. Young people need to be mentored and encouraged to explore the green path of practice. They need support, opportunities, friends, and a multigenerational community of practice partners. The vision I carry of a healthy and life-sustaining earth will take some time to accomplish. It is a cross-generational and cross-cultural project. We don't know how long we must invest in this path of practice. A very important part of following the green lifeway is inviting younger people along, showing them it is possible to nurture the green heart and live a life of conscious intention.

How Then Shall We Live?

In today's world, the pace of change seems to accelerate exponentially year to year. It is not easy to take the time to reflect on our actions, assess priorities, set intention, and build community. Mostly we fall short of our green hopes and ideals. Sometimes the rate of destruction seems to be speeding up right before our eyes. But it is also true that the rate of learning—the spread of information and new ways of doing things—is faster than we ever could have imagined ten or twenty years ago. Yes, people and nations vary considerably in their commitment to the new sustainability practices. But the overall momentum toward the green practice path is accelerating and headed in the right direction, urged on now by the most pressing matter of climate change.

I know only some pieces of what will be required in taking up these challenges. But I do know we need each others' voices and hearts as we deliberate about how to proceed. The green practice path will be fraught with difficulty; the obstacles are everywhere. We need to understand that these very obstacles are the path. We will all be called to deepen our green commitment to be ready for the complexities, the impossibilities, the world as we can't yet imagine it—both terrible and beautiful in its unfolding.

The Open Road:
The Global Journey
of the Fourteenth
Dalai Lama

Pico Iyer

Pico Iyer brings to his observations of the Dalai Lama not only their
friendship of more than three decades, but a novelist's eye, a journalist's
powers of analysis, and, although he is not a Buddhist, a serious
contemplative practice of his own. Iyer is undoubtedly our premier
interpreter of this unique and complex global figure. In his new book,
Iyer teases out the many sides and roles of the Dalai Lama, both private
and public, political and spiritual. Here, he discusses the Dalai Lama
in perhaps his primary identity—as a Buddhist monk.

A monk is a figure of fascination to some of us, even of inspiration,
precisely because (in theory, at least) he turns his back on what most
of us find important and chooses to interpret success, wealth, power
only inwardly, seeing the self as more of an instrument than an end
per se. Where some of us try to make a name for ourselves, he begins

by discarding his very name, and where some of us try to follow the news, he roots himself in the old, through which he can make sense of everything new that happens. The Christian monks I know who gather in their cloisters on Sunday evenings to watch John Cleese movies, the Tibetan rinpoches who have no patience for Western-ers' careful pieties, can afford to be irreverent only because their sense of what they owe reverence to is so precise and so sharp.

I often felt that the heart and soul, quite literally, of the Dalai Lama's life existed in precisely the parts that most of us couldn't see. "The truth," as Meister Eckehart put it, "is that the more ourselves we are, the less of self is in us." Like the most impressive experts in any field, the Dalai Lama tempted us to forget that he had studied for eighteen years and faced an oral examination by thirty scholars of logic, thirty-five doctors of metaphysics, and thirty-five experts on the Noble Path; indeed, his warmth and everyday humanity meant that many of us spoke to him as if he were truly one of us—no one asks the pope whether he has dreams of women or what makes him angry. Yet the fact remained that, like every Tibetan Buddhist monk, he was bound by more than 253 different vows.

I asked the Dalai Lama once how things had changed for him since the last time we'd met in his room, and he said, "Less hair, I think, both of us," to get rid of all reserve at the outset, and broke into gales of wholehearted laughter. Then he answered my question, saying that nothing much had changed except for a small problem with his throat. "And my spiritual practice," he went on, "not much. But as usual, I carry it."

Nowadays, he said, as a result of ongoing studies and the new requirements that came with each new teaching, "my daily prayer, especially what I have to recite and go through, that normally takes about four hours."

"Every day?"

To answer, he took me through his day: meditation, prostra-tions, reciting special mantras; then more meditation and more prostrations, followed by reading Tibetan philosophy or other texts; then reading and studying and, in the evening, "some meditation—

evening meditation—for about one hour. Then, at eight thirty, sleep. Most important meditation. Compulsory meditation for everyone— even some birds. The most important meditation not for nirvana, but for survival!"

A joke, or course, to defuse the onerous sound of the activities and to bring in everyone, even those birds, and yet what I was brought up against again was an almost unimaginable otherness at the center of him. Most of what he did, I was reminded, was invisible.

I have spent much of my adult life in monasteries, interested in watching how these often-silent revolutionaries turn the world in- side out, subverting our assumptions, rooting themselves in what can't be seen, and then disappearing at regular intervals behind the sign that says, Monastic Enclosure. Please Do Not Enter. The Greek word *askesis,* from which *ascetic* comes, refers to the training of ath- letes, and monks are, at least in principle, spiritual athletes who put themselves through almost unfathomable training practices to make their minds as sharp and effective as the bodies of professional sportsmen are.

On Mount Hiei, behind Kyoto, near where I write this, so-called marathon monks embark on prolonged stretches of meditation and, in a few cases, go for days on end without sleeping, spending every night, all night, racing along the narrow paths of the sacred moun- tain, a dagger at their side; they have sworn they will take their own lives if they drink a single glass of water or eat a crust of bread in the course of nine days. At the end of their ordeal, the monks of Mount Hiei look as if they've passed through death itself and emerged at the other end like human candles, illuminated outlines of themselves, aglow (photographs are taken of them after their intense austerities, as if to record the inner equivalent of a three-minute mile). On Mount Hiei, a monk is said to be able to hear ash dropping from a stick of incense in the next room; in Catholic hermitages, according to the Benedictine brother David Steindl-Rast, an ascetic aspires to a state in which a "drop of spring water" is full of flavor.

When we see the Dalai Lama pick out from a crowd a face he has not seen for fifty years or recover a statement he heard thirty years before, what we are seeing, in effect, are the fruits of his long exercises in collecting himself, the ways he has brought his attention to a point in meditation so that it burns as a magnifying glass might burn a piece of paper in the sun. Students at the Gyuto Monastery in Tibet, to take an almost random example, used to have to memorize six hundred pages just to gain admission to the monastery and then embarked on learning another twenty-five hundred pages by heart, apart from all the other chants and recitations they had to master. The purpose of such exercises is not just ritualistic; it is a way of sharpening the mind so that it opens out into what might seem a gigantic filing cabinet or computer hard drive (thus the Dalai Lama, for example, when talking about rural development around the world, will, as in Taiwan in 2001, recall the mayor of Shanghai in 1955, who—with impressive prescience, as the Dalai Lama sees it— told him that he was devoting as much energy to developing the villages around Shanghai as to the city center, so as not to deepen the gap between rich and poor). This is not magic but—the whole point, really—something anyone can choose to do if it may be of help.

You can see all this in the way the Dalai Lama speaks. Monks tend to be sparing with their words, precise—few "um's" and "er's"— because they have cut away everything that is inessential and their words emerge from an abundant silence. Often the Dalai Lama will say nothing for what seems like minutes after I ask him something, and I can almost see him gathering himself and sorting through his mind to find the central principle.

He starts speaking slowly, usually, like a car in a residential neighborhood, and then gathers speed and continuity, as if accelerating onto the open highway, going back to develop points he's made before, picking up new examples and facts, often returning after an hour or so to offer an addendum or ignoring my next question to go back and amplify his previous answer. (One time he even used driving as a good practical example of how all the book knowledge in the world does not help until we practice—and the more we practice driving, the less dangerous it will become.) The answers tend to be rich, fully paragraphed, philosophical treatises, complete with subclasses and qualifications, and broken down almost visibly into points one, two, and three; though they end, very often, in some comical example that sets him off on gusts of infectious laughter and, to some degree, brings us back to earth. Humor in the Dalai Lama arises frequently from setting the world around us against the lofty principles he's just explained.

It's no coincidence, I think, that the Dalai Lama is often photographed peering down a microscope in some foreign lab; as with most of the monks I know, he tends to bring a concentration to things that means a large part of him is living below the surface. Often I will take something he's said to be almost a truism, solid and inert as it comes to me; but as soon as I go over my notes or start to think more about it, I realize that "the mind is its own master," say, has special and rich implications for those who believe that the mind is something different from the self; that mastery is a way of speaking of discipline and craft, as well as power; and that the very word *master* is the same word often used for the Buddha. A student at the Institute of Buddhist Dialectics, next to the Dalai Lama's house, one of its teachers told me, spends two years studying just four lines written by Tsong Kha Pa. He then spends the next four years on a single phrase.

When someone like the Dalai Lama says (as he constantly does, in a brisk, unhesitating way), "Impossible!" or "Impractical!" or "No problem!" or "Not important," what he is really doing is refusing to be distracted and reminding us what is central. And when he goes to meetings with practitioners of other religions, he's not just taking in the latest discussions and techniques in the field, but also becoming a deeper Buddhist, as he said in Vancouver, by talking to a Christian. Reading Saint John's account of the meeting between Mary Magdalene and Jesus after the Resurrection, talking on the parable of the mustard seed and the Transfiguration before a group of Christians in London, the Dalai Lama moved many of his listeners to tears, even as he constantly, carefully stressed that Christianity and Buddhism were not just different ways of explaining the same truth and that to try to combine them was like trying "to put a yak's head on a sheep's body."

Indeed, even though all monks are committed to the same task deep down—as doctors or hospital construction worker are—the details of their practice are as different as their wildly divergent times and cultures. A Christian generally longs to be rooted in the home he's found in God; the Buddhist, more concerned with uncovering potential, is more interested in experiments and inquiries, always pushing deeper. In fact, Christianity works from very uncertain beginnings toward a specific end (redemption and a life with God); Buddhism starts with something very specific (the Buddha and the reality of suffering he saw) and moves toward an always uncertain future (even after one has attained nirvana). The image of the open road speaks for a perpetual becoming.

In either case, though, the monk aspires to bring the perspective of his silence into the chatter of the world, looking past events to all that lies behind them. Thus, when terrorists attacked the United States on September 11, 2001, the Dalai Lama lost no time in sending a letter of commiseration to George W. Bush and his people, and he did the same on the first anniversary of the attack. Yet he also took pains, true to his principles, to say that everything has a cause and that nothing will be resolved until the fundamental cause is taken care of. Simply to respond to violence with violence is like hitting a man in a hospital; he is unlikely to act kindly until he is made better. On the first anniversary of the attack, he reminded the U.S. president that in a world of flux, "today's enemies are often tomorrow's allies."

A doctor's religion may not be important, but which teacher he studied under is often of great importance, and the Dalai Lama always stresses the depth of his debt to Ling Rinpoche ("an acute philosopher with a sharp, logical mind and a good debater with a phenomenal memory") and, even more, of the closeness with which he attends to the figure he sometimes calls his boss. "As followers or students of this great teacher," he told the American Buddhist magazine *Tricycle* in 2001, speaking of the Buddha, "we should take his life as a model. His sacrifice—leaving his palace and remaining in the forest for six years. He worked hard to be enlightened. When the

Buddha started his teachings, he considered his audience's mentality, their mental disposition, then accordingly found teachings." It was hard, reading these words, not to think that the man delivering them had himself been forced to quit his palace in his twenties; had worked, day and night, for fifty years to try to bring light to a tangled situation; and when he appeared in public, was famous for being able somehow to communicate with small children, grandparents, atheists, and Christians alike.

Whenever I read about the Buddha's life, in fact, I felt a strange frisson of déjà vu, uncanny, which made sense only when I recalled that I had been watching someone who traveled so carefully in his footsteps. It was as if the Buddha, walking along his road, had left signs and messages for those who came after, to advise them how to get over that high gate or which was the best way to get around the large boulder in the middle of the road. Everyone ended up taking his own slightly different route, but the aim, as much as moving forward, was to offer what you had learned to those coming after. Once you have crossed the river, in the Buddha's favorite example, you can leave the raft behind. And the Tibetan Buddhists, true to this idea of progress, believe that there are fourteen fundamental questions ("Are the self and universe eternal? Are the self and the universe transient?") that even the Buddha left unanswered for those who came after to take on.

One of the striking things about Siddhartha Gautama was that after coming upon his enlightenment under the papal tree, he had no wish to spread his discoveries, since he didn't feel confident that they would be of use or interest to anyone else; the essence of his teaching, famously, was "Be lamps unto yourselves" and "Seek no refuge but yourself." But when he became convinced that there might be some virtue in talking of his own experience, he spent the last forty-five years of his life ceaselessly traveling across the Gangetic Plain, among the new cities that were coming up there in a time of flux that also brought, as one biographer, Karen Armstrong, writes, a sense of "spiritual hunger." Although he engaged in public debates, he repeatedly shied away from cosmic questions as distractions, perhaps, from the main concern.

"Forget about next life," I once heard the Dalai Lama say on a tape, as I was browsing in a bookshop within his temple. "This very life should be useful to others. If not, at least no harm."

"I do not give knowledge," the Buddha said. "If you can believe anything, you get caught in that belief or distraction." Zen monks famously took this distrust of images to such an extreme that they burned buddhas to keep themselves warm in winter and said, "If you meet the Buddha along the road, you must kill the Buddha."

The correspondences between the teacher and his far-off student were sometimes so startling that I did not know whether to call them coincidence or continuity or a mixture of the two. The Buddha is said to have had his first moment of insight when his nursemaids left him alone as they went to watch an annual ceremonial plowing of the field, and he noticed that some young grasses had been torn up for the ceremony, destroying insects and their eggs. No television interviewer who has seen the Dalai Lama break off an answer because he's noticed a bird falling to the ground outside and wants to tend to it will be surprised. When the Buddha practiced austerities, all he achieved, in the dry accounting of Karen Armstrong (once a nun herself and now a scholar of religions), "was a prominent rib cage and a dangerously weakened body." When the Dalai Lama tried to become a vegetarian for twenty months around 1965, he contracted hepatitis B and almost died, his doctors telling him, as his mother had done, that his Himalayan constitution could not survive without meat. The Buddha is said to have cried out in pity when he heard of a yogic master who had spent twenty years learning to walk on water (he could just have taken a ferry and used his energies for something else); the Dalai Lama has said that "the best thing is not to use" any magic powers, not least, perhaps, because they take most of us away from what is more sustaining.

Even Thomas Merton, during his visit, was struck by how "always and everywhere the Dalai Lama kept insisting on the fact that one could not attain anything in the spiritual life without total dedication, continued effort, experienced guidance, real discipline." In later years, however, the Dalai Lama has begun talking even more about "hard work," "determination," the importance of not giving up. Indeed, it's not uncommon to see tears come to his eyes, even in a huge arena, when he speaks of the Tibetan poet-saint Milarepa, say, meditating and meditating for years in a cave, or of any of the great Tibetan figures who almost killed themselves in their exertions. (I remembered how a tear had come into his eye even when my wife, Hiroko, once said that she had tried, really had, to learn from his books, but it was difficult.)

One other thing moved him to tears, even in public, I heard from an American monk who had been living in the Dalai Lama's monastery for twenty years. That was when someone asked, during a public address, "What is the quickest, easiest, cheapest way to attain enlightenment?" And, the Californian monk went on, "these days in the East there's nearly always someone who asks that question."

Every monk is the same monk in that he is working to dissolve his sense of self, in part by surrendering to something larger; and every monk is a radical insofar as he works from the root (*radix* in Latin). For the Buddhist, though, this has especial truth, since his first concern is the interior landscape, where awareness or its obscuration lies; faith for him is really self-confidence and prayer a form of awakening latent energies.

The Dalai Lama is, in these respects, truly just another monk, "a little bit anxious," as he confessed to me, when he has to give a talk before senior monks, many of whom have much more time for study than he does, and obliged to spend months doing "a lot of homework." He comes to important meetings in flip-flops (for interviews he generally sheds his shoes and sits cross-legged in his chair, sometimes holding his interlocutor's hand), and when he's backstage at a modern theater, I have seen, he eagerly cross-questions technicians as to how the lights work. "Utilize modern facilities," is his practical position, "but try to develop a right kind of attitude." It seems apt that he has a remarkable memory for dates and faces but is altogether less good with names.

It's a happy aspect of his circumstances that he takes as his political model a Hindu (Gandhi), works very closely with many Christians (Desmond Tutu, Vaclav Havel, Jimmy Carter), and lives in a country (India) that has the world's second-largest Muslim population. Many of the scientists he collaborates with may pride themselves on having no religion at all. Yet even as he has made dissolving distinctions his life's work, he is careful not to speak for a "world religion," if only because we need different approaches and different languages, as it were, to deal with the different kinds of people there are in the world. "Sometimes," I heard him say in Europe, "people, in order to have closer relations [with other traditions] stress only the positive things. That's wrong! We have to make clear what are the fundamental differences." In almost the next sentence, though, he added that whenever he saw an image of the Virgin Mary, he was moved: which human being does not have a mother?

Because of the "fast pace of life" in the West, he told me once, monks in the East may have a small advantage over their counterparts in the West when it comes to meditation (though no sooner had he said this than he remembered some Catholic monks he'd visited in France who seemed unsurpassable in their single-pointed concentration); yet Buddhists, he said, perhaps had something to learn from Christians and others when it came to social action and bringing the fruits of their practice out into the world. As he said that, I recalled how Bono, the ardently Christian lead singer of the group U2, had been asked in 1990 to write a song for a Tibetan Freedom Concert and had come up with a haunting ballad about how we share "one love, one blood, one life, you've got to do what you should," and yet concluded again and again, "we're one, but we're not the same." The song had become one of the group's talismanic anthems, which I'd heard sung in the dusty Current Event café in Dharamsala, and was a favorite at modern weddings. And yet, Bono always stressed, the song was about divisions, inherent differences—the fact that we can never be as one as we would like.

Every monk is the same monk insofar as he journeys into a similar silence and a parallel darkness—the blackness behind our thoughts we find in meditation—and every monk is the same monk as every lover is the same lover: it doesn't matter whether the object of your devotion is called Angela or Jigme or Tom, whether she existed in Sappho's time or right now. Yet every monk is most the same monk because his journey into solitude, community, and obedience is a way, really, for him to bring something transformative to the larger world, in the attention he brings to it.

"Be not *simply* good," as Thoreau wrote in his first letter to Harrison Blake. "Be good for something."

Perhaps the most moving moment I ever witnessed in Dharamsala came in 1988, when I was invited, during the Tibetan New Year celebrations centered on the Dalai Lama's temple, to stand in on one of the meetings the Dalai Lama holds with Tibetans who have just arrived, after treacherous flights across the mountains, to see him again. Many of these people had risked their lives traveling three weeks across Himalayan passes in midwinter to meet with him for a few minutes and then would cross back over the mountains, perhaps never to see him again.

The people who were gathered in the room, maybe thirty or so, were strikingly ragged, their poor clothes rendered even poorer and more threadbare by their long trip across the snowcaps. They assembled in three lines in a small room, and all I could see were filthy coats, blackened faces, sores on hands and feet, straggly, unwashed hair.

When the Dalai Lama came into the room, it was as if the whole place began to sob and shake. Instantly, among almost all the people assembled on the floor, there was a wailing, a convulsive movement, a release of all the feelings (of hope and fear and concern and relief) that had been building inside some of them for more than thirty years. The man sat before them, seeking them out with shrewd, attentive eyes, and none of the adults before him could even look at him.

"Even we cannot watch this, often," said the Dalai Lama's private secretary, who had stood by his side imperturbably, as calm as the monk he once was, for almost a quarter of a century at that point. The Dalai Lama sat firmly in the middle of the tumult, though later he would tell me that although "generally sadness is manageable," even he was sometimes moved to "shed a tear" when he saw all the hopes that these people brought to him and all that they had suffered.

"Sometimes we try to find someone else to do this for us," the secretary whispered to me where we stood. "It's just too much."

The Dalai Lama tends to be more brusque with Tibetans than he is with Westerners, partly because he knows that this is what they expect of him, and partly because he knows that they would be discomfited by too much familiarity from their godhead. But now he went down the lines, greeting each person in turn, asking (I could guess) where this person came from, how things were in her local area, what might be done to help. Each person, in answer to the questions, looked down or just began to howl and shake with sobs.

Only a few children sitting in the front, the smallest in the party, answered the questions, their high, piping voices telling him they came from Kham, or their father was a farmer, or the trip had taken them twenty-three days. Only the children had not been storing up their hopes for all these years, with only this one chance to release them. Then, after making sure that all the refugees would be properly looked after and given new homes here if that was what they wanted, the Dalai Lama told them to keep their spirits up and their hearts intent on how they could help others.

The four hours every morning of meditation were, I saw now, straightforward compared with the house those foundations supported.

The Art of Losing: On Writing, Dying, and Mom

Ruth L. Ozeki

"Letting go" is a spiritual practice much recommended these days. In letting go, we feel uplifted, open, yet still in control. But life's true challenge, says the novelist and essayist Ruth Ozeki, is the art of losing, so much more painful, involuntary, and real. In this beautiful memoir/contemplation about losing her mother, she fulfills the writer's mission to—although "it may look like disaster"—write it!

Last year, I was asked to give a talk at the annual donor-appreciation dinner for the Zen Hospice Project in San Francisco. I'm a great admirer of the Hospice Project's work, so I accepted without hesitation. When they asked me to provide a title for the talk, I thought it would be easy. I'm a writer, so I would talk about writing, and since this was for the Hospice Project, I would talk about death. I'd been thinking a lot about both writing and death, as I'd quite recently lost my mother and was using writing as a way of working with my feelings of grief and loss. So I sent the organizers an e-mail proposing this title: "The Art of Losing: On Writing, Dying, and Mom."

I have to admit, I was kind of proud of my title. I thought it was subtle and literary, but not too flashy. The phrase "art of losing" is from a favorite poem of mine by Elizabeth Bishop, called "One Art." It's a sad, brave, beautiful poem about both death and writing, and I was happy because I could start my talk by reading it. Beginnings are important, and as a Buddhist woman writer, I like to pay tribute to my women ancestors.

But the Zen Hospice organizers came back to me with a polite counterproposal. They asked me to consider instead "The Art of Letting Go."

Losing. Letting go. The difference in nuance is interesting, right? Actually, I thought it was kind of funny. *Losing* does sound awfully negative, and even Buddhists don't want to be losers. And I certainly didn't want to make anyone at that particular dinner feel like a loser. The event was a tribute, a way of saying thank you to all the kind people who gave to the Zen Hospice Project and helped make their work possible. That kind of giving is not about losing. It is all about amply, generously, and joyously letting go.

So the organizers knew better and I agreed, but I continued to think about the difference between losing and letting go, and the degree to which they are interchangeable or not. Elizabeth Bishop's poem offers a lens through which to look at this question.

One Art

The art of losing isn't hard to master;
so many things seem filled with the intent
to be lost that their loss is no disaster.

Lose something every day. Accept the fluster
of lost door keys, the hour badly spent.
The art of losing isn't hard to master.

Then practice losing farther, losing faster;
places, and names, and where it was you meant
to travel. None of these will bring disaster.

I lost my mother's watch. And look! my last, or
next-to-last, of three loved houses went.
The art of losing isn't hard to master.

I lost two cities, lovely ones. And, vaster,
some realms I owned, two rivers, a continent.
I miss them, but it wasn't a disaster.

—Even losing you (the joking voice, a gesture
I love) I shan't have lied. It's evident
the art of losing's not too hard to master
though it may look like (*Write* it!) like disaster.

Clearly, this is a case where "losing" and "letting go" are not
interchangeable. "The art of letting go isn't hard to master" makes
for lousy poetry, failing both rhythmically and rhetorically. What
makes the original line and the poem so strong is loss—the stark,
uncontrollable, and increasingly disastrous quality of the losses it
enumerates in such a casual, almost nonchalant tone. It's the unsettling disparity between the tone and the turbulence of feeling that
makes the lines quiver and sing.

So what is the difference between losing and letting go? What
makes losing feel like such a disaster? On an obvious level, it's about
control. When I let go, I'm in control; when I lose, I'm not. Letting go
is a willful act; losing, a violation of my will. The poet's assertion of
her art, her will, over her losses heightens the poignancy of her poem,
because in the poem, she both is and is not in control. Beneath the
surface tension of her careful lines lies disaster.

My Zen teacher, Norman Fischer, is fond of noting that the
world is a disaster, but he is a poet, like Elizabeth Bishop, so perhaps
this is just something that poets notice. Of course, being a Zen teacher,
he tempers this by pointing out that the world is simultaneously magnificent. Maybe it's precisely these unbearable and irreconcilable
tensions between magnificence and disaster, between chaos and

control, between loss and letting go, that give birth to both poems and religions.

Dividing the Bones

My own introduction to religion and poetry came when I was very young. My mom's father was a poet and Zen practitioner, and the very first memory I have, as a small human being, was of watching him sit zazen with my grandmother. I was very little, maybe three years old, and growing up in New Haven, Connecticut. My grandparents came to visit us on their way back to Japan. It was the first time I'd met them. We lived in a tiny house with no spare bedroom, so they were given my parents' room, while my parents slept on the couch. I remember being very excited about these two strange people in the house, who must be very powerful to displace my parents, the most important people in the world. I remember their clothes smelled funny, probably like incense, now that I think of it.

The first morning was filled with suspense. My mother was in the kitchen, cooking, and she must have sent me to call my grandparents to breakfast. I remember approaching the closed bedroom door with enormous trepidation. Perhaps I knocked, or maybe I didn't. It was perfectly silent on the other side. I imagine I must have felt a grave sense of responsibility—I had been given a duty to discharge, and Asian people, even very small ones, are nothing if not dutiful. So perhaps it was this innate sense of duty that compelled me to turn the knob and open the door.

Nothing in my entire three years of living had prepared me for what I saw. My grandmother and grandfather were sitting on the floor, on either side of the bed, with their legs crossed and their eyes half-closed, rocking gently back and forth.

Now, you have to remember that this was New Haven, Connecticut, in the 1950s. People didn't sit on the floor cross-legged with their eyes half-closed, rocking back and forth. This was not San Francisco. It was not the East Village of New York. Seated on the floor like that, they were my height exactly. We were at eye level, only their eyes were shut.

Mine, on the other hand, were wide open. I stood there for a moment, then I backed out of the room and ran full tilt into the kitchen, where I told my mother what I had seen.

And here's the funny part. My mom must have tried to explain to me that they were meditating, which, of course, meant nothing to a three-year-old. So when I didn't understand, she went and got my Daruma doll. Daruma is the Japanese name for Bodhidharma, the monk who founded the Zen lineage in China and who sat for nine years, gazing at a wall, in silent meditation. Japanese Daruma dolls are round and red and shaped like rice balls, with no legs or arms, and big, blank, white circles where their eyes should be. Mine had a curved bottom so it would rock, and the idea was that even if you tried to push it over, it would always regain its balance.

So, my mom set my Daruma rocking back and forth, and she told me he was meditating, the same thing my grandma and grandpa were doing. Then she explained that Daruma had been a really good meditator. In fact, he had been such a good meditator and had meditated for so long that his arms and legs had fallen off. And the reason he had no eyes was that he had gotten sleepy while he was meditating and so he had cut off his eyelids.

This was my introduction to Zen, and thanks to Mom's explanation, I developed an association in my mind between Zen meditation, blindness, and grave bodily disfigurement. For the rest of my grandparents' visit, I kept fearing I'd walk in and find them sightless and limbless, rocking gently back and forth.

In time I got over it, and much later on, when I started sitting zazen myself, Mom was mystified. She called the posture "squatting on the floor." She never understood why I would choose to squat on the floor and stare at a wall for days on end, when I could be reading a good book. She saw me as the Buddhist equivalent of a born-again Christian.

Like many second-generation Japanese kids in America, my mom had little connection with her Japanese roots. In Hawaii, where she had grown up, she was sent to Christian church while her parents practiced Buddhism. When World War II broke out, my grandfather was interned in Santa Fe, my grandmother was left behind in Hawaii, and my mother was put under house arrest in Michigan, where she was attending graduate school. After the war, my grandparents moved back to Japan. My mom moved to the East Coast to continue her studies, and she saw her parents very rarely. My grandfather passed away shortly after their return to Japan, and by the time my grandmother died, at the age of ninety-three in an old-age home outside of Tokyo, Mom hadn't seen her for many years.

When she called me in New York to give me the news of my grandmother's death, my mom told me that she couldn't go to Japan to attend the funeral. It would be a Buddhist ceremony, she said, and she had a bad leg—arthritis or something—so she wouldn't be able to squat on the floor during the service. She was afraid she would be an embarrassment to the family if she were forced to use a chair, and she asked me if I would go to the funeral in her stead.

So I went to Tokyo, to my aunt's house. My grandmother had already been cremated by the time I got there, but I arrived in time for her funeral ceremony at the family temple and her interment in the family grave. Before we left for the temple, my aunt took me into the parlor, where she was keeping my grandmother's remains. She showed me the urn, which I dutifully admired, then she went to the kitchen and brought back a small Tupperware container and a pair of wooden chopsticks, the disposable kind that you get with take-out sushi. I watched as she lined the Tupperware with one of my grandmother's fancy handkerchiefs, opened the urn, and started poking around inside with the tips of her chopsticks like she was trying to fish a pickle from a jar.

I was surprised to see that the remains were bones instead of ashes and to watch my aunt picking them out and packing them in Tupperware. But most of all, I was surprised to hear her name each bone as she moved it. "This is a piece of your grandmother's skull. This is a bit of her rib. . . ." When she had transferred several bones, she snapped the top onto the container, burped it to remove the extra air, and handed it to me, instructing me to take the bones home and give them to my mother.

I didn't realize it at the time, but this was a custom—not the Tupperware part, but the rest of it—called *honewake,* or dividing the bones, which is often practiced when a person's family lives in different places. It's also practiced when a woman dies, so that her parents can have some of her remains, as a consolation, while the rest are buried with her husband.

To make a long story short, I came back from Japan with the bones and a large box of my grandmother's belongings, but for one reason or another, I didn't get around to bringing them to my mom for several years. She and I had grown apart, much as she had grown apart from her parents. I was busy with my career, a marriage, a divorce, and talking about death is never easy. She knew I had her mother's bones. I kept hoping she'd ask me about them, but she never did, and I didn't want to bring up the subject. So the bones sat on a shelf in my closet, a skeleton that haunted me for years.

At the time, I was working as a television producer, but I wanted to make an independent film of my own. I was interested in exploring my Japanese heritage and had started writing down little snippets of family history, stuff that I'd heard from my mom and from my grandmother over the years, and it quickly became clear to me how much I didn't know. There were these great, gaping holes of missing information, and I felt a deep sense of loss and regret that I could no longer ask my grandparents anything because they were dead. At the same time, I felt an increasing compulsion to make something out of what remained.

What remained were my grandmother's bones, the fragments of stories, and the duty I'd been given by my aunt to discharge—and as we've established, I am nothing if not dutiful. But more powerful than that, I had a mandate from the dead.

This might seem strange, but that's what it felt like. As though I had a mandate from my dead Japanese grandparents to engage with the world creatively. My grandfather, in addition to being a haiku poet, was also the first official photographer for Volcano National Park on the big island of Hawaii. I had grown up surrounded by his landscapes and his words: his black-and-white photographs, painstakingly hand-colored by my grandmother, and his book of poems with their beautiful, calligraphed paintings and scrolls. When I was little and just starting to write poems and take pictures myself, my mother used to say that I was just like my grandfather. She used to shake her head ruefully and marvel at how her father's love of the arts had skipped a generation, bypassing her, only to end up in me. It made me feel very proud whenever she said this, and she said it often, as though to make sure I would remember. I had only met my grandfather that one time when I was three, but I felt some kind of transmission had occurred. And my grandmother's bones had completed the process. Her bones were the seal to the mandate.

What grew from this was a documentary film called *Halving the Bones*. It was the first narrative effort I dared put out into the world, and it's made from stories—stories of my grandparents' lives, my grandmother's death, and delivering her bones to my mother; stories of World War II, my grandfather's internment, and the dissolution of their family; stories of loss and coping with loss. I tell some of the stories. My mother tells others. The ghost of my grandmother tells still more.

At the end of the film, after I've finally handed the bones over to my mom, I ask her what she wants me to do with them, and she tells me her wishes. It's a nice scene. Before giving them to her, I'd transferred the bones to a pretty Japanese tea canister and ditched the Tupperware, so Mom is sitting there in her living room with the little can of bones on her lap. She laughs at the Tupperware story and professes her fondness and admiration for the tea can. She opens it and inspects every bone, peering at each one, exclaiming over the beauty of their shapes, their surprising hues and shades of color. She whispers to the bones, as if to her mother. And in the end, after closing up the can and patting it contentedly, she tells me what she wants me to do with my grandmother's bones, and hers, after she dies.

I'll tell you what she said, but first I should explain that this was a turning point in our relationship. Making the film with my mother, engaging in this creative and collaborative storytelling project, helped us to reconnect. It gave us the excuse to spend time together, and get to know each other again, and learn to talk about the important matters of life and death. It was as if our relationship were somehow reknit from the bones of my grandmother, so much so that when my mother was diagnosed with Alzheimer's, and then my father died, I decided to bring her to live with me so I could take care of her myself. I think this decision was only possible because of the closeness we'd found, but in addition, making the film—writing, shooting, editing, putting it out into the world—forced me to think deeply about loss and the many ways we lose people and the choices involved. My choice was simple: I didn't want to be half a world away from my mother when she died.

I think there's a powerful link between creativity and death. We make things because we lose things: memories, people we love, and ultimately our very selves. Our acts of creation are ways of grappling with death: we imagine it, struggle to make sense of it, forestall or defeat it. When I sat down to write this essay, I realized that all my work—in film or on the page—has ultimately been about dying, and I know I'm not alone. These media are, quite literally, mediums, the means of traveling to the other shore. They are our imaginative transport to the land of the dead. We learn things there and then return what we learn to the living. This journey is undertaken by anyone who has ever told stories, from Homer to Dante to Elizabeth Bishop. To tell stories is to practice of the art of losing. As Bishop says, it is one art.

THE ART OF LOSING

It wasn't always easy to care for my mom. It became clear pretty quickly that she couldn't live on her own, but my mother, like most mothers, had a serious stubborn streak, so I was prepared for the worst. But to my surprise, in 1999 she packed a tiny suitcase with a toothbrush, two bathing suits, and a pair of pajamas, and declared herself ready to come home with me and my husband to a remote island in British Columbia. She lived there with us in a little house just down the road from ours, pretty much until she died in November of 2004.

To care for a parent with Alzheimer's is to practice losing every day. I wrote a lot during that time, which was part of my practice. These are some entries from my blog.

AUGUST 17, 2003

So, my mother said to me the other day, "When I die, are you going to start renting out this house I'm living in to other people?"

"I haven't thought about it," I replied, hedging. Obviously I still don't like it when she talks about dying.

"Well, you should take the washer-dryer up to your house before you rent it to anyone."

"The washing machine?"

"Yes," she said. "I don't know why you put it in this house. You have to come all the way down here every time you want to do your laundry."

"We put it down here so we could all share. . . ." We put it down here so we'd have another excuse to hang out with you. We put it down here because we are afraid you'll become bedridden and incontinent.

"Well," she said, "that's very nice of you, but after I die, I don't want to have to worry about you not having a washer-dryer."

"Mom," I told her. "Please." She's had Alzheimer's since the mid-1990s, she's just been diagnosed with what looks like jaw cancer, and she's eighty-nine years old. She has enough on her mind without worrying about our laundry.

"So, you'll take it back up to your house?"

"Mom, when you die, I'm burying the washer-dryer with you."

"Don't be silly."

"I don't want to have to worry about your dirty clothes when you're in heaven." (I don't really believe in heaven and neither does she, but I know she will humor me.)

"Clothes don't get dirty in heaven," she said, staring at a tall

Douglas fir outside the window. "Clothes are always clean in heaven."

"They are?"

"Yes. They have angels there who do all the laundry. Now, isn't that a lovely tree? What kind of tree is that?"

MAY 25, 2004

A lot has happened. My mother turned ninety last month, and we had a little birthday party for her.

"How old am I?" she asked me.

"You're ninety, Mom."

Her eyes widened. "I am! That's unbelievable! How can I be ninety? I don't feel ninety."

"How old do you feel?"

"Forty."

She was perfectly serious.

I laughed. "You can't be forty. Even I'm older than forty."

"You are?" she exclaimed. "That's terrible!"

"Gee, thanks."

She shook her head. "You know, I must be getting old. I just can't remember anything anymore." She looked up at me and blinked. "How old am I?"

Later on, I asked her, "How does it feel?"

"What?"

"When you can't remember things. Does it frighten you? Do you feel sad?"

"Well, not really. I have this condition, you see. It's called os . . . oste . . ."

"You mean Alzheimer's?" I said, helping her out.

She looked astonished. "Yes! How on earth did you know?"

"Just a guess."

"I can never remember the name," she explained.

"Of course not."

"It affects my memory."

"And that's why you can't remember."

She frowned and shook her head. "Remember what?"

"There's not a single thing I can do about it," she told me, when I reminded her. "If there was something I could do and I wasn't doing it, then I could feel sad or depressed. But as it is . . ." She shrugged.

"So you're OK with it?"

She looked at me patiently. "I don't have much choice," she explained, "so I may as well be happy."

DECEMBER 8, 2005

Dear Norman [Fischer],

The other day you asked me to write something for the Hospice Project grief workshop that you will be leading. So, here goes.

My mom died one month ago today. She had three terminal conditions: Alzheimer's, cancer of the jaw, and ninety years of living. Her death should have come as no surprise, but of course, when she died in my arms, I was astonished.

How can this life, which has persisted here on this earth for over ninety years, be over? Just like that? This strange new state of momlessness is inconceivable to me. It is new and foreign, a condition I've never experienced in my own forty-eight years of living.

I've been taking care of my mom for the last ten years, so my grieving is minute and quotidian. When I go to the grocery store, I find myself searching for things that are soft and sweet (she loved chocolate, and she had no teeth) or beautiful, bright things (she loved flowers, but her sight was failing). Then I remember that she isn't here anymore, and I'll never again see her face light up when I come into her room or hear her exclaim over the color of a leaf or a petal or the sky. For the first couple of weeks, I just stood in the ice cream aisle, stunned and weeping.

When I think about her death from her perspective, mostly I just feel relief. She was beginning to suffer a lot of pain and confusion, and I believe she was ready to go. But when I think about it from my point of view, it breaks my heart. Maybe that's selfish. I don't know. All I know is that I miss her like crazy.

I miss her thin little fingers. I miss holding her hand. I miss twirling her wedding ring around so the tiny chip of a diamond sits back on top.

I've tried so hard to be strong for her. When she was diagnosed with Alzheimer's, our roles began to switch. I took over caring for her, and slowly she became dependent on me. In the end, I was feeding her and changing her, and she was calling me Mom. Alzheimer's is an achingly long way to say good-bye, but I had to be strong, I thought. It would only confuse and upset her to see me cry.

Then, a few months ago, I had to take a trip and leave her for a couple of weeks. I went to tell her, knowing that she might die while I was gone, and as I sat on the bed next to her, the tears just came and there was no stopping them. I tried not to let her see, but of course she noticed. She's my mom, after all—it's her job to notice these things. She put her arm around me, put her head on my shoulder, and although she'd pretty much stopped using language by then, she made these sweet, singing, momlike noises meant to comfort me. And it worked, and I felt better, and when I left, we were both laughing. So that was good. My grieving gave her something that she could do well, something she could succeed at, and that made her happy. It let her be the strong one for a change.

They say every death is different, and I think every occasion of grief is different, too.

When my dad died, I was angry because he was angry and despairing. He did not want to die. He wasn't ready. I was in charge of his health care, but I couldn't do a damn thing to prevent or forestall this utterly unthinkable and unacceptably terminal outcome. I was mad at him for his lack of readiness, and I was furious at myself for my impotence and lack of compassion. After he died, I couldn't think of him without a lot of pain and anger and confusion and despair, and a sense of having failed him. I couldn't look at his picture without feeling my insides twist. I wanted to look away. And I did. I remember I drank a lot, too, in order to get through it. I took his death very personally.

It was different with my mom. We'd had lots of time together, and we were both as ready as we could ever be. And I wasn't drinking. I quit two months before she died. I'd done the drunken death-and-grieving thing once, and it was lousy. I didn't want to do it again. I wanted to keep my wits about me. I didn't want to run away.

The last thing I promised my dad was to take care of my mom. He knew she had Alzheimer's, and he was tortured at having to leave her behind. So for ten years now, I've been fulfilling my promise to him. And this has been good, too. His request gave me something that I could do well, something I could succeed at, and this has made me happy.

So I'm grateful to my parents for dying in my presence and for teaching me their two different ways of how it can be done. It is hard work, dying, but after watching my mom and dad, I realize that we're built to do it.

Grieving is hard work, too, but again, I guess we're built to do it. We come equipped with hearts to break and eyes to cry with. We have brains to hold the memories and stories, and voices to tell them with. We have the capacity to love and heal.

Now, a month after my mom's death, I'm not crying in the grocery store so often anymore. Instead, when I think of my mom, I buy a sweet and offer it to her, and then I eat it (she hated wasting perfectly good food). I bring home flowers and admire them through her eyes. I take walks for her by the ocean and look at the sky.

So that's a little of what it's been like. Thank you so much, Norman, for asking me to write this. It helps to have a place to put the feelings.

With love,
Ruth

Negotiating with the Dead

If creativity is a way of offsetting or coping with loss, then perhaps writing—our written language—exists on account of, or to account for, our mortality. If we were not able to count our days and to foresee our termination, then why would we bother to write things down? If we could not envision the world without us, then why would we feel the need to leave bits of ourselves, these words, behind? And if we were not compelled to hold on to our dead, then why would we keep them alive in stories? Why would we feel the need to speak to them or for them? Why would we grieve? Why would we need history at all?

The act of telling a story is an act of negotiating with the dead, to use Margaret Atwood's wonderful phrase from her book of the same title. You could argue, as she does, that all stories are about dying. Storytelling is about the ticking of the clock. It's about "once upon a time." And stories, written down, have unique qualities that set them apart from other art forms. Unlike painting, stories are time-based—they unfold through time. Unlike the performance of a play, they persist—they survive their enactment. Unlike music, they are literal. Stories literally reenact time passing. They have a beginning, a middle, and an end. They are born, they live, and then they die, and every time you participate in the writing or reading of a story, you are participating in that same cycle. Pretending. Rehearsing, if you will.

Stories are messages from the nether land, the land of the dead, and writers are the future dead, calling back to the living. In the publishing business, there's a saying: "The only good author is a dead author." For those of us still living, this statement is a bit problematic, but at least we can take some consolation in knowing that the best may still lie ahead. And to be fair, you can see the publisher's point. Authors are, hands down, the most unreliable link in the production chain. They are moody and capricious. They can be preening prima donnas or stubbornly reclusive, puffed up or crippled by doubt. Often they have bad habits, like drinking or philandering or bad hygiene. Generally, these are not people you want in key roles in your production team. And when you think about it, the saying is quite true. The majority of the books and stories that we read—the good ones, anyway, the ones that linger and continue to haunt us— were written by dead authors. Language, this medium of story, is an inheritance we receive from the dead, and when we practice the art of telling stories, we do so in the tongues of the dead, calling them back to life.

Which brings us back to Elizabeth Bishop's poem, "One Art." Bishop's art is the art of losing, which, like any art, must be practiced and *will* be practiced whether we like it or not. But in the final stanza, she intrudes upon her very last line with a private, parenthetical imperative:

. . . It's evident
the art of losing's not too hard to master
though it may look like (*Write* it!) like disaster.

"*Write* it!" she commands herself. Write it! Write your loss, because for a poet this disaster that we call life—and it truly is a disaster, when you think about it—can only be transformed into magnificence through the practice of this one art. It is through poetry that Bishop practices the art of losing and transforms each loss into a poem, which is a kind of liberation, a letting go. And through the poem she leaves behind, postmortem, she shows us all how to make the journey and to effect this transformation, too.

I spent ten years losing my mom, little by little, day by day, but during that time, I wrote books, letters, e-mails, blog postings, stories, journal entries, and poems. While I was writing this essay, it hit me that, by following a dead poet's injunction, I've been turning loss into letting go. Now, almost three years since my mother died, I read what I wrote when the pain was strongest, and I feel the pain again, but less so. The suffering, too, has changed, and yet instead of relief, I feel a quick stab of grief at the diminishment—and then I have to laugh, realizing that even loss can be lost and grieved for.

One last thing. I promised to tell you Mom's instructions regarding the disposal of her mother's bones. What she told me was this: she said that when she died, after her cremation, she wanted me to take her bones, along with my grandmother's, back to Hawaii and throw them all in the ocean.

I confess, I haven't done that yet. I'm not quite ready to let go.

Detours from Reality

Ezra Bayda

While the Buddhist path promises an end to suffering, there's a lot of hard work required to get there. Perhaps the most important part of the practice is becoming acutely, even painfully, aware of all our neuroses and tricks— the ways we cause ourselves and others suffering, the clever ways ego sabotages our spiritual progress (for enlightenment is ego's greatest fear). Here's the Zen teacher Ezra Bayda with a look at three of the ways we get trapped.

One of the greatest hindrances to living a more awake life—a life of satisfaction and appreciation—is that we spend most of our time lost in the mental world. We are literally addicted to our thoughts, whether we are planning, fantasizing, worrying, dramatizing, conversing, or whatever. If we are honest, isn't it true that most of our time is spent spinning in thoughts?

There are three habitual grooves where most of us get caught spinning in the mental world: analyzing, blaming, and fixing. These conditioned patterns are detours from being present to reality, and taking any one of them guarantees that we will perpetuate the story line of "me."

ANALYZING

When a difficult situation arises, one of our first reactions might be to ask why. We analyze the situation by asking, "Why is this happen-

ing?" "Why am I depressed?" "Why am I so tired?" "Why am I anxious?" and so on. We ask why, in part, because we want certainty; we
want to maintain the illusion that our lives are guided by certainty
and logic. We want to avoid the anxious quiver of the present moment, the discomfort of not having ground under our feet. We think
that through analysis we can uncover why we think the way we do,
why others are doing what they're doing, or why something happened the way it did. We think this mental understanding is necessary for our comfort. But, most of the time, does asking why on this
level give us much real clarity or satisfaction? Don't we usually end
up just spinning in circles? Granted, when we uncover our believed
thoughts—those repeated thoughts that we have a habit of taking as
reality—we can sometimes see how these thoughts impact our emotional reactions, but most often, the reasons we come up with are, at
best, only marginally accurate.

I once visited the Catacombs of Paris, where the bones of six
million dead bodies are piled neatly along a mile-long corridor, deep
beneath the streets. I imagined how many times in the lives of all of
these people the question "Why is this happening?" was asked—the
vanity of thinking we can actually figure life out. There was an apt
inscription carved in the walls: "Silence, you mortals. Great vanity—
silence."

From a practice perspective, the real question is not why but
what—"What is my life right now?" Or even better, "What is this?"
This question moves us out of the mental world into the experiential. The question "What is this?" is really a Zen koan. The Zen koan
is traditionally a question that a teacher gives to a student, but koan
questions cannot be answered with the conceptual or analytical
mind. In fact, a koan such as "What is the sound of one hand clapping?" is specifically meant to baffle our normal thinking mind and,
in so doing, allow us to experience the spaciousness of the nonconceptual. Asking, "What is this?" serves as the perfect koan because,
like any koan, there is no way you can answer it by thinking or analyzing. In fact, the only answer to this question is the actual experiencing of the present moment itself. The only answer is "Just this!"

Right now, ask yourself, "What is this?" To answer, simply feel the breath going in and out. Feel the air in the room. Feel the tension in your face. Feel the energy going through your body. Experience a felt sense of the overall body posture. Experience "just this!"—the simple quality or texture of the moment.

Gutei, a ninth-century Zen master, would often respond to students' questions by simply raising his index finger, saying nothing. Instead of getting an answer, students would be forced into being present with their own experience. Can you imagine the frustration of coming to talk to a teacher, expecting the comfort of intellectual clarity or psychological insight, and being met only with silence? However, even if we did find it frustrating, that silence can be an invaluable teacher. Instead of conceptualizing, instead of asking why, students would have to face the "what" of their experience. They could no longer use their thinking to escape what was happening *right now*.

Rather than holding together the me, we can begin to turn away from the comfort of fixed identities—identities that are held in place by our thoughts. Every time we have a thought about ourselves— "I'm the kind of person who . . ." or "I'm like this because . . ."—we solidify the concept of a me. On a subtle level, even beliefs such as "I'm a Democrat" or "I'm an American" feed the I-as-a-me. But to see through these artificial mental identities allows us to stop identifying exclusively with the little self and connect more and more with a larger sense of life.

Naturally, when difficulties arise in life, we look for answers, because we prefer the comfort of black-or-white thinking. We continue to hold on to the notion that we can figure life out; yet, the fact is we'll never figure life out by asking why. Most often, we just don't know.

My mother told me a story about her father at the end of his life. He was a very religious and humble man, well respected in his Orthodox Jewish community. From his sickbed he requested a prayer book so that he could recite the Friday night prayers.

Everyone tried to tell him it was not Friday night, but he persisted

in his request. Finally someone got concerned about his seeming lack
of clarity and went to ask the rabbi for advice. The rabbi understood
that my grandfather knew he was about to die and told them they
should honor his request and gather around him for the prayers,
which they did. Shortly after he finished praying, he passed away. The
knowing that my grandfather tapped into is not readily accessible to
the thinking mind, nor can the mystery of what life is ever be explained by easy formulas or by what we think of as "knowledge."

My wife, Elizabeth, and I recently visited the concentration
camps at Auschwitz-Birkenau. The hardest part, much more than
the verbal descriptions of the systematic cruelty and horror, was see
ing the piles of baby clothes and the photographs of the individual
human faces, especially the mothers and children clinging together
as they got off the train, not knowing that they would be dead within
a few hours. All the lives cut short. The completely arbitrary nature
of it. Even the most comprehensive practice overview can't explain
or make sense of something like this. Platitudes such as "There is no
life or death," or "Within emptiness everything is perfect just as it
is," are hollow words, denying the basic fact that within life there is
inexplicable suffering. We can do our best to learn from it, but there
are no easy solutions, no overarching explanations. The experiential, rather than any mental explanation, is what opens and transforms us—such as seeing the piles of baby clothes and letting the
image etch itself into our hearts.

Even to look for profound spiritual wisdom may be a detour;
much of what passes for profundity may be just confusion that's
well stated. To accept that we really know very little may be uncomfortable, but it will certainly bring us back to this basic fact: that only
through returning again and again to the "what" of our experience
itself—the physical experience of what our life is right now—can we
enter into and live from the nonconceptual understanding that is
the basic essence of our being. Like it or not, it is exactly where we
must go if we wish to stop our attempted escapes and detours from
what is real.

Blaming

The second equally fruitless detour is *blaming*. We continually fall into the trap of looking for someone to blame. Some of us may be very aware of this pattern, while for others, it is so subtle or hidden that we don't even realize we are doing it. Either way, blaming has a very compelling quality; it has a certain juice or power, almost like an addiction. Yet justifying ourselves and blaming others can keep us spinning in the mental world for hours, days, or even years. But if we look closely enough, we'll see that blaming is primarily a defense against feeling the anxious quiver of our own experience.

For example, say we're criticized and have an emotional reaction such as hurt. It's very likely that past hurts will reinforce our present feelings, and our reaction may hit us much more deeply than the present situation warrants. But in order to avoid feeling the painful emotional reaction, we immediately move into the defensive strategy of blaming and self-justifying. We defend so that we don't have to feel the pain of unworthiness or rejection that the criticism triggers. In blaming, we focus on the perceived faults of the other to detour away from having to direct our attention inward, which we fear might be extremely uncomfortable.

The practice countermeasure to blame is to directly face the pain we are trying to avoid. This is not a mental process; it involves feeling the pain, residing in it, as the *physical* reality of our life. I'm talking about doing something very straightforward yet very difficult, which is to cut through the story line of blame and instead stay in the present moment of our experience. We simply don't want to do that. Yet this is where the sense of separateness, of the "me-ness," transforms into awareness.

To enter the present moment of hurt, ask yourself what that hurt actually feels like physically. Remember, the word *hurt* is just a concept. Although as a mental concept it may seem very complicated or overwhelming, as an actual physical experience in the body, it becomes very specific. Again, we're back to the koan question "What is this?" Is there an ache in the heart, queasiness in the belly, or an overall heaviness or rawness in the body?

Whatever you experience when you feel hurt or any other emotion, the practice is always to bring awareness to the energy coursing through the body rather than thinking or analyzing. If thoughts arise, notice them, but rather than getting caught in the story of me, especially the story of blame, keep awareness focused on what is felt in the body. You could also include awareness of sounds or other aspects of the environment outside of the skin boundary—this will help keep the experience from becoming too narrowly focused on "me and *my* body."

Please be clear that I'm not talking about wallowing in our feelings, which is what we usually do when we believe all our thoughts about being wronged. Instead, I am describing how to actually feel— fully feel—the physical reality of the present moment. With awareness, our suffering becomes more porous, and the energy of life can naturally flow through us. Refraining from the mental fixation of blaming is an absolute prerequisite to experiencing the sense of connectedness that we truly are. Blaming always separates; it always disconnects. In fact, when we're caught in blaming, the sense of me-ness is never more solid.

Fixing

The third major detour is *fixing*. When a problem arises, we almost automatically ask, "How can I fix it?" We instinctively feel the need to find the safety and comfort that come from taking whatever is "wrong" away.

What do you usually do when a difficulty arises? Think about this for a moment. Look at your own patterns. Is your strategy, for example, to withdraw or close down in order to avoid dealing with hardship? Or perhaps you have a more aggressive strategy, such as meeting your difficulty head-on in order to take care of it right away. Or maybe your strategy is to worry obsessively or to bury yourself in diversions. We can even use meditation as an escape, by trying to bypass our problems with an artificial sense of calm.

All of us need to become aware of our own strategy of escape, our own specific patterns of trying to "fix" our experiences. It's a given that we don't want to feel discomfort, but since it's inevitable, we have to learn how to address it. This is the blue-collar work of practice. It's not particularly exciting but is inwardly intense nonetheless. That's why the quality of perseverance is of key importance, because we have to learn to just *stay,* even when our experience is not pleasing us in the ordinary sense. Put simply, the solution is never about fixing but rather about staying—especially staying with the fear of helplessness and the loss of control.

Here's a small, mundane example. One day on a recent trip overseas, Elizabeth and I knew that the next day we had a lot of connections to make, between a boat ride, a bus ride, a train ride, and two flights. We also had a lot of luggage, so I knew the logistics would be difficult. That night I woke up, and my mind started going over the scenarios for the next day. Feeling anxiety, my mind went right to the question "How can I fix this?" The answers that came back were pretty much surface thoughts, such as "Maybe we should take a cab instead of a bus," or "Maybe we should ship some luggage."

This question about how to fix the situation was not necessarily an escape, because on an objective level something could certainly be done to make the trip less complicated. However, the real issue was that the question "How can I fix this?" took on an emotional urgency. This urgency turned what could have been an objective approach to simplifying logistical problems on the trip into an attempt to avoid facing the fear of the loss of control. My practice in this situation was to see clearly where I was caught in the believed thoughts of dread and to then stay present with the visceral experience of anxiety. As always, the practice is to stay with the "what," the physicality, of our present-moment experience.

We all have experiences like this on a regular basis, where we get caught in the three major detours, asking, "*Why* is this happening? Who can I *blame*? How can I *fix it*?" We need to watch ourselves take these three escapes time and again, and see if we understand how to implement the practice countermeasure in our differing situations. Again, the countermeasure is "just this"—raising the question "What is this?" in order to cultivate a willing curiosity toward the immediacy of our experience.

Even though staying present with our discomfort is counterintuitive—that is, it goes against our natural instinct for comfort and safety—it is ultimately the only path that offers real freedom. That we will detour off this path by spinning in the mental world is a given. Yet such detours offer no real escape from our sense of anxiety and unease. Residing in the anxiety, without trying to fix or change the situation, is always difficult, but it also provides a potentially fruitful learning opportunity. Our difficulties can mold us, and our biggest difficulties—the ones we want to avoid the most— offer us the greatest opportunity to break through the protected cocoon of a separate me. Only by opening directly to our experience itself will we ever tap into the sense of connectedness that is the essence of who we are.

Time and Again ⤵

Adam Frank

Of all the building blocks of conventional reality, time seems to us the most solid. The past is behind us, the future is ahead, and we're all living together in the present. Yet is time an objective reality at all, or simply another concept through which we construct our world? Buddhism's great philosopher of time is Dogen, founder of the Soto school of Zen. The physicist and Zen practitioner Adam Frank compares Dogen's view with the Western world's evolving understanding of time.

An ancient buddha said:
For the time being stand on top of the highest peak.
For the time being proceed along the bottom of the deepest ocean.
For the time being three heads and eight arms.
For the time being an eight- or sixteen-foot body.
For the time being a staff or whisk.
For the time being a pillar or lantern.
For the time being the sons of Zhang and Li.
For the time being the earth and sky.
   —EIHEI DOGEN (*The Time-Being*, translated by Kazuaki Tanahashi and Dan Welch)

For the time being, my knees are killing me. It's the second day of the *sesshin*, a seven-day meditation intensive at the Rochester Zen

Center, and I'm in big trouble. The stiffness in my legs has not gone away. I'm hot, tired, and clammy under the brown robe. Worst of all, I cannot find my way into a deeper, more concentrated sitting. I'm not engaged in meditative absorption. I am not breaking through to insight and enlightenment. Instead I'm stranded, left with nothing but the pain in my legs and my endless, exasperating thoughts. The bell marking the new meditation round fades, and I sit staring straight into a thirty-five-minute death march of boredom and discomfort. As a theoretical physicist, I'm fairly well versed in human speculation about time and its subtle nature. Now I'm getting a lesson on its not-so-subtle nature. Time, that most elusive and slippery concept, has abruptly jumped from the realm of the abstract into the domain of the concrete. And all that concrete is crushing my knees.

Every culture in every era has its own way of understanding and making use of time. From Stonehenge to the digital chronometers staring down on Times Square, humans have always woven their idea of time into the organizational fabric of their societies.

Contemplative practice, on the other hand, takes us beyond our mere concept of time and forces us to engage with it directly. For better or worse, the flow of moments is the raw material of meditation. The nature of time is also central to the work of physics as it attempts to reveal the fundamental laws shaping physical reality. The dialogue between science and the contemplative tradition of Buddhism is still a relatively new addition to the contentious four-century-old "religion and science" debate. The first wave of that dialogue, focusing on relatively silly New Age enthusiasms for quantum physics, has passed (at least one hopes) among those who take the conversation seriously. Now the real work (and fun) can begin. Any attempt to understand *if* and *where* points of contact exist between the great investigative traditions of contemplation and science requires an open mind, sharp skepticism, and perhaps a little taste for mischief. Given the centrality of time in both the Buddhist and the scientific worldviews, it just may be the right place to begin a search for authentic parallels between them.

Buddhism's essential insight on time's passage is its fundamental lack of substance. As Shunryu Suzuki put it, "You may say, 'I must do something this afternoon,' but actually there is no 'this afternoon.' At one o'clock you will eat your lunch. To eat your lunch is, itself, one o'clock." In his great work *Uji*, or *The Time-Being*, the thirteenth-century Zen master Eihei Dogen drew a direct link between time, being, and the self. For Dogen, they were all of a piece, unfolding through a present that is essentially dynamic and creative, an elemental self-revelation of all that is. "The way the self arrays itself is the form of the entire world," says Dogen. "Thus the self setting itself out in array sees itself. This is the understanding that the self is time." Dogen's writings are nuanced and complex, but the lightning bolts of illumination in his description of time can strike even a novice reader like myself.

When Dogen says, "Time runs from present to past," it can seem nonsensical, but as Kazuaki Tanahashi writes in his introduction to *Moon in a Dewdrop: Writings of Zen Master Dogen*, "Time, according to Dogen, is experienced moment to moment; actual experience happens only in the present. Past was experienced in the past as the present moment, and future will be experienced in the future as the present moment." But past and future always collapse into the experiencing of now, for that is all there is. Tanahashi continues, "Yet past is remembered as past in the present moment as future is expected as future in the present moment. Each moment carries all of Time." Time can only disclose or unfold itself in our now, and as it does, all of time and all the world unfolds, too. They cannot be separated. We stand in the center of what Dogen calls "arraying ourselves" as simultaneous observers, participants, and creators. Fields, grass, flowers, and wind always appear in the "now" that is ever one and ever renewing. Dogen has a word for this unity: being-time, or *uji*. To be is to be time. "As the time right now is all there is," Dogen writes, "each being-time is without exception entire time." In the context of Dogen and, perhaps, much of Buddhist understanding, the presence of the present is the only time you have.

• • •

As the meditation round continues, I struggle to find a way into this elusive present moment. The silence is broken by a flock of geese honking sharply as they fly overhead. I can almost feel the birds' smooth trajectory through the autumn sky and the infinitely subtle dance of forces that turn air and wings into the grace of flight. Not just above, this dance is everywhere: in the light reflecting off the wall in front of me; in the gamboling atoms that constitute each breath. Then, suddenly, my instincts as a scientist become a part of my effort. The universe revealed so powerfully through physics flows in its own way, and for an instant it fills the room. That universe, as it has played out for generations of scientists before me, offers a very different but equally startling vision of time.

Physicists, too, must do away with culturally conditioned notions of time. The deepest revolutions in physics have often turned on a radical reenvisioning of time. From Newton to Einstein, rethinking time has led to conceptual earthquakes that have shaken science to its foundations, razing the prevailing sense of what is both real and true.

Nowadays our planet is tiled with time zones, and we meter moments into ever-finer intervals for everything from sports to commerce to communications. A new kind of time has emerged over the last few centuries, which in one sense can be considered the creation of a single man. It took Isaac Newton just a few years to reinvent the world with his radically new physics, and Newton started his revolution with time. Most people associate Newton with his theory of gravity. But before he could even formulate his ideas of falling apples and orbiting planets, he had first to imagine a framework, a stage, on which to build the most basic description of forces and their effects. To accomplish this, he created what we now call Newtonian "mechanics," a universal description of the interplay between matter and motion. Resting at the base of this mechanics, this new theory of physics, was a powerful new vision of time.

Newton imagined the flow of time to be absolute and universal.

Time was like a smoothly flowing river running through all creation with unwavering constancy. Ten minutes on my watch must be the same as ten minutes on yours, no matter where or when in the universe we may be. Time for Newton was separate and unique. It stood apart from people and events and animated his equations as a kind of omnipresent heartbeat against which all change, in all places, could be measured with infinite precision. In a very real sense, Newton's time was God's time.

While others such as Galileo and Descartes preceded him in developing the new physics, it was Newton's powerful vision, resting on an absolute time, that truly set the Scientific Revolution in motion. The Industrial Revolution followed close on its heels, as precision-timed machines made from Newtonian mechanics transformed human life. In the sky, planets moved with clockwork predictability through their orbits. On Earth, men and women in burgeoning cities clocked into factories for their perfectly metered workdays. In both pure physics and the organization of human society, time became an innate property of an objective reality. The time we now experience in our socially structured daily lives is, for the most part, Newtonian time.

The geese honking overhead continue on their southward path. I listen as their calls fade into the distance. The *zendo* returns to its deep, collective silence. Then the monitor slides from her cushion, pads quietly to the altar and retrieves the *keisaku,* the "wake-up" stick, as I like to think of it. Whack! Whack! The sound of her quick strikes to the shoulders of my fellow meditators reverberates through the zendo. Each sharp strike connects the stick, their backs, and my ears. Each staccato crack draws the room together in a web of relationship—a matrix of events, sound, and attention—breaking the silence and the silent flow of moments.

In 1905, Einstein published his first paper on relativity. In just a few pages, he swept away Newton's absolute time. In its place, the young Einstein showed us the counterintuitive truth that time is malleable. It can bend and stretch. To truly understand the nature of physical reality, Einstein found that his theory needed to merge time and space into a larger whole. The understanding that time could flow at different rates in different frames of reference arose as Einstein attempted to understand the universe as an interconnected web of "events" strung together by light waves. Time and space, separate and uniform, disappeared for him and no longer served as an unchanging bedrock for physics.

How does time's relativity show itself? Everything in Einstein's theory depends on "observers" who measure events. The motion of these observers (or their location near a massive object like a planet or a black hole) forms the key to linking time and space. To be concrete, consider my round of sitting as an "event": it has duration, a beginning and an end, that can be measured with a clock. Everyone in the zendo is an observer. Any one of us could, in theory, look at the zendo clock and see that the sitting lasts thirty-five minutes.

In Newton's universe those thirty-five minutes are absolute. Everyone, everywhere in creation, will experience the same thirty-five-minute interval, no matter where they are or how they move relative to each other. Not so for Einstein's new world: a Zen monk–turned-astronaut traveling past the Earth at near the speed of light will look at the zendo and note something quite different. Instead of thirty-five minutes, our astromonk will clock the round at more than four hours. If he tries to time his own sitting to ours, he will stay in meditation for 241 of "his" minutes. (And I thought my legs hurt.)

The stillness in the zendo returns. I hunker down, trying to forget the pain in my knees, and just follow my breath. But with every sound, every rasping scrape from people shifting slightly or breaking into a cough, my focus is shattered, and I return to agonized thoughts about pain, about the duration of the sitting, about anything, everything. The wind rises, and I hear leaves in the trees rustle. In response, a quieting thought slides across my attention. Who hears the leaves? I can imagine the physics, leaf brushing against leaf, the flow of wind converted to acoustic energy radiating through the air, but what of the essential presence that animates hearing the sound? What is the difference—is there a difference—between the sound and the hearing?

Physics, by its nature, deals with objective external realities. Einstein offered a deeper vision of how that reality could be described. But Einstein always imagined a universe of phenomena that exist independently of human action, agency, or consciousness. The "observers" in Einstein's theory can be anything marking the duration of an event: whether a zendo-bound roshi or a subatomic particle whizzing through the atmosphere, it makes no difference. No self-awareness is required.

If we want to take the vision of the true and real that physics offers and compare it with the subjective realities revealed by contemplative practice, we must never forget this fundamental difference. Retaining a firm grasp of the distinction is particularly crucial when we understand time through the lens of the other great revolution of twentieth-century science—quantum physics.

In the first years of the 1900s, physicists developed increasingly powerful instruments to probe the atomic and subatomic realms. The data from these experiments revealed a world apparently not governed by laws familiar to scientists until then. To describe this new world, scientists were forced to invent an entirely new set of physical laws that came to be known as quantum mechanics. The list of examples of quantum weirdness is long. Here are a few:

- A particle trapped in the nuclear version of an impenetrable box can escape by spontaneously disappearing from the inside and reappearing unbound on the outside.

- A single electron traveling around an object seems to take two paths at the same time.

- Two atoms separated by light years can each somehow manage to always know what the other one is doing.

These are all sharp departures from what we think of as the "ordinary" behavior of things. Quantum Buddhism's essential insight on time's mechanics reveals a world that is nothing if not bizarre. As the great Danish physicist Niels Bohr once said, "Anyone who is not shocked by quantum mechanics does not really understand it."

Ironically, except for in the all-important moment, no great revolution in our understanding of time came with the development of quantum mechanics. It is only at the precise moment that this quantum stuff is measured that things get weird. It's as if the act of taking a measurement—the explicit moment of observation—triggers a profound switch in the behavior of quantum systems. At the instant a quantum system is measured (or observed), physicists must stop using one set of rules and switch over to another—something unheard of in every other branch of physics. Out of that one instant of weirdness alone, countless popular books on science and Buddhism have been launched.

The apparent intrusion of conscious observation into the objective realm of physics has led many writers to claim that physics has affirmed the discoveries of Buddhism, Hinduism, mysticism, and whatnot. Since, some argue, Buddhism emphasizes consciousness rather than matter as the fundamental ground of existence, then it must be true that quantum mechanics, with its "measurement problem," recovers this emphasis and therefore confirms the realizations of Buddhism. This has been a particularly popular theme with New Age audiences, as exemplified by the maddeningly silly film *What the Bleep Do We Know!?* or Deepak Chopra's profoundly misinformed writings on the subject. But neither physics nor Buddhism is that simple.

With a few notable exceptions—B. Alan Wallace (however much I may disagree with his conclusions), the astrophysicist Piet Hut, and the physicist Vic Mansfield, to name three—most writings on Buddhism and science are at best misguided and at worst so deeply wrong that they drive practicing physicists like me to breathe into a paper bag to stay calm. Their failure is an attempt to substitute wishful thinking for the hard work of rigorous thinking. By misconstruing the *questions* quantum mechanics raises (about time and measurements and reality) as answers that jibe with Buddhist tradition, they sidestep the most creative and fascinating part of investigation: not knowing where you may be led. But these failures serve an important function by demonstrating how a sincere dialogue between science and spiritual practice can go terribly wrong. Making tidy claims about tidy connections between science (à la quantum physics) and Buddhism (or some version of "Eastern mysticism") fails to do either one much justice. Indeed, such claims fail utterly to hit the essence of what makes both science and contemplative practice so dynamic, so interesting, and ultimately, so worth our effort.

My knees begin sending out alarms to neighboring body parts. Now it's my back and ankles that are on fire. How much longer can this stinking round last? I start wondering whether Tibetan or Insight Meditation intensives have shorter rounds and longer breaks. Maybe they serve chocolate pudding at dinner, too! The intensity of the discomfort is so bad it forces me to focus deeply on my breathing just to get to the frontmost edge of the pain. For a moment, it works. On each out-breath, the fire in my knees recedes to some distant place. Then, amazingly, these moments hold. They expand and open on their own. The agonizing march of seconds is gone, folding in on itself as my breathing expands to fill the field of attention. Without thinking about it, I am suddenly exploring the flow of moments with a quiet directness. It is new and different and graceful. Then someone coughs, and my attention shudders again. The moment breaks, and I come back to the pain and the slow crawl of seconds. Still, I have to smile. No doubt about it, that was pretty cool.

Clearly, we must acknowledge the differences between science and contemplative traditions like Buddhism. One can say that in meditation practice, one seeks to rediscover and confirm truths that have already been affirmed and refined by tradition. In science, one builds on the discoveries of the past, but progress is made by finding new truths and thus falsifying previous views. Yet, on a direct and personal level, are the approaches toward truth so fundamentally different? As the ninth-century Zen master Rinzai taught, "Place no head above your own." That is a sentiment I could easily use with my astrophysics graduate students. Likewise, regardless of what we read or are told about practice, it's our own encounter, our own experience unfolding in time, that matters. For the student—and we are always students—*it is always new to us.* Tradition guides, but experience teaches.

There is an even deeper issue, however, that touches the core notion of truth in each domain: Does it make sense to evaluate conclusions reached through a subjective investigation of the mind by holding them up to the scrutiny of the putatively objective physical sciences, or vice versa? The evolutionary biologist Stephen J. Gould once used the term *nonoverlapping magisteria* to describe the idea that science and religion have separate domains and each should be happy to leave the other alone. Should this be our approach? If we are talking about contemplative practice and not some blind adherence to scripture, then I am not so comfortable with such clean and tidy boundaries. I learn things through both practice and science. Can they really have nothing to do with each other? Still, their means of investigation are so different that one should be justifiably suspicious of overlapping, conjoined claims of truth or falsehood. So, where does that leave us?

Here, it is important to remember the role of time and history. For more than four hundred years, all discussion about science and religion meant debate between science and Western monotheism. The advent of the Buddhist perspective on this discussion is still fundamentally new. There is a profound difference between arguing whether Genesis is compatible with Darwinian evolution and asking how understanding gained in contemplative practice relates to understanding gained in scientific practice. (Of course, many scientists would argue that, in fact, nothing is gained in practice, but that is part of the new debate.) The first wave of the discussion, the silliness of "quantum Buddhism," has passed, or at least one hopes. Now perhaps we can begin the hard work. The first step is deciding what—if any—are the appropriate questions that can be asked and answered about comparing two such complex, subtle, and different traditions.

Perhaps, going forward, what will matter most will be an exchange of metaphors allowing us to enliven what is already known (contemplation) and point us in new directions for what is not known (science). If this were possible, such a dialogue would be fascinating. But perhaps there is even further to travel. I am no roshi, and I can imagine getting smacked upside the head by those who have invested far more hours on the cushion than I, but I say, put it all on the table. The scholars of religion Elaine Pagels and Robert Sharf have each argued that at any moment in history, religions will selectively choose to emphasize certain aspects from their own traditions and to ignore others to serve current needs, and in that way they remain vital. Pagels calls this "creative misreading." Thus no single "correct" understanding handed down through history ever exists, and there are always new ways to see, new things to learn. If Dogen is right, then we know what we know only in the moment, for there is nothing else. The truly creative response to questions of the true and real exists in that single, unified moment; we cannot know beforehand where it will take us. Perhaps each tradition should remain radically open-minded and radically skeptical.

Finally, the bell rings. I've made it. The round of sitting is over. It seems to take me forever to unfold my stiff, numb legs and stand up. I draw a deep breath and let the exhaustion drain out of me. There is exhaustion, yes, but excitement, too. In the midst of all that hard work something new has discovered itself within the unfolding moments. The bell rings again, telling us that it's time to file out to lunch. For a moment, I want to linger. Do I have to leave my new sense of time on the cushion? Or can I bring it with me in to the meal, then out into the world, and then everywhere after? Only time will tell.

This Very Mind, Empty and Luminous

The Dzogchen Ponlop Rinpoche

It is fitting to conclude this book with a teaching from the Vajrayana tradition of Tibet. Vajrayana, or tantric, Buddhism, sees itself as fruitional—it starts not with suffering, the beginning of the path, but with enlightenment, the fruition. In this teaching by the Dzogchen Ponlop Rinpoche, one of the leading Tibetan teachers in America, we are offered the true nature of mind—the true, enlightened nature—and learn it is available to us at this very moment.

Only when we have a genuine, abiding desire to free ourselves from suffering and all its causes does our spiritual journey begin. That original desire is very potent and very real. It is the basis upon which we enter the path that will lead us to our goal. Yet from the point of view of the Vajrayana, or tantric, school of Buddhism, there is no place to go on that path, no end of the road where we will one day satisfy our thirst for liberty. Why? Because the very thing that we are looking for—freedom, wakefulness, enlightenment—is right here with us all the time.

There is a story in the tantric meditative tradition of Mahamudra about a farmer who owns a buffalo. Not realizing that the buffalo is in its stable, the farmer goes off in search of it, thinking the animal has strayed from home. Starting on his search, he sees many different buffalo footprints outside his yard. Buffalo footprints are everywhere! The farmer then thinks, "Which way did my buffalo go?" He decides to follow one set of tracks, and they lead him up into the high Himalayas, but he doesn't find his buffalo there. Then he follows another set of footprints that lead way down to the ocean. However, when he reaches the ocean, he still doesn't find his buffalo. It is not in the mountains or at the beach. Why? Because the buffalo is back home in the stable in his yard.

In the same way, we search for enlightenment outside ourselves. We search for freedom high up in the mountains of the Himalayas, at peaceful beaches, and in wonderful monasteries, where there are footprints everywhere. In the end, we may find traces of the great Tibetan yogi Milarepa's enlightenment in the caves where he meditated, or hints of the Indian pandit Naropa's enlightenment at the bank of the River Ganges. We may find signs of the enlightenment of many individual masters in different towns, cities, or monasteries. What we will not find, however, is the one thing we are looking for: our own enlightened nature. We may find someone else's enlightenment, but it is not the same as finding our own.

No matter how much you may admire the realizations of the buddhas, bodhisattvas, and yogis of previous times, finding your own freedom inside yourself, your own enlightenment, your own wakefulness, is much different. When you have your own realization, it is like finding your own buffalo. Your buffalo recognizes you, and you recognize your buffalo. The moment we meet our own buffalo is a very emotional and joyful moment.

In order to find our own enlightenment, we have to start right here where we are. We have to search inwardly rather than outwardly. From the Vajrayana point of view, the state of freedom, or enlightenment, is within our mind and has been from beginningless time. Like our buffalo comfortably resting in its stable, it has never left us, although we have developed the idea that it has left home. We think it is now somewhere outside, and we have to find it. With so many footprints leading in different directions, so many possibilities for where it could be, we may start to hallucinate. We might think it was stolen by a neighbor and is gone forever. We start to have all kinds of misconceptions and mistaken beliefs.

To summarize this, we can say there is nothing called "buddha" or "buddhahood" that exists outside of one's mind. We can say the same for samsara; it does not exist apart from one's mind. That is why Milarepa sang,

> Nirvana is nothing imported from somewhere else
> Samsara is nothing deported to somewhere else
> I've discovered for sure the mind is the buddha

From the point of view of the Mahamudra and Dzogchen traditions of Vajrayana Buddhism, there is nothing within samsara—our state of dualistic confusion—to be relinquished, discarded, or left behind. And nirvana—the state of enlightenment—is not a place we go to from here. It is not a place found outside of where we are right now. If we wanted to renounce samsara, leave it behind physically, where would we go? To the International Space Station, the moon, or Mars? We would still be within samsara. So how can we leave samsara behind?

What we are trying to leave behind is duality, the mind of confusion, our perpetual state of suffering. Physically, yes, you can leave your hometown and go to some secluded place such as a mountain cave or a monastery. Your body will be somewhere else, but will your mind be in a different state? How your mind functions when you are in a mountain cave, a monastery, or at home is what determines whether you are in the state of samsara or nirvana.

According to the Vajrayana teachings, enlightenment is right here within our mind's nature. That nature is what we are trying to discover and connect with. It is what we are trying to recognize, realize, and perfect. The entire journey on this path is trying to discover the nature of our mind as it is.

How can we recognize this nature of mind? The experience of

awakening, of complete enlightenment, can be arrived at through many different methods. The methods of the three vehicles of Buddhism—the Hinayana, the Mahayana, and the Vajrayana—all lead to the same goal. The difference is not in the result achieved but in the time it takes to reach that result and in the methods used. Only the Vajrayana is said to possess the methods that can lead to the realization of the true nature of mind in one lifetime. In the Vajrayana liturgy, this way of achieving the state of wakefulness is called attaining "complete enlightenment in one instant." When we take the instructions to heart, when we employ the methods properly, stage by stage, and when we focus on the path and do not drift onto any sidetracks, this awakening can take place in any minute. One moment we can be a totally confused, ordinary sentient being, and the next we can be a completely enlightened being. This outrageous but very realistic notion is known as sudden enlightenment, or "wild awakening."

THE PATH OF DEVOTION

The tantric path is sometimes known as the path of devotion. With the eye of devotion—toward our guru, our lineage, and our instructions—we can see the true nature of mind. What role does the guru play in our journey to find enlightenment? On the one hand, it is said that enlightenment is right there within you, and on the other hand, it is said that there is no enlightenment without devotion to the guru or lineage of enlightened masters. It sounds a little contradictory.

Why is devotion so important? How does it work? Devotion is a path, a skillful means through which you develop basic trust—trust in your own enlightened heart, trust that your mind is totally, utterly pure and has been right from the beginning. Trusting in that truth is what devotion is. You come to see the truth of your own enlightened heart through the guru and the lineage. Your relationship with your guru is personal, yet it is also beyond the personal. It is so close that you feel like you can control it, yet at the same time you realize it is beyond your control. It is similar to your ordinary relationships—with your spouse, friends, and family—yet it goes beyond them. If you can work with the relationship with the guru, it opens a door to working with every relationship in the world. It becomes a great vehicle for transforming your negative emotions and suffering.

The point here is that the guru simply plays the role of a mirror. When you look in a mirror, your own face is reflected back to you. The mirror does not reflect itself. It shows you whether your face is clean or dirty or if you need a haircut. The mirror is unbiased; it reflects positive and negative qualities equally clearly.

In the same way, when you look at the guru with devotion, you see both your positive and negative qualities. You see your failures, your struggles, your disturbing emotions arising, just as you see dirt on your face in an ordinary mirror. At the same time, you see beyond the surface impurities—which can simply be washed away. You see your true face, your actual reality, which is the perfectly pure nature of your mind.

What happens, though, if you are sitting in front of the mirror in a room that is dark? The mirror still possesses the potential to reflect, and you still possess all those qualities to be reflected. But if there is no light, you could sit there in the dark for ages and nothing would happen. You would never see anything. Therefore, it is not enough just to sit in front of the mirror. You need to turn on the light. In this case, the light is the light of devotion. When this light is on, and when the mirror of the guru is in front of you, you can see the reflection of your own nature of mind very clearly and precisely—yet in a nonconceptual way. That is the role of the guru and the lineage in our enlightenment. The guru is not the creator of your enlightenment. He or she is simply a condition for attaining your own enlightenment.

The mirror does not turn on the light for you. It does not bring you into the room and tell you to sit in front of it. It doesn't say, "Look here!" The mirror is just a mirror occupying a certain space. You have to enter the room, turn on the light, walk toward the mirror, and look into it. So who is doing the job here? It's us. We are activating this relationship.

Some traditions say that you have to be passive to receive divine grace or to have mystical experiences, but here it is the opposite. To invoke the blessing of the lineage, you have to be active. Everything is done by you; the guru is simply a condition, a mirror, that you have chosen to keep in your room. That mirror did not mysteriously land there, you know. You selected it and placed it there through your own efforts.

The lineage instructions are also not the creator of your enlightenment. They are simply another condition. They are powerful and profound tools that you must employ. Instructions are like directions for getting where you want to go. The instructions, the directions, play an important role, but not more important than your own role in initiating and taking the journey. You play the more active role on the path. You act on the directions. They give you all the information you need—which way is the safest, which is a little bit risky, and which is the fastest but most hazardous. However, if you take no action, then eons from now you will still be wandering around without reaching your destination.

We have full power to decide the course of our personal journey. This is the Buddhist view. Even from the perspective of Mahamudra and Dzogchen, you are the center of the path, and your enlightenment depends on your own effort. It does not depend on anyone or anything outside of you.

USING MIND TO DISCOVER THE TRUE NATURE OF MIND

The basic nature of our mind, and the basic nature of all phenomena that we perceive as being external to our mind, is luminous emptiness. In other words, all forms, sounds, and so on, as well as all thoughts and emotions, are appearing yet empty, empty yet appearing. There are various approaches to discovering this nature of mind that is with us all the time.

From the Mahamudra-Dzogchen point of view, we first look directly at the appearances of thoughts and emotions and ascertain their emptiness. Their nature of appearance-emptiness is easy to see, because such mental forms are fleeting and insubstantial. Once this is seen with confidence, then we look at external appearances. Having penetrated the nature of thoughts and emotions, seeing the true nature of the outer world—the external objects that appear to our sense consciousnesses—is much easier. We see that they are equally empty.

In the Hinayana and Mahayana approach, the order is reversed. We first focus our analysis outside and ask, "How is form empty? How is sound empty? How is smell empty?" and so on. Through reasoning, we discover that the true nature of all these forms is emptiness. Once we find that the nature of all perceived objects is empty, we conclude that the nature of the perceiving subject is naturally empty as well. Subject and object exist only in dependence upon one another.

From the Vajrayana point of view, it is easier and more straightforward to analyze your mind first. Your own mind is very clear to you—you know your thoughts and emotions very well, and you experience them directly. They are not hidden from you. They are not something you have to discover through analysis. Your emotions and thoughts are right there in front of you, so when you look at them, your examination is experiential.

When we analyze a form or sound, or turn our mind to the metaphysics of seeds and sprouts, it is conceptual, an academic exercise. We come to "know," but our knowing is not direct knowledge. Therefore, from the Mahamudra-Dzogchen point of view, that approach is regarded as indirect analysis. It is not a direct experience. For this reason, the Hinayana and Mahayana stages of the path are called the "causal vehicles." They cause us to have, or lead us to, the direct experience later. The methods of the causal vehicles will bring us to that experience at some point, but not right now.

Mahamudra-Dzogchen uses the approach of direct analysis, which is known as the "analytical meditation of the simple meditator," or *kusulu.* This does not mean *simple* in the sense of being intellectually deficient, but *simple* in the sense of being intellectually uncomplicated.

The Hinayana and Mahayana approach to analysis is known, on the other hand, as the "analytical meditation of the scholar," or *pandita*, which is theoretical or scholarly analysis.

While the scholarly approach is necessary, if used alone, it does not bring us direct experience right away. The analysis of the simple meditator, in which we begin by looking at our immediate experiences of mind, is very clear and brings direct experience to everyone. Using this method, when you look closely at a thought or emotion, you can see its nature of inseparable luminosity and emptiness. You do not find any solid or substantially existent thing. The reason you do not find anything solid is that, on the absolute level of reality, nothing exists in that manner. Therefore, when we look for it, we do not find it.

True emptiness, however, is not just "not finding" something. If, for example, you searched your home to see if there was an elephant somewhere in your house and you did not find any elephant, would it mean that elephants do not exist? No. There are elephants living in zoos and in the wild.

Simply searching for something and not finding it is not the kind of analysis that leads us to the genuine experience of emptiness. To arrive at the true experience of emptiness, we must base our analysis on looking at something we do see, that appears to us to exist, whether that is an external or internal object. When we analyze that object, let's say an elephant, we look at it in order to discover its true nature, its fundamental reality. We look for that nature by thoroughly analyzing the existence of the elephant and each of its parts—ears, trunk, eyes, great body, legs, and tail—until we exhaust our looking. At that point, we come to the conclusion that we cannot find the true existence of this solidly appearing being. Nevertheless, we can see, smell, hear, and touch this empty-yet-appearing elephant. That is the method of analyzing that leads to the experience of emptiness.

In the same way, when we look directly at a thought or emotion, it is hard to find anything solid. We may be experiencing strong anger, but when we look at those intense feelings of aggression, we can't really pinpoint them. We can't really identify what they are. We may not even be certain why we are angry. After a while, our anger dissolves. One moment, we can barely speak or breathe because we are so enraged. In the next moment, the fury is gone, leaving nothing behind. Even if we want to maintain our anger so we can continue tormenting our rival or foe, it is too late. Our empty-appearing anger is gone. In truth, it was never there in the first place.

ORDINARY MIND

The actual point of all our efforts on the spiritual path, whether we are studying, meditating, or engaged in socially oriented activities, is to return to the genuine state of our mind, the inherent state of wakefulness, which is very simple and completely ordinary. This is the goal of all three vehicles, or *yanas,* of the Buddhist path.

The Hinayana school calls this state egolessness, selflessness, or emptiness. The Mahayana school calls it the great emptiness, or *shunyata,* freedom from all elaborations, all conceptuality. It is also known as the emptiness endowed with the essence of compassion, or as *bodhichitta,* the union of emptiness with the qualities of compassion and loving-kindness. Further, it is known as buddhanature, or *tathagatagarbha,* the essence of all the buddhas, the "thus gone ones." In the Vajrayana, it is called the *vajra* nature, or sometimes the vajra mind or heart, which refers to the indestructible quality of awareness. In Mahamudra, it is called ordinary mind, or *thamal gyi shepa,* and in Dzogchen, it is called bare awareness, or *rigpa.* The meanings of all these terms point to the most fundamental reality of our mind and phenomena, which is luminous emptiness. All is empty yet appears, appears yet is empty.

While many different methods are taught to reach this ordinary state of mind, the methods themselves can appear to be anything but ordinary. In some sense, they are extraordinary rather than ordinary, abnormal rather than normal, and complex rather than simple. The Hinayana path of personal liberation, for example, is known for its many detailed instructions for practice and postmeditation conduct.

For monastics, there are the customs of shaving one's head and putting on beautiful robes, which are rituals prescribed in order to lead the practitioner to the realization of selflessness.

In the same way, followers of the Mahayana system for realizing the great emptiness undertake the *paramita* practices, the six transcendent actions of generosity, discipline, patience, diligence (or exertion), concentration (or meditation), and discriminating knowledge (or *prajna*). In the Vajrayana, there are many complex practices, such as the visualization of deities and mandalas, which lead to the realization of the vajra mind.

So with all these practices, are we getting any closer to the natural state? Since it is natural for our hair to grow, the Hinayana practice of continually shaving our heads seems unnatural. It is also not the normal custom of society. In the Mahayana, there are many highly conceptual and occasionally "counterintuitive" methods for purifying negative states of mind, such as breathing in the impurities of the minds of others in *tonglen* practice. In the Vajrayana, in contrast to the Hinayana practice of shaving off our hair, we not only visualize extra hair, but we also imagine extra heads, extra arms, and extra legs.

Why do we do this, when such methods seem to take us further and further away from an ordinary, normal, and simple state of mind? There must be a reasonable explanation! The answer is simply that in order to reach the level of ordinary mind, to truly arrive at the basic state of simplicity, we have to cut through our habitual, dualistic pattern of labeling some things as normal and others as abnormal. If we have too much fixation on normalcy, on day-to-day convention, we have to cut through that to experience our mind as it truly is.

Therefore, in order to break through and transcend such solid, dualistic notions, we create "abnormal" situations to practice with on the path. In the deity yoga practice of the Vajrayana, you might be visualizing yourself in the form of an enlightened being with multiple heads, arms, and legs when you suddenly realize that you have no idea who you are—which is a wonderful experience. We usually have too many preconceived notions about who we are and about the world "out there." We are so caught up in the process of labeling that we never see beyond the surface of those labels to the nonconceptual reality that is their basis.

When we work with profound and skillful methods like those of the Vajrayana path, they cut through the very root of our dualistic concepts. With these methods, we rely on concept to go beyond concept, on thought to go beyond thought. A good example of this is a bird taking off from the ground. When the bird wants to fly, it has to either run a little bit or push down against the ground so that it can leap up. It has to rely on the earth to go beyond the earth—to leap into the space of sky. In the same way, we have to rely in the beginning on dualistic concepts in order to leap into the space of nonconceptuality or nonduality.

This is what all these teachings do for us. Through words and concepts, they point out the nature of phenomena, which is emptiness beyond words and concepts. If, when Buddha realized the true nature of mind and the world, he had never spoken about it, never communicated his wisdom to us through words, we would have no way to enter this profound path.

When it comes to the Mahamudra-Dzogchen tradition, however, the masters of these traditions introduce ordinary mind, or bare awareness, with utmost simplicity. Such a master might say to a student, "Look, a flower. Do you see it?"

The student will say, "Yes, I see the flower."

The master will say, "Do you see the beautiful sunshine outside today?"

The student will say, "Yes, I see the beautiful sunshine today."

Then the master will say, "That's it."

Normally we feel that our perceptions, thoughts, and emotions are too ordinary to mean much. Just seeing a flower or the sunshine on a beautiful day is too simple to be profound. As meditators we want whatever is profound, and so we look past our mundane experiences. We are looking for something that is extraordinary. Something big. We want the *maha*, or "great," religious experience that we know is out there somewhere in a mysterious place called "the sacred world." However, whenever we try to look outside, that is the point at which we depart from our own enlightened nature. We start walking away from the natural state of our mind—the basic state of Mahamudra and Dzogchen. "Looking outside" does not mean that we literally leave our home and go look in our neighbor's backyard, or that we pack our bags and catch a bus for the next town, or shave our head and enter a monastery. Looking outside means *looking outside whatever experience you are having right now.*

Think about it from the perspective of your own experience. What do you do when an aggressive thought suddenly arises? You might try to stop that thought, deflect its energy by justifying it, or even correct it—change it from a "negative" thought into a "positive" one. We do all these things because we feel that that thought, just as it is, is not good enough to meditate on. We will meditate on the next pure thought we have; or even better, we will rest in the essence of the gap between our thoughts, the very next one we recognize. In this way, we continually miss the moment that we are awake now. The problem is that we will never catch up to the wakefulness of the next moment, the wakefulness we will have in the future. If aggression is here now, then that aggression is at heart, in its very nature, vividly awake, empty, and luminous. As our simple-minded master of Mahamudra and Dzogchen might say, "Do you see it? That is it."

You may prefer to meditate on the Buddha rather than on your emotions. The Buddha is always perfectly relaxed and at ease; therefore, you feel very comfortable. When you are meditating on your emotions, you may start to feel slightly anxious and uncomfortable. You may think that your mental health is at risk or that the environment of your mind is not in a sacred, uplifted, or spiritual state. It is helpful to a certain point, at the beginning of our training, to meditate on pure objects like images of the Buddha, deities, or great masters. If, however, you get addicted to relying on such objects, there can be negative consequences. When you feel you cannot invoke the experience of sacredness or connect with your basic, enlightened mind through your everyday experiences of perceptions, thoughts, and emotions, you are developing a serious problem. Your emotions are as familiar, as commonplace, as sunshine and flowers, and that is great news for realizing ordinary mind. You have so many opportunities. Appreciate and take advantage of them.

What we have been looking for—the true nature of our mind—has been with us all the time. It is with us now, in this very moment. The teachings say that if we can penetrate the essence of our present thought—whatever it may be—if we can look at it directly and rest within its nature, we can realize the wisdom of buddha: ordinary mind, naked awareness, luminous emptiness, the ultimate truth. The future will always be out of reach. You will never meet up with the buddha of the future. The present buddha is always within reach. Do you see this buddha? Where are you looking?

Contributors

MARTINE BATCHELOR, the author of *Let Go: A Buddhist Guide to Breaking Free of Habits,* was ordained as a Buddhist nun in Korea in 1975 and studied Zen Buddhism under the guidance of the late Master Kusan at Songgwang Sa monastery until 1985. She edited the books *A Women's Guide to Buddhism* and *Buddhism and Ecology,* and is the author of *Principles of Zen, Meditation for Life,* and *Women in Korean Zen.* She coleads meditation retreats worldwide with her husband, the well-known author and Buddhist scholar Stephen Batchelor. They live in France.

EZRA BAYDA is a Zen teacher affiliated with the Ordinary Mind Zen School. A student of meditation for more than thirty years, he teaches at the San Diego Zen Center. He is the author of *Being Zen, At Home in the Muddy Water,* and *Zen Heart,* which is excerpted here.

PEMA CHÖDRÖN is one of America's leading Buddhist teachers and the author of many best-selling books, including *The Places That Scare You, When Things Fall Apart,* and *Start Where You Are.* Born Deirdre Blomfield-Brown in 1936, she raised a family and taught elementary school before being ordained as a nun in 1981. Pema Chödrön's root teacher was the renowned meditation master Chögyam Trungpa Rinpoche. Since his death in 1987, she has studied with Trungpa Rinpoche's son, Sakyong Mipham Rinpoche, and her current principal teacher, Dzigar Kongtrül Rinpoche.

GABRIEL COHEN is the author of *Storms Can't Hurt the Sky: A Buddhist Path Through Divorce,* as well as three novels, including *The*

Graving Dock, a mystery with a Buddhist subplot. He lives in Brooklyn and likes to meditate next to a lake in Prospect Park.

LIZA DALBY is an anthropologist specializing in Japanese culture. Her 1983 book, *Geisha,* was based on her experiences conducting fieldwork among these traditional entertainers. Dalby's most recent book is *East Wind Melts the Ice,* a memoir in the form of essays about Eastern and Western culture and seasonal sensibilities.

CHRISTINA FELDMAN is the author of a number of books, including *Compassion: Listening to the Cries of the World.* She is cofounder and a guiding teacher at Gaia House, a Buddhist meditation center in Devon, England, and a senior teacher at the Insight Meditation Society in Barre, Massachusetts.

NORMAN FISCHER is the founder and teacher of the Everyday Zen Foundation, whose mission is to open and broaden Zen practice through what he calls "engaged renunciation." Fischer practiced and taught at the San Francisco Zen Center for twenty-five years and served as abbot from 1995 until 2000. His latest collection of poetry is titled *I Was Blown Back,* and his most recent book, excerpted in this anthology, is *Sailing Home: The Spiritual Journey as an Odyssey of Return,* his reflections on Homer's *Odyssey* as a map of the human inner journey.

ADAM FRANK is a professor of astrophysics at the University of Rochester. He is author of *The Constant Fire: Beyond the Science vs. Religion Debate.*

NATALIE GOLDBERG is the author of eleven books, including the best seller *Writing Down the Bones* and *The Great Failure.* Her most recent book is *Old Friend from Far Away: The Practice of Writing Memoir,* excerpted here. She teaches workshops and retreats on writing as a spiritual practice and lives in northern New Mexico.

JOAN HALIFAX, PHD, is a Zen priest and anthropologist. For forty years she has worked with dying people and has lectured widely on the subject of death and dying. In 1990, she founded Upaya Zen Center, a Buddhist study and social action center in Santa Fe. In 1994, she founded the Project on Being with Dying, which has trained hundreds of health care professionals in the contemplative care of dying people.

THICH NHAT HANH is a renowned Zen master and poet, and founder of the Engaged Buddhist movement. The author of more than forty books, he resides at practice centers in France and the United States. Thich Nhat Hanh's newest book is *The World We Have: A Buddhist Approach to Peace and Ecology,* which is excerpted in this anthology.

OLIVIA AMES HOBLITZELLE is a writer, psychotherapist, and teacher. Throughout her career she has educated people in contemplative practices in a wide variety of settings: government agencies, businesses, hospitals, organizations, churches, and school systems. While teaching at the Mind/Body Medical Institute, she developed training programs in new approaches to health and healing through Harvard Medical School.

PICO IYER is an essayist, a travel writer, and a novelist, and his writing often addresses the theme of cultural identity in a global age. His books include *The Global Soul; Sun After Dark;* and excerpted in this volume, *The Open Road,* the result of more than thirty years of talks and travels with the Fourteenth Dalai Lama. He is currently working on a book about autumn in Japan.

LIN JENSEN is the senior Buddhist chaplain at High Desert State Prison in Susanville, California, and founder of the Chico Zen Sangha in Chico, California. He is a member of the Buddhist Peace Fellowship, and his book *Pavement* described his daily peace vigils sitting on Chico's downtown sidewalks. His latest book, which is excerpted here, is *Together Under One Roof: Making a Home of the Buddha's Household.*

WENDY JOHNSON has been practicing Zen meditation for thirty-five years and has led meditation retreats nationwide since 1992 as an ordained teacher in the traditions of Thich Nhat Hanh and Shunryu Suzuki Roshi. She was one of the founders of the Farm and Garden Program at Green Gulch Farm Zen Center in Marin County, California, and has been teaching gardening and environmental education to the public since the early 1980s. Since 1995 Johnson has written a gardening column for *Tricycle* magazine.

HIS HOLINESS THE SEVENTEENTH KARMAPA, Ogyen Trinley Dorje, is the spiritual leader of the Kagyu school of Tibetan Buddhism. In 1999, the then-fourteen-year-old Karmapa made international headlines with his dramatic escape from Tibet to India. He made his first trip to the United States in 2008, with thousands attending his public talks in New York, Boulder, Colorado, and Seattle.

STEPHANIE KAZA is a professor of environmental studies at the University of Vermont, where she cofounded the Environmental Council, a campuswide consortium on sustainability. She has been an active participant in Buddhist-Christian dialogue and served as president of the Society for Buddhist-Christian Studies. Her books include *Hooked! Buddhist Writings on Greed, Desire, and the Urge to Consume* and *The Attentive Heart: Conversations with Trees.* She is an avid bike commuter and enjoys cooking with local foods in her logo-free kitchen.

DZIGAR KONGTRÜL RINPOCHE lives with his wife, Elizabeth, in southern Colorado, where he directs Mangala Shri Bhuti, an organization dedicated to the teachings of the Longchen Nyingthik lineage of Tibetan Buddhism. He is the author of *It's Up to You, Uncommon Happiness,* and *Light Comes Through,* which has been excerpted here.

JACK KORNFIELD trained as a Buddhist monk in Thailand, Burma, and India, and is cofounder of the Insight Meditation Society and Spirit Rock Meditation Center. He holds a doctorate in clinical psychology and is the author of *A Path with Heart; After the Ecstasy, the Laundry;* and excerpted here, *The Wise Heart: A Guide to the Universal Teachings of Buddhist Psychology.*

DAVID LOY is the Besl Professor of Ethics/Religion and Society at Xavier University and a Zen teacher in the lineage of Koun Yamada. His books include *A Buddhist History of the West: Studies in Lack; The Great Awakening: A Buddhist Social Theory; The Dharma of Dragons and Daemons: Buddhist Themes in Modern Fantasy* (with Linda Goodhew); and *Money, Sex, War, Karma: Notes for a Buddhist Revolution,* which is excerpted in this anthology. He lives in Cincinnati with his wife, Linda, and son, Mark.

CALVIN MALONE was incarcerated in 1992 with a twenty-year sentence for aggravated assault. He began practicing Buddhism after he entered prison and started writing about his prison experiences shortly thereafter. He was instrumental in developing a postprison transitional program and makes *malas* (Tibetan prayer beads) for Buddhist prisoners around the country. Malone is currently working on a Buddhist novel and is up for early release in October 2009.

PHILLIP MOFFITT is the founder and president of the Life Balance Institute, a nonprofit organization devoted to the study and practice of spiritual values in daily life. In 1987, he left his position as chief executive and editor-in-chief of *Esquire* magazine to focus on his inner life. Moffitt teaches vipassana meditation at retreat centers around the country and holds a weekly meditation class in Marin County, California. He is a member of the Spirit Rock Meditation Center teachers' council.

KATHLEEN WILLIS MORTON has been practicing Tibetan Buddhism since the age of seventeen and holds a master of fine arts in creative writing from the University of New Orleans. She lives in Cambridge, Massachusetts, with her family.

RUTH L. OZEKI is a filmmaker-turned-novelist and the author of *All Over Creation* and *My Year of Meats*. She is a student of Zoketsu Norman Fischer and splits her time between New York and British Columbia, where she is working on a new book.

THE DZOGCHEN PONLOP RINPOCHE is a meditation master and scholar in the Kagyu and Nyingma schools of Tibetan Buddhism. He is the president of Nalandabodhi, a network of meditation centers, and founder of the Nitartha Institute, a course of Buddhist study for Western students. He is the author of *Wild Awakening* and *Mind Beyond Death*.

TOM ROBBINS is a renowned American novelist and essayist. Among his works are *Another Roadside Attraction* (1971); *Even Cowgirls Get the Blues* (1976); *Still Life with Woodpecker* (1980); and *Wild Ducks Flying Backward* (2005), a collection of essays, reviews, and short stories. The interview excerpted here was sparked by his *Harper's* magazine essay "In Defiance of Gravity," which argued for the essential place of humor in spiritual practice.

SHARON SALZBERG is a cofounder of the Insight Meditation Society in Barre, Massachusetts, and of the Barre Center for Buddhist Studies. Among her best-selling Buddhist books are *Lovingkindness: The Revolutionary Art of Happiness* and *Faith: Trusting Your Own Deepest Experience*. Salzberg's latest releases are *The Kindness Handbook* and *Unplug*, an interactive audio kit, both published by Sounds True.

RABBI RAMI SHAPIRO is the founder of One River, an educational institution promoting dialogue on religion, science, and ethics. He is a graduate of the Hebrew Union College–Jewish Institute of Religion and holds doctoral degrees in both religion studies and divinity. He has been a student of Zen since 1968.

JOAN SUTHERLAND is founder of the Open Source, a network of practice communities emphasizing the confluence of Zen koans, creativity, and companionship. Before becoming a Zen teacher, she worked as a scholar and teacher in the field of archaeomythology, as well as for nonprofit organizations in the feminist antiviolence and environmental movements.

PEGGY ROWE-WARD and LARRY WARD are ordained dharma teachers who were married by Thich Nhat Hanh at his practice center in Plum Village, France. Peggy is the coauthor of *Making Friends with Time.* Larry can be heard periodically on the National Public Radio broadcast "Brother Thây." Together, they direct the Lotus Institute, a nonprofit organization dedicated to cultivating the mind of love.

ALAN WEISMAN is the author of five books, including the best seller *The World Without Us* and *Gaviotas: A Village to Reinvent the World.* His reports from around the world have appeared in *Harper's,* the *New York Times Magazine,* the *Atlantic Monthly,* and other publications, as well as on National Public Radio.

JOHN WELWOOD, PHD, is a psychotherapist who has been a student of Tibetan Buddhism for more than thirty-five years. Although not explicitly autobiographical, his essay in this anthology traces his own journey through his twenty-year marriage. His books include *Journey of the Heart, Toward a Psychology of Awakening,* and *Perfect Love, Imperfect Relationships.*

Credits

Phillip Moffitt, "Mindfulness and Compassion: Tools for Transforming Suffering into Joy." Reprinted from *Dancing with Life* by Phillip Moffitt, copyright © 2008 by Phillip Moffitt. Permission granted by Rodale, Inc., 33 East Minor Street, Emmaus, PA 18098.

Kathleen Willis Morton, "The Blue Poppy." From *The Blue Poppy* by Kathleen Willis Morton, © 2008 by Kathleen Willis Morton. Reprinted with permission from Wisdom Publications, 199 Elm Street, Somerville, MA 02144 USA. www.wisdompubs.org.

Ruth L. Ozeki, "The Art of Losing: On Writing, Dying, and Mom." From the March 2008 issue of the *Shambhala Sun.*

The Dzogchen Ponlop Rinpoche, "This Very Mind, Empty and Luminous." From the May 2008 issue of the *Shambhala Sun.*

Tom Robbins, "Wisdom of the Rebels." From the July 2008 issue of the *Shambhala Sun.*

Sharon Salzberg, "The Kindness Handbook: Communication." From *The Kindness Handbook: A Practical Companion* by Sharon Salzberg, copyright © 2008 by Sharon Salzberg. Used by permission of Sounds True, Inc., Boulder, CO. www.soundstrue.com.

Rabbi Rami Shapiro, "Where Is God When Stick Hit Floor?" From the Spring 2008 issue of *Buddhadharma: The Practitioner's Quarterly.*

Joan Sutherland, "Koans for Troubled Times." From the Spring 2008 issue of *Buddhadharma: The Practitioner's Quarterly.*

Peggy Rowe-Ward and Larry Ward, "Love's Garden." From *Love's Garden: A Guide to Mindful Relationships* by Peggy Rowe-Ward and Larry Ward, © 2008 by Peggy Rowe-Ward and Larry Ward. With permission from Parallax Press. www.parallax.org.

Alan Weisman, "Cranes in the DMZ." From the Introduction to
The World We Have: A Buddhist Approach to Peace and Ecology by
Thich Nhat Hanh, copyright © 2008 by Alan Weisman. With per-
mission from Parallax Press. www.parallax.org.

John Welwood, "Intimate Relationship as a Spiritual Crucible."
From the November 2008 issue of the *Shambhala Sun*. Adapted
from a talk given at the California Institute of Integral Studies in San
Francisco. © 2008 John Welwood.

Also from the editors of the *Shambhala Sun*

• • •

In the Face of Fear: Buddhist Wisdom for Challenging Times
Edited by Barry Boyce and the editors of the *Shambhala Sun*

Most of us have never experienced such deep anxiety and uncertainty in the world; this anthology of Buddhist teachings offers an antidote. How we react to the ups and downs of life makes all the difference, and Buddhism offers a wealth of wisdom and practices to help us maintain a stable, wise, and helpful state of mind no matter what happens. *In the Face of Fear* features the greatest contemporary Buddhist teachers and writers—people renowned for addressing precisely the problems we're facing today—including the Dalai Lama, Pema Chödrön, Thich Nhat Hanh, Chögyam Trungpa, Sylvia Boorstein, Jack Kornfield, Norman Fischer, Jon Kabat-Zinn, Sharon Salzberg, and many others.

Available from bookstores or from www.shambhala.com.